SONG NOI

The REVERB series looks at the connections between music, artists and performers, musical cultures and places. It explores how our cultural and historical understanding of times and places may help us to appreciate a wide variety of music, and vice versa.

reverb-series.co.uk
SERIES EDITOR: JOHN SCANLAN

Already published

SONG NOIR
TOM WAITS
AND THE SPIRIT OF
LOS ANGELES

ALEX HARVEY

REAKTION BOOKS

For Joey

Published by Reaktion Books Ltd
Unit 32, Waterside
44–48 Wharf Road
London N1 7UX, UK
www.reaktionbooks.co.uk

First published 2022
Copyright © Alex Harvey 2022

Printed and bound in Great Britain by
TJ Books Ltd, Padstow, Cornwall

A catalogue record for this book is available from the British Library
ISBN 978 1 78914 663 9

Contents

Duke's Coffee Shop and the Tropicana Motel, Santa Monica Blvd, West Hollywood, c. 1980s; Waits's infamous place of residence during the 1970s.

Introduction:
Crawling down Cahuenga

I really became a character in my own story.
I'd go out at night, get drunk, fall asleep underneath
a car. Come home with leaves in my hair, grease
on the side of my face, stumble into the kitchen,
bang my head on the piano and . . . chronicle
my own demise and the parade of horribles
that lived next door.

– Tom Waits, 1982[1]

T
hese days the nearest any fan can get to the presence of
Tom Waits is the 'Crawling down Cahuenga' tour, an annual
pilgrimage around the places in Los Angeles associated
with the legendary Californian singer-songwriter. Waits has not
performed a full public concert for over a decade and left Los
Angeles back in 1984. However, as such a fan-driven heritage trip
indicates, Waits is intimately associated with the city's identity and
history. Namechecking a line from the title track of his album of
1980, *Heartattack and Vine*, the 'Crawling down Cahuenga' tour
ushers devotees round sites of interest like Canter's late-night deli
on Fairfax Avenue, which Waits frequented, or Sunset Sound studios, where he recorded his albums in the 1970s and '80s. The
music writer David Smay organizes the tour to underline LA's central importance for Waits: 'he's really entwined with the city in a
way that few musicians are. Obviously, a lot of musicians came to
LA and started their careers here. Not that many wrote about Los
Angeles the way he wrote about it and not the parts of LA he's
writing about.'[2]

Song Noir examines the formative first decade of Tom Waits's career, when he lived, wrote and recorded nine albums in Los Angeles, from his soft, folk-inflected debut, *Closing Time* (1973), to the radically abrasive, surreal *Swordfishtrombones* (1983). Waits was able to mine an extraordinarily rich seam of the city's lowlife locations, characters and noir associations. He let the city feed and nurture his dark imagination. In response, Waits created a body of work that has helped define the sense of LA as a profoundly unsettling urban experience; a city of extremes; a site of dreams and violence, yearning and despair. At the very outset of Waits's career, back in the early 1970s, Los Angeles represented a wealth of musical and cultural influences that he could absorb and reflect in his songwriting:

You'd still hear music on the street. There were still panhandlers and buskers on the street in those days. I used to go down to a place called Ernie Francis's Parisian Room. You could see Redd Foxx down there or Jimmy Witherspoon, the blues singer. Shelly's Manne-Hole was still up on Cahuenga by the news-stand. I used to go out to the Palomino and hear Jerry Lee Lewis. Captain Beefheart was playing at the Golden Bear in Huntington Beach. Richard Pryor was playing clubs in those days. Taj Mahal played at a place called the Ash Grove. There was a whole rockabilly scene back then. Levi and the Rockats. There was a gospel scene. There was Musso and Franco's Grill [*sic*], the Nuart Theatre, the Cinerama Dome, the Ivar Theatre, Canter's Deli, The Pantry, Felipe's, Wallachs Music City . . . was a big music store on Sunset and Vine, The Continental Club was out in Silverlake; that was a big Latin club. I used to go there. Schwab's Drugstore was still around. MacArthur Park was on Sixth and Alvarado. I remember the summer they drained that lake in MacArthur Park. They found countless skeletal remains, firearms, and vehicles. Swords and knives. Fifth and Main downtown was pretty wild. It was like Mexico City at the time.[3]

Song Noir looks at how Waits combined these contemporary Los Angeles experiences with the spoken idioms of Beat writers such as Jack Kerouac and Charles Bukowski. Drawing on the legacy of jazz-blues rhythms, he explored the city's literary and film noir traditions to create his own powerful, hallucinatory dreamscapes. As a young songwriter in LA, Waits learned to mix the domestic with the mythic. He turned his quotidian, autobiographical details into something more disturbing and emblematic. The result was a vision of Los Angeles as the warped, beating heart of his nocturnal explorations: an American nightscape which resembled the warm, dark compulsion of narcotics. For much of his time in LA, Waits chose to live in the Tropicana Motel. This unsanitary West Hollywood motel was his literal and metaphorical home, somewhere which was hardly a place of rest but, instead, a location where Waits could set his personal preoccupations within the rhythms of the city's seedy underbelly. William Burroughs, sent by *Rolling Stone* in 1980, captured its decayed, noir ambience. 'There is a kidney shaped swimming pool in the courtyard. On the patio are rusty metal tables, deck chairs, palms and banana trees: a rundown Raymond Chandler set from the 1950s. One expects to find a dead man floating in the pool one morning.'[4]

The dilapidated Tropicana had already reached cult status within rock 'n' roll circles for its cool sleaze by the time Waits checked into his two-room apartment in 1976. Earlier residents had included Jim Morrison (who wrote his dystopian hymn 'LA Woman' there), Led Zeppelin and Van Morrison. Visiting New Wave bands from the East Coast or the UK, such as the Ramones, The Dickies, Blondie and The Clash made it the focus of their stay, drawn by Waits's residence, his life of dissipation on show. An evening in with Waits, who didn't have his own tv set, was recalled by the Tropicana motel's office manager, Loren Pickford:

> I was doing the night audit and in came Tom. 'I want to watch Spartacus on tv,' he said. About that time a girl walked in. I didn't think she was a prostitute, so I rented her a room. Two minutes later her pimp pulls a gun on Nick Lowe from Rockpile. I'm calling the sheriff, and I got Tom Waits on the floor, rocking back and forth with a bottle of cognac. Right then four gay Filipinos came in. I gave them the room next to the office and, not 15 minutes later, they are having an orgy in there, banging on the walls. Meantime the sheriff pulled up and there's a big confrontation in Nick Lowe's room. At that point a Mexican guy pulled in with his six kids in a car. While they're in the office, his car caught fire. Went up like a torch. He starts crying. The four guys are still banging on the wall. The cops are arresting the pimp. And lastly, I got Tom Waits yelling, 'I love the scene of Spartacus on the hill.'[5]

In his crammed apartment, half-buried under a stash of records, girlie magazines and empties, with junkies and pimps for neighbours, Waits publicly enacted his stage persona, that of a jazz-Beat musician, whose own life was in tune with the poetry of the streets. *Song Noir* shows how Waits's Tropicana residency represents the high watermark of his LA legend, the time that he deliberately set about living the life his songs described or the moment when his creative inter-penetration of city and selfhood became almost complete.

In the mid- to late 1970s Waits was at the centre of a small, bohemian LA circle of musicians, performers and party animals. They moved as a pack from the Tropicana to sober up over coffee next door at Duke's, a celebrated diner, before spending their nights drinking and performing inside (and outside) the Troubadour, where Waits had made his breakthrough.

A young visitor to Los Angeles in the 1970s witnessed the scene outside the famed venue:

> As I went out of the double doors, which open straight out onto the street, there was Tom Waits with a bagged beer bottle in hand, fag in mouth, leaning on a dusty old Cadillac. I acknowledged him and slunk back into the rounded edge of the doorway to watch 20 minutes of crazy drunken street theatre play right out in front of me. Someone gave me a swig of beer. I just pretended I was waiting for a cab. Tom was in full character (or maybe it is just him) shouting out to all the players, leering at the women, cursing out the times in his guttural drawl. Soon he had a little coterie around him, hanging on his every word, evading the flailing arms.[6]

Waits's main sidekick and 'conspirator' was Chuck E. Weiss, a good-time guy from Denver, who loved his drugs and tall tales. Weiss was made famous by Rickie Lee Jones, Waits's girlfriend at the time, in her hit single the serenade 'Chuck E.'s in Love'. Waits had also paid Chuck E. a tribute in the track 'Jitterbug Boy' on the album *Small Change* (1976). The song showcases Wait's favoured early persona, that of a button-holing boozer who bends your ear with ever more outlandish stories. The track's subtitle, 'Sharing a Curbstone with Chuck E. Weiss, Robert Marchese, Paul Brody and the Mug and Artie', pays homage to his LA circle and underlines his need to self-mythologize, his attempt to turn the literal into the mythic. According to Rickie lee Jones, Waits had 'a cult-like ability to gather people around him; his inner circle of friends felt privileged and treated newcomers with secret signs and phrases. His charisma, his compelling spirit, we all wanted to be a follower of Tom Waits.'[7]

Out carousing with his boys at night, Waits attracted increasing numbers of female fans. They would camp out on the open porch of his bungalow, waiting for their hero's early-hours drunken return. 'People came looking for me and calling for me in the middle of the night.'[8] The real Tom Waits had begun to resemble 'Tom Waits'. His lush life turned into a kind of prison: his performing persona, one that drew on so many of the city's influences, hardened into a mask, threatening to restrict his musical growth. This book charts the way Waits's LA life became more of a trap than a means of escape; how his stark, melancholy musical portraits of Americana, with its diners and drunks, strippers and shysters, started to feel repetitive and mannered. It was partly a personal trap, as Los Angeles also embodied the demons bound up with Waits's complex relationship with his alcoholic father, Frank.

Song Noir concludes by examining how Waits found a way to outgrow the city with which he'd developed such a love-hate relationship. While writing the soundtrack to Francis Ford Coppola's *One from the Heart* (1981), a movie about the importance and fragility of romantic love, Waits met and married a woman whom he hailed as his only true love – Kathleen Brennan. With her crucial support, Waits broke away from his Los Angeles associations, friendships and identity to forge a new path in his music and life. He gave his wife full credit for turning his life around: 'I'm alive because of her. I was a mess. I was addicted. I wouldn't have made it. I really was saved at the last minute, like *deus ex machina*.'[9]

Brennan helped give Waits the confidence and support to venture into unknown territory. *Swordfishtrombones*, the last of his albums to be recorded in Hollywood, took him a great distance away from his LA influences. In the album's geographical references (Australia, Hong Kong, New York, Fellini's Rome) and, more importantly, in its radical harmonic variations, Waits created his own 'world music'. Surreal, disturbing, moving and original, his work

Waits's crammed apartment at the Tropicana, photograph by Mitchell Rose, in *Rolling Stone* magazine, January 1977.

could embrace anything. In the words of his cherished literary mentor, Jack Kerouac, Waits knew 'there was nowhere to go but everywhere.'[10]

However, even though he sloughed off his LA life, like a snake shedding its old skin, reinventing himself as a 'global' artist, Waits left behind a peerless musical legacy. His great songs of Los Angeles continue to embody the dark, urban poetry of this lonely city. Tracks such as '(Looking for) The Heart of Saturday Night', 'Eggs and Sausage (in a Cadillac with Susan Michelson)', 'Tom Traubert's Blues', 'Muriel', 'Burma-Shave', 'Blue Valentines', '$29.00', 'Heartattack and

Vine', 'On the Nickel', 'In the Neighborhood' and 'Frank's Wild Years' transformed the City of Angels into Waits's own mythic, melancholy terrain; his 'song noirs' remain extraordinary lyrics of longing and loss.

1

Riding with Lady Luck

I was conceived one night in April 1949 at the Crossroads Motel,
in La Verne, California, amidst the broken bottles of Four Roses,
the smoldering Lucky Strike, half a tuna salad sandwich and the
Old Spice.

– Tom Waits, 1986[1]

Tom Waits, like his early hero Bob Dylan, felt a compulsive need to reinvent his past. He turns the prosaic details of his family origins into a founding myth, an act of self-creation. For his 'un-immaculate conception' Waits imagines a typical motel, that classic American place of transience and seedy assignations. Alcohol is present in this creation of the embryonic young Tom; the 'broken bottles' of bourbon intimate an altercation or fight. Such masculine debris is balanced by the savoured feminine mystique of 'Four Roses'; the 'smoldering Lucky Strike' cigarette could be smeared in lipstick, given its noir imagery. Waits completes his forensic scene of love and crime with the squalor of a half-eaten sandwich and the smell of deodorant cream; the lovers' appetite moves from food to sex. He adds another mythic element, naming his motel 'Crossroads', the place in blues legend where a Faustian pact with the Devil gains unrivalled musical genius. Waits pays homage to (and subtly aligns himself with) the spirit of Robert Johnson, iconic 'king of the Delta blues'.

In another ironic flight of fancy about his entry to the world, Waits mentions that the great singer Leadbelly 'died the day before I was born. I like to think I passed him in the hall and he banged into me and knocked me over.'[2] Waits ties himself into the story of another blues legend; he grounds his identity and music by association with a foundational, Old Testament-like, father figure: 'Leadbelly was a river, a tree. His twelve-string guitar rang like a piano in a church basement. The Rosetta Stone, for much of what was to follow.' Leadbelly's music 'contained all that is necessary to sustain life, a true force of nature'.[3]

Adding to his imaginary, un-immaculate conception, Waits also created mystery over the real circumstances of his birth. Was he born in Park Avenue Hospital, Pomona (as recorded in the *Pomona Progress Bulletin*), or not in a hospital at all, as he announced at a concert?

I was born at a very young age in the back seat of a yellow cab in the Murphy Hospital parking lot in Whittier, California. It's not easy for a young boy growing up in Whittier. I had to make decisions very early. First thing I did was pay, like a buck eighty-five on the meter. The only job I could land was as a labor organizer on the maternity ward for a while. I got laid off, a little disenchanted with labor.[4]

While his comment is a comic riff on the myth of early development, it also upholds a sense of Waits being self-created, of owing his survival in the world to himself. Perhaps his parents didn't quite make it to the maternity ward. Rather more likely, Waits found the idea of entering the world already on the move, the earliest possible image of restlessness, deeply appealing. The cold, prosaic truth is that Thomas Alan Waits was the second child of schoolteachers Jesse Frank and Alma Waits, who lived at 318 North Pickering Avenue in Whittier, a middle-class suburb of Los Angeles. Its main claim to fame is being the home of Richard Nixon. Whittier was so quiet a backwater that Hollywood chose it as a stand-in for a 1950s suburb in the movie *Back to the Future*. Sheltering under the San Gabriel Mountains, Whittier is part of the Inland Empire, a vast, suburban network of LA that sounds vaguely sinister. With anonymous, identical stretches of fast-food outlets, garages, bars, motels and gas stations, it was a place to leave or to kick against. In 'Putnam County' Waits sings of somewhere under a night sky, which resembles a pin cushion; bright stars prick the heavy darkness, which envelops the land like a drug.

Frank and Alma Waits were new to this warm, young land, first-generation Californians. Alma's family came from upright Norwegian stock who had settled in Grants Pass in Oregon. Jesse Frank Waits had descended from wilder Scottish and Irish ancestry in Sulphur Springs, Texas. Named after the infamous outlaw brothers Jesse and Frank James, Frank would prove to be 'a tough one, always an outsider', as Waits stated. 'All the psychopaths and all the alcoholics are on my father's side of the family. On my mother's side we have all the ministers.'[5]

Frank Waits had come to the Golden State to work the abundant orange groves, which dominated the landscape around southeastern Los Angeles in the 1940s. He became a high-school Spanish teacher, combining his love of drinking with a taste for sentimental Mexican songs. To have such a nonconformist figure as Frank for his father was a difficult, confusing legacy. Waits was naturally far more attracted to his father's roving boozing than his mother's strait-laced churchgoing. 'I remember my father taking me into bars when I was very young. I remember climbing up a barstool like Jungle Jim, getting all the way to the top and sitting there with my Dad. He could tell stories in there forever.'[6] But, although Frank drank to excess and refused to conform to suburban norms, he could also lay down the law in the most pre-emptory way. Waits recalled his father threatening that if Tom ever grew a greased-back duck-tail haircut like Elvis, he'd kill him. Waits was eight at the time.

In contrast, Alma Waits was a 'very put-together, suburban matron', according to musician Bill Goodwin, who played with Waits in the 1970s. Whenever visiting his mother, Tom's gruff voice would 'go up a few octaves in her presence' – as a mark of respect.[7] Throughout his career, Waits would try to balance his father's hard-drinking, libidinous abandon with his mother's softer domesticity. He often seeks out musical dichotomies. In *Orphans*, a collection of songs of 2006, Waits starkly divides his progeny into '*Brawlers*', '*Bawlers*' and '*Bastards*'. It's as if his musical offspring perpetuate the opposition of his parents' antithetical personas.

A love of music seems to be about the only thing Frank and Alma shared. 'My Mom came from a big family and they were all very musical. She had three sisters and they all sang in four-part harmony.'[8] Frank played in a mariachi band at night and his station wagon's radio was permanently tuned to *ranchera* songs, broadcast from Mexican border stations. Waits fondly recalled being taken to see Los Tres Ases, a 1950s *trio romantico*, at LA's Continental Club, as well as visits to his father's parents' home, still surrounded by orange groves. He relished the way his wider family were eccentric to the point of strangeness: 'Uncle Robert . . . was a blind organist in a Methodist church in La Verne, California. After they tore the church down he took the pipe organ into his living room. I remember listening to him play the organ. As his eyesight began to fail his performance seemed to drive into more interesting places.'[9]

Waits's own demolition of a wall in his tiny Tropicana Motel bungalow to accommodate an upright piano takes on a sense of family orthodoxy. His trademark growl was acquired by imitating Uncle Vernon's rasping voice, which had been caused by a throat operation. Doctors forgot to remove the scissors and surgical gauze, which, Waits claimed, Vernon choked up over Christmas dinner years later. The journey from his parents' new-build home in Whittier, southeast of LA, to La Verne was a short drive. But for an eight-year-old, it seemed an intoxicating shift away from the suburbs to the country, crossing the railroad as the landscape changed. 'We were always waiting for trains to pass. And the magic for that as a kid, hearing the bell . . . and counting the cars as they go by and I knew we were getting further out of town when I could smell horses . . . it was like perfume to me.'[10]

'Kentucky Avenue', a ballad from *Blue Valentine* (1978), celebrates Waits's life in Whittier and his boyhood friends: Ronnie Arnold, Bobby Goodmanson, Eddie Grace, whose Buick had four bullet holes in it, and Charley Delisle, to be found at the top of an avocado tree.

I grew up on a street called Kentucky Avenue, in Whittier, California. My dad was teaching night school at Montebello. I had a little tree fort and everything. I had my first cigarette when I was about seven years old. It was such a thrill. I used to pick them up right out of the gutter after it was raining. I used to repair everybody's bicycles in the neighborhood. I was the little neighborhood mechanic. There was a guy called Joey Navinski who played the trombone, and a guy called Dickie Faulkner whose nose was always running. And there was a woman called Mrs Storm. She lived with her sister. She used to sit in her kitchen with her window open and a twelve-gauge shotgun sticking out of it . . . so we took the long way around.[11]

'Kentucky Avenue' isn't, of course, direct autobiography; it's a re-imagined evocation of a composite American childhood. Whittier was a quiet suburb of greater Los Angeles, but the idyll Waits recalls has the idealized tragicomedy of Mark Twain's Missouri. The boys are all furtive, restless and reckless – as much Tom Sawyer as real friends. Waits, like Twain, revels in this mix of boyish transgression and petty criminality; adults and the law exist to be mocked or flouted in minor ways. Mrs Storm must be avoided lest she stab you with a steak knife and rattlesnakes are to be killed with a trowel. In the song Waits combines the 'real' Kentucky

Avenue with the Mississippi Delta when it ends with an imaginary trip to New Orleans, hopping a freight train. Waits blends his Californian suburb with the mythic landscape of the blues; his desire to escape from suburbia mixes with Huck Finn, lighting out for the territory.

Waits also uses Whittier as the location for another 'origin' story, the birth of his musical self. He was taught to play the guitar by an older boy, Billy Swed, a school dropout. At the age of twelve, Billy drank, smoked and lived with his mother in a trailer by a mud lake with tyres sticking out of it, 'blue smoke, dead carp and gourds as big as lampshades'.

> You could get lost trying to find their place – through over-grown dogwood and pyracantha bushes, through a culvert under a freeway and canyons littered with mattresses and empty paint cans . . . Billy's mother was enormous. I would look at her and then at the door to the trailer . . . How could Mrs Swed ever get through that door? As an eight-year-old I remember thinking that Mrs Swed was like a ship in a bottle, and she would never be able to leave. Somehow the trailer, the swamp, and Mrs Swed all came out of Billy's guitar in a minor key. It was New Year's Day after a week of heavy rain when I went back to their spot to see them again, but Billy and his mother were gone. But the secret knowledge of the chords he taught me was to outweigh all I learned in school and give me a foundation for all music.[12]

Waits was small for his age and odd-looking. His wild, sticking-up hair and pigeon-toed walk due to a bad leg meant he was picked on at school. The experience gave him an early sense of empathy for outsiders or misfits. One friend called 'Kipper', who was confined to a wheelchair, 'had polio, [and] we used to race to the bus stop every morning'.[13] 'Kentucky Avenue' ends with a prayer of restitution. The song's narrator promises to free the boy's legs from their braces and remove the spokes from his wheelchair, as an act of redemption. Waits also suffered from a heightened aural sense for a few months – the slightest sounds could become a deafening roar. 'I'd put my hand on a sheet and it would sound like a plane going by. Or like loud sandpaper.'[14] For a while he believed himself to be emotionally disturbed.

One event transformed Waits's sense of the world and his place in it. In 1959 Frank Waits abruptly moved out of the family home in Whittier, never to return. Tom was nine. 'After Frank left home, the family kind of hit the wall and cracked up and it went by the wayside,' Waits admitted to his biographer, Barney Hoskyns. 'It was an extreme loss of power and totally unpredictable, I was in turmoil over it for a long time.'[15] In his spoken-word track, 'Frank's Wild Years', from *Swordfishtrombones* (1983), Waits creates a parallel protagonist called Frank, who lives in greater Los Angeles, just like his own father. Fictional Frank settles in the San Fernando Valley and sells office furniture. Sharing Frank Waits's frustration with the conformity of suburban life, the fictional Frank rebukes his wife by indulging in his wild years. Such behaviour, the song suggests, is like a nail driven into the forehead of his wife. One night Frank buys extra gasoline on his way home. Dousing everything in the house, he sets it alight and, watching from a short distance, Frank laughs to himself as his home burns to the ground. 'Metaphorically,' as Hoskyns emphasizes, 'Frank Waits did exactly that.'[16]

> Most entertainers . . . have some type of wounding early on. A breakup of the family unit . . . sends them off on some journey, where they find themselves kneeling by a juke box, praying to Ray Charles. Or you're out, looking for your Dad, who left the family when you were nine, and you know he drives a big station wagon and that's all you got to

go on. And in some way, you're going to be a big sensation
. . . and somehow it will be this cathartic vindication or
restitution.[17]

As a teenager, Tom found himself literally kneeling at the
altar of Ray Charles, obsessively playing his songs and dreaming
of the redemption, which might come if he, too, could become
such a voice. Young men, growing up with an absent or missing
father, can fall into a cycle of searching for and rejecting male
role models. This will become a recurring pattern during Waits's
LA years.

Waits's parents were divorced quickly, and the ever-roving
Frank was soon involved with another woman (he'd marry three
times). Young Tom's attitude to his father taking up with another
woman can be glimpsed in 'Frank's Song', an early sketch for
'Frank's Wild Years'. There's a raw misogyny in its outburst against
women, who take away the male protagonist and break him.
Women's claws hold a man against his will and cause him to lose
his mind. But the song can also be interpreted in an alternative way.
If the voice is Frank's, then the woman with claws, from whom one
must escape, is Alma, with her restrictive domesticity and clinging
religiosity. Waits displays a complex ambivalence about his father's
behaviour: anger at betrayal of the family is contradicted by a
romanticized admiration of Frank's lush life. This fed into and
directly informed Waits's work. 'When I think back on it, my Dad
was an alcoholic then. He really left to go sit in a dark bar and drink
whatever . . . He was a binge drinker. There was no real cognizance
of his drinking problem from my point of view. He removed himself – he was the bad tooth in the smile and he kind of pulled
himself out.'[18]

Waits would often adopt the similar persona of a garrulous
barfly when he performed, composing songs about men who
needed to sit in dark bars and drink. In interviews Waits has stated

how his father's flight or absence made him want to age prematurely, to become the male adult in his household, creating an appearance, posture and opinions to match. 'After my father left we struggled a bit. And I was the man of the family,' he told Patrick Humphries. 'I was at home with these three women, my mother and two sisters, I grew up without a father, and although they were there, I was on my own a lot.'[19] He admitted that 'I wanted to be an old man when I was a kid. Wore my granddaddy's hat, used his cane and lowered my voice. I was dying to be old.'[20] The cane gave him a distinctive walk and identity. As a teenager, Tom would prefer to stay indoors at his friends' houses, talking to their fathers about masculine subjects like lawn mowers and life insurance. He'd check out their jazz and Sinatra albums (the 'other' Frank in his life). 'I'd end up sitting in the den talking to their Dads. Eventually they started putting on records, so I was listening to old timers' stuff. I felt like an old man when I was about 12, and I couldn't wait to grow old.'[21]

It was as if he was building an identity from the shards or fragments his father had left behind: 'When you come from a broken home you'll always feel attracted to things that are broken. You want to find something that's broken and then put it all together. You're going to feel sorry for that broken radio and that broken guitar.'[22]

In 'Soldier's Things', a moving elegy on *Swordfishtrombones*, there's a list of odd, unwanted or broken items left behind in a bric-a-brac store. Notably there's a radio, which simply needs a fuse. One of Waits's most treasured possessions was a Heathkit radio his father had built as a technician during the Second World War. The story of the son re-animating Frank's abandoned belonging, an object from which music would emanate, feels almost too Freudian. By 'fixing it' for the family, Waits becomes the man in the household, and the one who brings forth music. It was a way of replacing his father and holding on to his memory.

After the divorce Alma left the Los Angeles area and moved Tom and his two sisters south to Chula Vista, a trim, uniform suburb of San Diego, only 32 kilometres (20 mi.) from Mexico. Frank remained in Los Angeles teaching. Tom saw him only occasionally, when his father would drive down to pick him up and cross the border at Tijuana. For Waits, these rare paternal excursions were entries into another world: 'a place of total abandon and lawlessness. It was like a Western town, going back 200 years – mud streets, the church bells, the goats, the mud, the lurid, torrid signs. It was a wonderland, really, for me, and it changed me.'[23] During these Mexican trips Waits began to think of music as a possible future calling. 'Hearing a *ranchera* on the car radio with my Dad' was a first epiphany. Henceforth Waits would associate music with nonconformism and an escape from suburban identity:

> If you went to a restaurant in Mexico with my Dad he would invite the mariachis to the table and give them two dollars a song. Then he would wind up leaving with them and we would have to find our way back to the hotel on our own, and Dad would come home a day later, because he fell asleep on a hilltop somewhere looking down on the town.[24]

Waits particularly responded to how the Mexican experience of music was woven into the fabric of life, not reserved for a special occasion or performed only in licensed premises.

> I've always thought that, in Mexican culture, songs lived in the air. Music is less precious and more woven into life. There's a way of incorporating music into our lives that has meaning: songs for celebration, songs for teaching children things, songs of worship, songs to make the garden grow, songs to keep the devil away, songs to make a girl fall in love with you.[25]

As a musician in LA, Waits would choose to live in areas with a similar feel, places where he could hear music on the streets. 'Where I live in LA I go to the liquor store and there's a guy standing on the corner with an accordion and a guy with an upright bass.'[26]

Waits's trips to Mexico with Frank were infrequent, his father an absent figure throughout his teenage years. Waits's deepening interest in music led him to follow a series of iconoclastic male characters whose tastes and influence he could copy. One such model was the charismatic figure of DJ Bob 'Wolfman Jack' Smith, whose rasping voice, with its growls and howls, introduced soul and R&B classics direct from a radio station south of the border. Waits 'listened to Wolfman Jack every night, the Mighty 1090. 50,000 watts of Soul power.' To Waits, Wolfman seemed to be sharing something personal, talking man to boy. 'I thought I had discovered something that nobody else had, that nobody was getting this station, and nobody knew who this guy was, and nobody knew who these records were [by].'[27] Actually, thanks to the power of its transmitter, a generation of American youth had grown up to Wolfman's broadcasts. George Lucas (who also came of age in 1960s California) paid the DJ a tribute by giving him a speaking role in *American Graffiti* (1973), his rite-of-passage film.

One night, in late 1962, Waits downed a bottle of cough syrup, jumped into a powder-blue Lincoln convertible and, as if in a scene from *American Graffiti*, drove to Balboa Stadium in San Diego where James Brown was performing with his Famous Flames and managed to get through the fence with the aid of some wire-cutters. He told Mick Brown in 1976 that he 'hadn't had such fun since'.[28] It was another Californian musical epiphany: 'It was like putting a finger in a light socket. He did the whole thing with the cape. He did "Please, Please, Please." It was such a spectacle . . . you couldn't ignore the impact of it in your life. Everybody wanted to step down, step forward, take communion, take sacrament, they wanted to get close to the stage and be anointed with his sweat.'[29] 'It was like you'd been

James Brown at the Sports Arena in San Diego, 1967. When Waits saw James Brown perform in San Diego, he described it as 'an epiphany'.

dosed or taken a pill. I didn't recover my balance for weeks. It was like a revival meeting with an insane preacher at the pulpit talking in tongues.'[30]

While still at school, Waits set up a band called The Systems, a surf and soul trio, playing standards like 'Hit the Road, Jack' and

'Papa's Got a Brand New Bag'. He later dismissed these earliest efforts as purely imitative: 'white kids trying to get that Motown sound'.[31]

However, as Waits's junior high school was predominantly African American, it made sense that his musical influences were mainly Black: James Brown, New Orleans R&B, Wilson Pickett, the Four Tops, the Temptations, Ray Charles. The exception was Bob Dylan, whom he saw perform in a gym at San Diego State College in December 1964. 'Here's a guy like Dylan onstage with a stool and a glass of water, and he comes out and tells these great stories in his songs. It helped unlock the mystery of performance.'[32] Bobi Thomas, who shared the same high school as Waits and a room during his early LA days, recalled first spotting Waits sitting cross-legged on the grass with a guitar. 'He was singing Bob Dylan songs. He was really affecting that little boy look that Dylan had on the first album. He even wore a cap like Dylan did in the beginning.' Even the way Waits walked was memorable. 'That guy's got music in him . . . The easy way he moved, the way his shoulders swayed from side to side, his shoes clicking down the walkway.'[33] By the time Thomas noticed his freewheeling strut, Waits had already dropped out of high school in his mind, dreaming of life on the road. 'I wanted to go into the world. Enough of this! I didn't like the ceilings in the rooms. I didn't like the holes in the ceilings . . . and the long stick used for opening windows.'[34]

With such distaste for school and a declared need to take care of his mother and sisters given his father's absence, Waits was already working part-time at fourteen. He has listed a string of dead-end jobs: bartending, changing tyres at a gas station, driving taxis and ice-cream vans, selling vacuums and encyclopedias. Some of these he may have actually done. His most celebrated job (starting out as a lowly dishwasher) was at Napoleone's Pizza House, at 619 National Avenue in National City. A rough, blue-collar place south of San Diego, National City was known for its 'Mile of Cars',

Napoleone's Pizza House, National City, where a young Waits worked, listened to Ray Charles on the jukebox and eavesdropped on the clientele's conversation.

a strip of automobile outlets. For Waits it meant escape from his 'respectable' Chula Vista home into a Runyonesque adult world of pool hustlers, drunken sailors, travelling salesmen and small-time gangsters. 'Vinyl white-booted go-go dancers' would appear in the early hours of Saturday morning, pursued by packs of drunken sailors.[35] 'Hookers would come in, grab and play with me.'[36] Waits celebrated Napoleone's as his own school of life. It peopled his imagination with a rich cast of characters: the bleary-eyed sailor in 'The Ghosts of Saturday Night', for example, who dreams of a waitress with Maxwell House eyes and hair yellow as fresh scrambled eggs.

National Avenue provided his first list of lowlife joints to commemorate in song: Golden Barrel, Escalante's Liquor, Mario's Pizza, the Westerner (where Hank Williams once played), Phil's Porno, Sorenson's Triumph motorcycle shop, Berge-Roberts Mortuary, Wong's Chinese. 'Wong would tell me to sit in the kitchen, where he's making up all this food [to take back to Napoleone's] . . . It was the strangest galley; the sounds, the steam, he's screaming at his co-workers. I felt like I had been shanghaied. I used to love going there.'[37] Waits was inked with his first tattoos at Iwo Jima Eddie's Tattoo Parlor – one image displayed the name 'Nighthawks', a local car club (and title of his third album). He pretended he'd been tattooed with 'the full menu of Napoleone's Pizza House on my stomach. After a while they dispensed with the menus, they'd send me out and I'd take my shirt off and stand by the tables.'[38] Sal Crivello, Napoleone's co-owner, recalled when Waits 'was in high school about 16 years old. He was shy at first, but that was just because he was young. He washed dishes and then he became a cook. He was an excellent worker. He made good pizzas.'[39] Waits liked to boast he was 'dishwasher, waiter, cook, janitor, plumber; everything. They called me Speed O'Flash. Sundays I'd come in at 6am, and wash, buff and wax the floors.'[40]

Waits's time at Napoleone's was richly formative. During long nights of pizza and beer he'd listen to its rough clientele, mobs of sailors lining their stomachs before moving on to the bars and brothels. He'd hear their trash talk and slang phrases, their lustful dreams and sad delusions, and he'd stash it all away. 'I started writing down people's conversations as they sat around . . . When I put them together, I found some sort of music hiding in there.'[41] For five years the would-be apprentice knelt at the altar of Ray Charles. 'I worked on Saturday nights and I would take my break, and I'd sit by the jukebox and I'd play my Ray Charles. It was just amazing what he absorbed and that voice . . . "Crying Time", "I Can't Stop Loving You", "Let's Go Get Stoned", "You are My Sunshine" . . . That's all there was on the restaurant's jukebox.'[42] He had to figure out how to get from where he was sitting, in apron and paper hat, 'through all the convoluted stuff that takes you to where you're coming out of that juke box'.[43]

An answer to the question of how to become a songwriter was provided by the iconic, rebellious Catholic writer Jack Kerouac, patron saint of adolescent misfits. Appearing to Waits like a kindred spirit, Kerouac had immersed himself in the squalor and poetry of poor American lives in the 1940s, in search of mystical epiphanies and moments of 'Beatitude'. And so, in the late 1960s, Waits discovered an intense personal passion for the Beats; primarily for Kerouac and Allen Ginsberg, later for Gregory Corso and William Burroughs:

> I found them as a teenager and it saved me. Growing up with-out a dad, I was always looking for a father figure and those guys sort of became my father figures. Reading *On the Road* added interesting mythology to the ordinary and sent me off on the road myself with an investigative curiosity about the minutiae of life.[44]

The Beats renounced what they saw as comfortable 'bourgeois' conventions; the closed, smug sterility of the American nuclear family. Instead, they asserted solidarity with the poor, the oppressed and the Black communities. Sal Paradise, in *On the Road*, wanders through a Black neighbourhood in Denver, 'wishing I were a negro, feeling that the best the white world had offered was not enough ecstasy for me, not enough life, joy, kicks, darkness, music, not enough night'.[45] Waits tracked down all Kerouac's writings he could find, even pieces in laddish magazines such as *Cad* and *Rogue*. He was responding to Kerouac's palpable reality; how his characters, though idealized as 'holy outcasts', had the texture of lived experience. As a writer and role model, Kerouac was alive; 'he bled, he sweated, he fucked, he drank too much and wrote about it all.'[46] A central element of the Beat credo was the need for total honesty in the representation of their personal experience. Without it, any attempt to get at truth or reality would be doomed to fail. This is partly why Kerouac was so influential for a generation of disaffected youth. It wasn't only that he rejected the social conformity of post-war suburban America. The example of his literary insights and life could be adopted and incorporated into the core of one's being. 'It's like when you buy a record, and you hold it under your arm and make sure everyone can see the title of it . . . I felt I'd discovered something so rich and I would have worn it on the top of my head if I could have.'[47] Copying his hero, the teenage Waits, along with his friend Sam Jones (later namechecked on *Nighthawks at the Diner*), tried to hitchhike out of California 'to see how far we could go in three days, on a weekend'.[48] The closest they got to a bona fide *On the Road* moment was when they ended up stranded in a freezing Arizona small town one New Year's Eve. Broke and hungry, they found themselves ushered into the warmth of a Pentecostal church:

> They were singing, and they had a tambourine, an electric guitar and a drummer. They were talking in tongues and then they kept gesturing to me and Sam; 'These are our wayfaring strangers here.' So, we felt kind of important. And they took up a collection, gave us some money and bought us a hotel room and a meal.[49]

Waits describes this adolescent Beat adventure as 'the most pivotal religious experience' he ever had. Kerouac, like many U.S. writers, was in thrall to the search for transcendence.[50] His 'mystical' longings sometimes reduce his representation of American street life to mere layers that need to be peeled off in order to find an inner spiritual reality. But Waits was less interested in Kerouac's religiosity than his melancholy cityscapes, full of the marginal or displaced, and the teeming social life he evoked: 'impressions of America, the roar of the crowd in a bar after work, working for the railroad; living in cheap hotels; jazz'.[51] To an aspiring songwriter, someone so obsessed with lyrics that he'd pinned Dylan's words onto his bedroom walls, Kerouac showed how vocabulary could be like an instrument; good writing was cool and auditory. Waits loved the way Kerouac had considered himself 'a jazz poet, using words the same way Miles Davis uses his horn. And it's a beautiful instrument. He had melody, a good sense of rhythm, structure, color, mood, and intensity.'[52] Although Waits was influenced by other American writers (Carson McCullers and Flannery O'Connor with their love of the grotesque, Damon Runyon and Nelson Algren with their world of petty criminals and sinners), it was Kerouac's writing that validated his experience. It allowed him to understand that Napoleone's, where a 'nighthawk' could pick up late-night scraps of conversation to piece together anonymous lives and make them worthy of recognition, could be celebrated as a world in its own right.

In typical Waits fashion, by the time he had become a passionate advocate of the Beats their influence was on the wane, or had been absorbed by counter-cultural figures such as Ken Kesey (he chose Neal Cassady, Kerouac's muse, to drive the bus filled with his 'stoned' followers, known as The Merry Pranksters and captured in the documentary *Magic Trip*) or The Grateful Dead with their acid-fuelled improvisations. Waits, who preferred alcohol and George Gershwin or Jerome Kern's melodies, had little time for the Hippies. He was content to be a misfit: 'I was kinda lost in the Sixties. I didn't go to San Francisco until the whole of the flowers and love bit was over and when I did go, I was looking for the City Lights Bookstore and the ghost [of] Jack Kerouac.'[53] Out of sync with his contemporaries, Waits preferred to seek out blues legends such as Mississippi John Hurt and Reverend Gary Davis. Seeing Lightnin' Hopkins play at the Heritage Club in San Diego was like 'watching birds land on a wire and take off again. Simple and very moving,' Waits declared. 'He was doing . . . "Black Snake Moan" . . . I just thought "Wow. This is something I could do." I don't mean I could play guitar like him. I just mean this could be a possible career opportunity for me.'[54]

The Heritage folk club on North Mission Beach, a bohemian part of San Diego, was the venue for Waits's first public gig. He started by covering bluesmen or impersonating Ray Charles, but soon

Heritage coffeehouse, Mission Beach, 3842 Mission Blvd, San Diego, 1972.

introduced his own songs. The Heritage's owner, Bob Webb, who shared Waits's love of the Beats, recalled that, although 'Tom's repertoire consisted of covers, he certainly wasn't traditional either in his choice of music or his performance style. He was already performing his own material . . . People just about begged me to hire him.'[55]

Waits had chosen to work as a doorman at the Heritage because he aimed to play there: 'I was sitting incognito, in the inner sanctum of this club, hobnobbing, doing some low-level social climbing. I knew one day I would perform myself, but I was trying to soak up as much before I did, so I wouldn't make an ass of myself.'[56] Lou Curtiss, a musicologist, remembered how, on slower nights, Waits had a bigger crowd hanging out with him on the sidewalk than inside listening to the music. 'Sometimes it was more fun standing outside gabbing with Tom than being inside the place. He was great to talk to. He'd have books by Kierkegaard. He was getting into pretty heavy philosophy as well as Kerouac and all that stuff.'[57] Being the doorman suited Waits; he could be part of the scene but also an observer. He'd bring his books, coffee and cigarettes and put his feet up. 'I'd read my Kerouac and watch the cars go by and I felt just like I was on fire and I had a reason to live. Sitting there, my own ordinary life was just lifted out of that and I was all dusted with something sparkling.'[58]

Waits described his appearances at Southern California clubs such as Escondido's In the Alley, La Mesa's Bifrost Bridge and San Diego State University's Back Door as rolling around 'in the bowels of a small folk music circuit'.[59] However, as an aspiring singer, he would soon make his way to Los Angeles. His intentions are transparent in songs like 'So Long I'll See You'. He sings about a certain Tom, who must leave; outside his Buick is already waiting. Behind an easy-going, bohemian facade, Waits was focused on escaping his Chula Vista suburban existence and knew he had to move back to LA to make it. He could see the future in San Diego. His ex-classmates worked at a Lockheed plant or joined the U.S. Navy. Surfer beach culture wasn't something he valued: 'I disavow any knowledge of surfing. I don't know the first thing about surfboards. Which way you ride it, or what side is up, and I don't want to learn.'[60]

Waits's early work obsessively circles themes of escape and entrapment; his songs feature dreamers longing to break away, adventurers who grasp freedom by escaping or those who fail to make the break and become lost to themselves. 'Ol' '55', Waits's first song on his first album, *Closing Time*, is a hymn to movement. Leaving his lover at dawn, a young man experiences an epiphany of freedom, embodied in his car and the I-5 highway. He feels more fully alive as he drives with the sun rising; 'Lady Luck' must be riding with him. 'Old Shoes (& Picture Postcards)' is also straight from this template of a restless young man breaking away from love or commitment to discover himself on the road. This time the image of a tearful girl merges with that of the sun. Ricocheting from San Diego to LA, driving an automobile the size of a boat, Waits was delighted to be on the move. 'When I was 21, I was just happy to be on the road. Away from home, riding through the American night, y'know, out of my mind, wild-eyed about everything.'[61] As the child of divorced parents who lived 193 kilometres (120 mi.) apart, shuttling between two Southern Californian cities was second nature.

One trip to LA's Filthy McNastys, a sleazy Sunset Strip club, produced another epiphany. Waits watched a Puerto Rican singer called Sir Monti Rock III perform. Singing to bored businessmen, a sweaty Sir Monti stopped, grabbed his drink and hurled it at the wall, calling the suits 'a bunch of blood-suckers'. He launched into a rambling, 'psychotic confession – a cross between an execution and a striptease'.[62] Half preacher and half pimp, Sir Monti regaled the sparse audience with tales of Puerto Rican days, his life as a celebrity hairdresser and dreams of Hollywood stardom. He ended with an *a cappella* cover of 'I (Who Have Nothing)'. Waits claimed he knew at that exact moment he was in the right business.

Waits's trips to LA had a singular focus: Doug Weston's Troubadour Club. In the early 1970s it was the place in Southern California for any singer-songwriter to make their reputation. Located on West Hollywood's Santa Monica Boulevard (parallel to the more famous Sunset Strip), the Troubadour held live auditions ('Hootenanny' or open-mic nights) on Mondays, when a dozen acts would be showcased. The club had become fashionable in the 1960s, an LA version of a Greenwich Village folk-revival venue (Weston excluded electric instruments until 1967). Lowly A&R men, sleazy talent managers and rich major record label executives could all be found drinking, networking and looking for unsigned performers on these fabled Monday 'Hoot' nights. This was where Linda Ronstadt and Judy Collins had first performed, launching their careers; where Elton John had made his storming U.S. debut; where Steve Martin had taken the audience outside (showing them how to steal a car); and from where a drunken John Lennon had been ejected for hitting a waitress ('It's not the pain that hurts,' the woman said, 'it's finding out one of your idols is a real asshole').[63]

Eve Babitz, 1960s Angeleno wild child and socialite, recalled the club's heady atmosphere, its pre-eminence in LA's music scene: 'Gram Parsons and Mike Clarke (of the Byrds) drinking champagne and Wild Turkey, or Arlo Guthrie falling in love with one of the waitresses . . . Janis Joplin would sit in her nightgown with a pink Boa, by herself, drinking . . . Van Morrison glowered in corners and Randy Newman was all innocence and myopia.'[64] By the time Waits made his way to the Troubadour's cramped interior, typical 1970s singers who had patronized the club included James Taylor, Joni Mitchell, Graham Nash and Kris Kristofferson. Even accounting for music industry hyperbole, it was true that a debut at the Troubadour could make or break you. It was the first place Don Henley, of the Eagles, headed for on arriving in Los Angeles. 'I had heard about how legendary it was and all the people who were performing there. The first night I walked in I saw Graham Nash and Neil Young and Linda Ronstadt standing there in a little Daisy Mae kind of dress. She was barefoot and scratching her ass. I thought, "I've made it. I'm here. I'm in Heaven."'[65]

Waits was conscious of how success at the Troubadour would be crucial in developing a music career; a path to 'the cathartic vindication' he sought; a way to become the voice from the jukebox. 'At the Troubadour . . . Doug would go out onstage and recite The

Love Song of J. Alfred Prufrock . . . Anyone could get up. It got very thrilling because you would find people who'd hitchhiked to this spot for their twenty minutes . . . If you sold out at the Troubadour, that was it.'[66] However, although Waits travelled up to Los Angeles many times to take part in Hoot Night, he had difficulty getting on-stage. 'You arrive at the Troubadour at 10 in the morning and wait all day. They let the first several people in line perform that night.'[67] Knowing that, when he got the call, he'd only be allowed four songs, made him 'scared shitless. You can blow it all in 15 minutes.'[68]

After months of standing on the sidewalk with a collection of the hopeful and desperate, Waits was finally allowed to come inside and prove himself: 'It was frightening to hoot, to be rushed through like cattle. You see old vaudeville cats, bands that have hocked everything to come out here from the East Coast just to play the Troub one night.'[69] He described it as 'like a slave market. People sell their souls to get up and play. It's like the last resort.'[70] One Troubadour Hoot Night, when Waits played his short set, a talent manager called Herb Cohen was in the audience listening. Or rather not listening, since Cohen claimed: 'I was on my way to the toilet when I heard Tom.'[71] Cohen managed Frank Zappa, who summed him up as 'a little Jewish man that nobody likes who always wears nylon shirts – the acme of bad taste . . . and has a terrible reputation coast to coast'.[72] It was rumoured that this street-fighter kept a stash of grenades in the back of his car. Cohen had been a fixture on the LA music scene since the 1950s. He'd run a couple of folk venues: the Unicorn, which featured Beat poetry; and Cosmo's Alley, which showcased two stand-up artists, Lord Buckley and Lenny Bruce, revered by Waits. Buckley, whose 'voice parlayed black jazz argot to patrons of chic West Coast supper clubs', had died in 1960, worn out by booze, dope and neglect.[73] Bruce had also died a few years later, hounded for his heroin habit and prosecuted for obscenity. In addition to Zappa, Cohen managed an eclectic roster: Captain Beefheart, Linda Ronstadt and singer-songwriter Tim

Buckley. Convinced he'd found a new talent, Cohen approached Waits with his usual directness: 'When I came out of the toilet, I asked Tom what he was doing. And he said, "Nothing."'[74] 'Herb came over to me – very honest and upfront,' recalled Waits.[75] The two men agreed to meet the next day at Ben Frank's, a celebrated Sunset coffee shop, which had also been a hangout for Buckley and Bruce. Waits was well aware of the type of artistic management Cohen represented. 'I wanted – the tough guy in the neighborhood. And I got it.'[76] Just 24 hours later he had 'a songwriting contract and 300 dollars in my pocket'.[77]

With enough money to quit his nightshift at Napoleone's, Waits could move to live full-time in LA. No more going hungry, shuttling back and forth, living in his car or on the road. Waits was coming to the City of Angels to pursue his dream as in the old Hollywood movies he knew so well. Given his break, he grabbed it:

> I felt I'd snuck in through the back way. I got a songwriting contract. I was sitting at a bus stop on Santa Monica Blvd in the pouring rain. I'm scared to death . . . making 300 dollars a month. I didn't feel qualified. I'm used to taking on more than I can handle, biting off more than I can chew, just so I can find out how much it takes to break my back.[78]

Waits had been fascinated by the art of songwriting since he was a teenager, listening to the jazz melodies of Jerome Kern and George Gershwin or the Brill Building tradition, with songwriters turning out hit after hit for others to perform. 'You go sit down in a room and write songs all day. Then you get these runners and you get the songs out to Ray Charles or Dusty Springfield.'[79] Although he was to be paid a minimal amount for five songs a month, which Cohen would sell to other performers, it was a foot in the door, a way to move forward before disillusionment could set in. 'You bust your chops to get hold of something. Get chumped again and again to where you become

Tom Waits during his early years in Los Angeles, when he
moved to Eagle Rock, 1972, photograph by Ed Caraeff.

bitter and cold-blooded and suddenly someone's saying, "Okay
here." You can't offer any kind of rebuttal. You just have to take it,
along with the responsibility. That was frightening."[80]

Moving back to reside in Los Angeles for the first time since
he was ten, Waits found a cheap, tiny one-bedroom place, east of
Hollywood and close to where his father was living. In the early
1970s, Silverlake was much edgier and rundown than today, a mixed
Latino, Asian and gay neighbourhood, known for its loud, sprawling

street life. Waits filled the minuscule space with his upright piano, stacks of albums and books. By favouring the East Side of the city over the West, he'd chosen an area whose seamier side fitted with certain noir images of Hollywood, which he already had in mind:

> I live in a predominantly Mexican American neighborhood and I get along fine there. My friends won't come over. It's a hovel. My landlord is about ninety. He's always coming and asking if I live here. My neighbor up front is a throwback to the fifties, an old harlot. She wears these pedal pushers and gold-flecked spiked heels and has a big, bouffant hairdo. She has one of the worst mouths I've ever heard. I wake up to that. I need a place that is cluttered so I can see the chaos. It's like a visual thesaurus.[81]

Waits sought a version of the City of Angels not to be found in the fashionable 'country' canyons of Laurel and Coldwater, peopled by sensitive navel-gazers in denim. He was looking for the tawdry Tinseltown he'd read about in the pages of Nathaniel West's noir novel *The Day of the Locust* (1939). West's Hollywood is a circus of grotesque clowns and cowboys, 'the screw-balls and screw-boxes' of the movie industry; a carnival of fools as flimsy as the sets they inhabit. Even his retirees are filled with a terrible boredom.[82]

Nathaniel West was one of many writers whose influence Waits was absorbing at this time. According to Bobi Thomas, his San Diego schoolmate who had also moved to LA (their friendship turning into a brief affair), 'Tom would stay up till five or six in the morning reading. He was voracious. He'd tell me how inspired he was by reading some short story or other; and I think that was the source of his muse. Some writers go to movies to get that emotional power. I think Tom got a lot of it from books.' Waits would go to the Copper Penny diner in Hollywood where Thomas worked, sit at the counter and have 'cup after cup of coffee and fill page after page of prose. He wrote a sheet of paper for me one day that ended: 'she serves it up hot and with a smile that would fix a flat tire.' Alone in the flat, he'd 'sit for hours at the old upright, trying to get the songs out'.[83] In her presence, Waits would only play the music, never share his lyrics-in-progress. Thomas's account of their early LA days shows the importance Waits always paid to his use of language. The quality of his songwriting built his reputation; some of his earliest songs were sung by friends or other musicians. For a singer who could write his own material, early 1970s LA was the place to be. It was the laboratory for a new kind of artist, partly made possible by Dylan's astonishingly creative songwriting in the 1960s. Dylan had paved the way for a more personal mode of emotional reportage, witnessed in the music of Joni Mitchell, Neil Young and James Taylor, most of whose early 1970s albums were critical and commercial successes. The industry was on the lookout for singers who could also write. 'I caught that wave of songwriters garnering sympathy, under- standing and encouragement. For a while there, anybody who wrote and performed their own songs could get a deal there. So, I came in on that.'[84]

By 1972, Waits had become a Troubadour regular; his dishev- elled appearance fitted right into the venue's shabby bohemian-chic image. He liked its retro, 'show-biz' sense of occasion: 'They'd put a big picture of you in the window . . . They announced your name and picked you up with a spotlight at the cigarette machine and they'd walk you to the stage with the light. It was the coolest thing . . . like Ed Sullivan without Ed.'[85] Even at this stage Waits was creat- ing a persona. Thomas noticed that, although he wasn't a big drinker when out in LA with her, Waits made sure his stage character had 'a flask of whisky in his pocket at all times'. She saw how he 'intui- tively knew that the element of "show" was more than half of the game'.[86] Word circulated about his odd Beat persona, a sense of 'weirdness' that set Waits apart from other singer-songwriters. In his magazine, *Sunset Palms Hotel*, Michael Ford published 'Diamonds on My Windshield', a Waits piece influenced by Beat prosody: 'Tom had the soul of a saloon singer, right from the ground up. There was a persona there; it could have been a way of protecting himself from that sort of James Taylor/Jackson Browne sensibility. The persona was a kind of camouflage.'[87] Tom Everett, who saw early Waits performances, pointed out that none of the other singers were 'his age or showing up at hoot nights at the Troubadour. I was a little older than Tom, but I was younger than Kerouac would have been. Here was this guy channeling all that stuff . . . he was never going to be the fourth member of Crosby Stills and Nash.'[88]

The Troubadour was also the location for Waits's second encounter with Lady Luck. One night in 1972, while he was up on its prestigious tiny stage, David Geffen was among the throng of music-industry characters at the back of the club. 'He was singing a song called "Grapefruit Moon" when I heard him. I thought it was a terrific song, so I listened to the set. Here was an artist who could make some intriguing records. After the show I said that I was interested in him. He said "Well, I'll have my manager, Herb Cohen, call you."'[89]

At 29 David Geffen was already a powerful figure in the music industry. Starting out at the William Morris agency, he'd gone independent and become the reigning monarch of the Laurel Canyon scene. Geffen, together with Elliot Roberts (who became Neil Young's manager), had put together a roster of musical acts that defined the California sound: Linda Ronstadt, Jackson Browne, the Eagles and Crosby, Stills, Nash and Young (who, in an industry noted for self-indulgent temperaments, stood out for their monstrous egotism). Barney Hoskyns notes in *Hotel California*, his book on the 1960s and '70s LA music scene, how Geffen was the first to understand how these post-Woodstock, soul-searching white musicians could generate staggering amounts of revenue. 'Geffen had upped the stakes, turning back-porch folkies into Lear-jet superstars. He saw that there were millions to be made here – maybe as many as in the movie industry – and he fantasized about becoming rock's very own Louis B. Mayer, a biography of whom he had devoured as a teenager.'[90] Geffen was the definitive new type of LA entrepreneur. Denim-clad, with a haircut as hip as his vocabulary, he moved effortlessly between the suited world of boardroom executives and the laid-back milieu of long-haired musicians. He had founded Asylum Records as a sister label to Elektra (home for iconoclastic talents such as The Doors, and Iggy Pop and the Stooges). Asylum was promoted as an artist-friendly sanctuary from the money-grabbing world of corporate entertainment for sensitive souls like Joni Mitchell and Jackson Browne. When Geffen heard Waits's distinctive grainy voice singing 'Grapefruit Moon', he was already on the lookout for a 'significant artist. I really mean singer-songwriters. People who were self-contained.' Waits was just what Geffen claimed he wanted on Asylum. 'He didn't look like the kind of singer-songwriter performers of the day at all. He had his own voice, his own style, his own presentation, and his own seeming lack of interest in it all, but I was blown away by the songs and I loved the way he sang.'[91]

Initially, Waits was full of praise for the Californian *wunderkind* who struck a deal with Herb Cohen. 'David Geffen does a lot for his artists. He gets very excited about them. It's not just signing someone's life away, he's personally interested in them. In the record industry, most labels have a huge amount of artists – each has their biggies and hopefuls. But Asylum is still small. Each artist is treated like one.'[92] Within a year, Geffen completed a Hollywood *volte-face*, selling Asylum to one of the largest entertainment corporations, Warner Communications, for $7 million. Asylum's sanctuary was absorbed into the parent company. Record producer Paul Rothchild, who had produced The Doors' albums at Elektra, stated that 'when David Geffen enters the California waters as a manager the sharks have entered the lagoon. And the entire vibe changes. It used to be let's make music, money is a by-product. Then it becomes, let's make money, music is a by-product.'[93]

Asylum became Waits's home for a decade, but he never tried to fit in with the incestuous musical community of LA's Laurel Canyon scene. Singer-songwriters who slept with each other and wrote songs about it might be marketed as one big musical family, but Waits wanted no part of it, even as a bastard outlaw.

> It wasn't like I was adopted into a family and was going to be bathing with these people. The idea that you're on a label doesn't mean that we're breaking bread together every morning, and David Geffen's at the head of the table praying. I'm sure a lot of them were good friends and, if they weren't, they probably thought it was good to have it appear that they were good friends.[94]

Waits kept his distance from Asylum's country rock genre to develop his own musical identity. He conceived of his relationship to LA, the city that he was writing about, in profoundly different ways. 'I'm getting pretty sick of the country music thing . . . so much of it is really Los Angeles country music, which just isn't country, it's Laurel Canyon. It's very difficult to live a country frame of mind when you're living in LA, so I identify more with the sounds of the city.'[95] For Waits, life and material needed to be authentic, rooted in observable reality, not a projection of faux country rock, existing only in wannabe rock-star lifestyles. 'Country Rockers? Those guys grew up in LA – they don't have cow-shit on their boots, they just got dog shit from Laurel Canyon. They wouldn't last two minutes in Putnam County that's for sure. If somebody gets shot and killed there on Saturday night, the Sunday papers say he just died of natural causes.'[96] Waits's references to a re-imagined Putnam County would always be his benchmark for a mythical kind of gritty Americana; his personal 'Desolation Row'.

Closing Time, Waits's debut album for Asylum, shows few signs of the urban realism that marks his later style. It has an open-hearted sincerity, which makes it very much a work of its time. 'Midnight Lullaby' and 'Little Trip to Heaven' could be sung by the more anodyne sensibilities of James Taylor or Jackson Browne. However, Waits's voice immediately comes across as more lived-in or world-weary than his contemporaries'. His best songs already have the quality of fractured short stories; condensed, lonely tales of lost loves and abandoned dreams. 'Martha' shows a 23-year-old Waits assume the identity of a sixty-year-old man, who, surveying his life, finds something has eluded him. Waits presents himself as an aged Tom Frost, phoning long-distance his first sweetheart from forty years ago. He recalls quiet evenings from his love affair with Martha when he trembled close to her. The break-up feels as if it were yesterday. The image of the teenage Waits, old before his years, who liked to discuss Sinatra with his friends' fathers, comes to mind. The song, 'I Hope That I Don't Fall in Love with You' manages a complex blend of tenderness and cynicism. It's also the sound of a young man out of time, a lost soul hymning his loneliness. Another early Waits figure, who self-identifies as an old Tomcat, contemplates a woman sitting by herself at the end of the bar. The narrator runs through the gamut of a courtship, love affair and break-up without ever making his move. At closing time the woman goes off into the night, without a word being exchanged; the whole cycle of love and its discontents remains imaginary. The novella *In Love* (1954), written by LA screenwriter Alfred Hayes, has a similar male barfly endlessly talking about a failed love affair to a young woman, who, as far as we know, is not at all interested. Waits shares Hayes's noir-like sense of existential uncertainty; men and women constantly circle each other, failing to make any real emotional connection.

In 'Rosie', another song of dissatisfied yearning, Waits again chooses to call himself an old Tomcat. This time the first-person narrator, like a prowling feline, is out on the tiles, with only the moon for company. Such a late-night, past-closing-time atmosphere is amplified by the more bluesy piece 'Virginia Avenue'. A claustro-phobic sense of ennui with the clubs and bars closed at two in the morning haunts the narrator, who wanders down the deserted main drag, trying to ward off his inner demons. Waits claimed it was about a street in Reno: 'the only goddamn place I've seen dentures in pawn shop windows'.[97] The doomed outsider has seen all the town has to offer. It can't ward off a rising sense of his own dis-turbed mind. The only solution seems escape. The Greyhound bus could carry him away. But the blues, which he tries to leave behind, will always catch up with him.

The best track on *Closing Time*, 'Ol' '55', is a song of youthful liberation; an easy-listening *On the Road*; a Beatnik hymn to a beat-up Buick. Unlike *Closing Time*'s disillusioned, older protagonists, 'Ol' '55' features Waits as a sincere, joyous youth, who loves to ride 'lickety-splickly' in his battered automobile. The car, as always in Waits, offers a taste of freedom, a chance to cruise as the sun comes up. It's a classic Californian epiphany; dawn light steals across an open freeway as the narrator leaves his girlfriend's bed. Soulful guitar and piano melody echo a rolling lyric of celebration. Driving makes him feel alive and blessed. The chorus is a direct, unironic chant; a literal list of freeway, trucks and cars. The narrator's feelings of romantic conquest blend with his sense of movement; he joins the traffic flow as if he's merging with life, since movement and driving define LA existence. The song feels the automotive pulse of Los Angeles, a city once named 'Autopia', whose fresh-built 1950s free-ways were celebrated as emblems of individual liberty. 'The freeway system in its totality is now a single comprehensible place, a coher-ent state of mind, a complete way of life, the fourth ecology of the Angeleno' wrote architectural critic Reyner Banham in *Los Angeles: The Architecture of Four Ecologies* (1971).[98] This idea is echoed in Joan Didion's novel *Play It as It Lays* (1970), set in Los Angeles. Didion's alter ego, Maria, on the edge of a nervous breakdown, only finds escape from her anxieties in the giant network of the freeways:

She drove the San Diego to the Harbor, the Harbor up to the Hollywood, the Hollywood to the Golden State, the Santa Monica to the Santa Ana, the Pasadena, the Ventura. She drove it as a riverman runs a river, everyday more attuned to its currents, its deceptions, and just as the riverman feels the pull of the rapids in the lull between sleeping and waking, so Maria lay at night in the still of Beverly Hills and saw the great signs soar overhead at seventy miles an hour, Normandie ¼, Vermont ¾, Harbor Fwy 1.[99]

This existential restlessness, embodied in an idealization of the freeway, is central to LA's identity. It was something Waits found 'exhilarating'.[100] He explained to a UK journalist how the thrill

Hollywood Freeway (part of Route 101), with the City Hall tower and Downtown LA in the background, c. 1956. 'Autopia' was a proposed alternative name for Los Angeles. 'Ol' '55', on *Closing Time* 1973), has the chorus: 'freeways, trucks and cars'.

of America lay in setting out in the morning 'in a later model Ford', knowing 'the country is big enough that you can aim your car in one direction and not have to turn the wheel for seven days. There's a great feeling of flight there.'[101] 'Vehicular' freedom as the quintessence of the American dream is often present in his early songwriting. It's a rite of passage: 'The first car I had was when I was 14. It's kind of an American tradition. Getting a license is kind of like a Bar Mitzvah. It's nice to have a car, but in winter you gotta have a heater, especially when it's colder than a Jewish-American princess on her honeymoon.'[102] Introducing 'Ol' '55' in concert, Waits would recite a litany of the gas-guzzling models he'd driven, lingering over each name, as if it were an address book of old girlfriends. 'Had a 56 Mercury, a 55 Buick Roadmaster, a 55 Buick Special, a 55 Buick Century, a 58 Buick Super, a 54 Black Cadillac four-door sedan, a 65 Thunderbird, a 49 Plymouth, a 62 Comet.'[103] Such cars are visual emblems of 1950s and '60s Americana, the period of Waits's childhood and adolescence. He loves them as objects which, like some music he reveres, have been eclipsed or forgotten. They are like people, once full of shiny promise but who now have fallen on hard times. 'Climb aboard that Oldsmobile and let it take you for a ride . . . I like the large one that's almost half a block long. Bald tires, broken turn signals, several shades of primer.'[104] Waits locates a melancholy lyricism in the banal rhythms of postwar American life. Like Warhol, he fixates on commodities, which have an iconic lure and a throwaway emptiness. The producer of *Closing Time*, Jerry Yester, recalled going to help Waits 'buy his 52 Cadillac. It was like a work of art and he trashed it on purpose. There were newspapers in it and old paper plates and plastic forks. Beer cans. It was a mess. Kind of an Andy Warhol thing.'[105]

Jerry Yester had been David Geffen's suggestion as the studio producer for *Closing Time*, perhaps because he had successfully recorded Tim Buckley's classic album *Happy/Sad*. Yester, who had grown up in Burbank and played in Los Angeles folk clubs through-out the 1960s, immediately recognized Waits's originality, even in his earliest work. 'In early 72 no-one was doing stuff like that. "Virginia Avenue". Give me a break. And "Martha"? Who the hell was doing songs like that? No-one was writing them. Tom was. His writing gift was huge. And the way he played the piano, it was like Hoagy Carmichael, for Christ's sake.'[106] Yester claimed that he realized the potential of Waits's music from the first time he met him.

> He was in my living room playing the stuff. You'd have to be a dummy to miss it. All I had to do was keep out of the way. That was the whole point of the thing. With Tom and Tim Buckley – it was the same kind of case. The talent is so big that it's real easy to keep out of the way. I feel very fortunate I was there.[107]

Waits hadn't worked with a full backing group before making *Closing Time* and admitted he found it frightening to realize how much he had at his disposal. But Yester found him 'absolutely communicative with all the musicians . . . He'd put things in terms of metaphors and they knew exactly what he was talking about.'[108] Waits got on so well with the band that the entire album was recorded at the famous Sunset Sound Studio in under two weeks. Bill Plummer, who'd played bass with such jazz legends as Al Jarreau or George Shearing and on the Stones' *Exile on Main St*, thought Waits gave out a wonderful, relaxed sense that 'he was authentic about the whole thing. He had his cigarette there in the ashtray and all that kind of stuff. Just his appearance and demeanor and everything felt very real.'[109] *Closing Time*'s most astute reviewer was *Rolling Stone*'s Stephen Holden, who saw the depth of Waits's musical influences. His voice evokes 'an aura of crushed cigarettes in seedy bars and Sinatra singing 'One for My Baby', his songs and piano-playing perfectly parodying the lounge music sub-genre so that we wonder if he's putting us on or if he is for real.'[110]

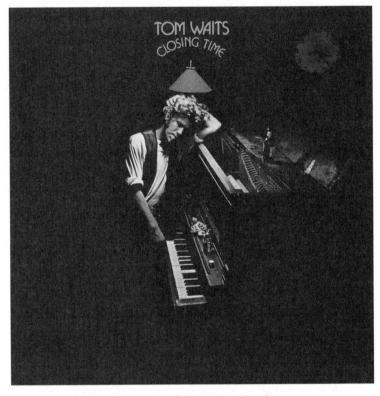

Front cover of *Closing Time* (1973).

The cover-sleeve photo of *Closing Time* shows Waits propped up by a battered, upright old bar-room piano, cluttered with debris – a beer bottle, a shot of whisky and an overflowing ashtray. The clock reads 3.22 a.m.; a single overhanging light picks out a weary musician. The atmospheric image looks back to his roots (a friend saw it as a 'conscious thank you . . . a total reference to the Heritage' in San Diego[111]) but it also points ahead to the jazz- and blues-based style that would dominate his early LA years. The moody instrumental title track, which ends the album, also anticipates a sound texture closer to his instincts. Waits later stated that he and Yester were pulling in different directions: 'If he had his way, he would have made it a more folk-based album, and I wanted to hear upright bass and muted trumpet . . . so that made it a little more uneven.'[112] Looking at Waits in LA, on the threshold of his career, the strength of his belief in his own latent ability is clear. Stephen Hodges, who was to tour with Waits, noted: 'Tom never bothered to play with anybody else. He had the balls and the inclination and the songs and the drive to just do it on his own from the very start.'[113] Waits, with typical self-deprecation, acknowledged how his younger self had the desire to set him on his way. 'I wasn't any good, but I was ambitious. I thought I was better than anybody and I sucked raw eggs. But you have to think that way.'[114]

2

Neon Buzzin'

I could hear everything, together with the hum of my hotel neon. I never felt sadder in my life. LA is the loneliest and most brutal of American cities . . . LA is a jungle.

– Jack Kerouac, *On the Road*[1]

The producer of *Closing Time*, Jerry Yester, believed it was during that album's recording that Waits first started to develop his 'skid-row image'. Waits enjoyed soaking up the street atmosphere in the seedy part of Hollywood where they were mixing the tracks. Taking an occasional break from the studio, Waits would hang out and observe the 'hookers and all the strange population down in Hollywood at that time'. Yester recalled one incident when Waits, who had been gone for an hour, returned, white and shaking:

I said 'Jesus Tom what's the matter?' And he said 'I just came onto . . . one of the most beautiful women I ever saw in my life. We were going to go up to her place and, right before, she said "You know I'm a man."'[2]

Aside from Waits's personal experiences of the seamier side of 1970s Hollywood, the discovery of Charles Bukowski's writing informed his vision of 'lowlife' Los Angeles. The alcoholic Bukowski was a bona fide, long-term Los Angeles resident whose dissolute tales and bar-soaked poetry had been deemed unseemly by the East Coast literary establishment and more or less ignored. Bukowski spent his brutal childhood in West Adams, a downtown neighbourhood constructed in the 1880s–1920s that had become notorious for its violent crime after the city authorities let it fall into neglect. Much of Bukowski's work is an attempt to exorcise the pain of his upbringing. Between the ages of six and eleven, his father assaulted him with vicious regularity, beating him with a razor strap. His body and face became disfigured with dreadful acne. He started writing at thirteen. When asked why he favoured a tight, direct style of writing, Bukowski replied: 'When you get the shit kicked out of you long enough and long enough and long enough, you will have a tendency to say what you really mean. In other words, you have all the pretense beaten out of you.'[3] He had spent his formative years on the road drifting throughout the USA, living as a tramp in dosshouses and wiping himself out with drink. Bukowski returned to live in his native LA in the late 1940s and, to survive, found work in the U.S. Postal Service as a mail courier and sorter. The job gave him 'the stink of LA' in his bones.[4] It provided the soul-destroying material (sadistic bosses, insane colleagues, years of exhausting tedium only made bearable by constant drinking and womanizing) for his first novel, *Post Office* (1971). In the late 1960s, Bukowski started writing *Notes of a Dirty Old Man*, a weekly piece for LA underground newspaper *Open City*. When it folded, Bukowski moved his column to *Los Angeles Free Press*, where Waits came across him. In *Bukowski: Born into This* (2003), a documentary on the writer, Waits spoke about how he had stumbled upon Bukowski's work almost by accident: 'I thought this was remarkable. This guy's the writer of the century and he's being published in this kind of street rag, which seemed kind of poetic and perfect . . . You felt that you had discovered him as well – that he wasn't being brought to you, but you had to dig and find him.'[5]

Many of Bukowski's stories and poems were written about the seedy neighbourhood haunts and darkened, rundown bars that Waits frequented. In *Confessions of a Man Insane Enough to Live with Beasts* (1965), Bukowski noted: 'An Alvarado Street bar is about as close to getting to Skid Row as you can get.'[6] Given Bukowski's work is a chronicle of the dark side of the Californian dream, the less-than-Golden State, it's obvious why the older man's writing deeply affected Waits. His own LA upbringing was a less extreme version of similar alcoholic suffering.

> My Dad spent a lot of time in the bars, so I was drawn to places like that – the dark places – my Dad drank in the afternoon . . . the fact that I hooked into [Bukowski] was because he seemed to be a writer of the common people and street people, looking into the dark corners where no-one seems to want to go – certainly not write about. It seemed like he was the writer for the dispossessed and the people who didn't have a voice.[7]

In *Post Office* Bukowski achieves a kind of existential noir, one which rests upon the anguished self-loathing of an alcoholic.

> I went into the bends. I got drunker and stayed drunker than a shit skunk in Purgatory. I even had the butcher knife against my throat one night in the kitchen and then I thought, easy, old boy, easy. Your little girl might want you to take her to the zoo. Ice cream bars, chimpanzees, tigers, red and green birds and the sun coming down on the top of her head, the sun coming down and crawling into the hairs of your arms, easy old boy.[8]

Never part of the Beats (though associated with them given his subject-matter), Bukowski became as important an influence on Waits in his LA years as his earlier literary love, Jack Kerouac. Both writers oppose the sentimental delusions of the American dream; both use their work to puncture the false comforts and conventional values of the middle class. But whereas the rhythms of Kerouac's prose seek a Whitmanesque sense of rapture by piling up lengthy, ecstatic sentences, Bukowski's use of language is terse, laced with a brutal, mordant wit. 'The blankets had fallen off and I stared down at her white back, the shoulder blades sticking out as if they wanted to grow wings, poke through that skin. Little blades. She was helpless.'[9] Combining Kerouac's lyricism and Bukowski's harsh humour, Waits used both to shape his view of the world and his art. Both are imaginary father figures: 'I guess everybody, when you're young and you enter the arts ... [finds] father figures. For me it was more profound because I had no father figure – no operating father – so I found other men that supplied all that for me. I was looking for those guys all the time.'[10]

After the compromise of *Closing Time*, Waits was determined to be truer to his vision of himself as a Beat poet and work in more of a jazz idiom. The new album would contain songs depicting the street life he'd absorbed from reading Kerouac and Bukowski and observed at first hand in Los Angeles. Waits had long revered *Poetry for the Beat Generation* (1959), a record on which Kerouac declaimed his looping, rhythmic prose over simple jazz chords played by pianist Steve Allen. Waits told Jack Tempchin, a San Diego songwriter, about planning something similar, as 'he was getting more and more into this Beat thing.'[11]

Jack Kerouac at a poetry reading in New York, 1958.

55

The title of his new album came directly from Kerouac. Waits was driving with his friend, Bob Webb, first down Alvarado Street and then cruising along Hollywood Boulevard, mirroring the Beat writer's restless search for kicks and inspiration. In Kerouac's novel *Visions of Cody* (1972), his protagonist is 'hurrying for the big-traffic-ever-more-exciting, all-of-it-pouring into-town-Saturday night'.[12] Webb remembered how he and Waits were

> struck on Kerouac's concept of wanting to be at the center of Saturday night in America. We got caught up in that literary notion and decided that each of us would create something around the theme. I drove home and stayed up all night writing a short play about some denizens of a backstreet poolroom. Sometime after I left, Tom picked up a guitar and wrote the lyric and music for *The Heart of Saturday Night*. He had it the next day.[13]

Like Waits, David Geffen wasn't convinced by the 'folk' direction on *Closing Time*, believing the singer-songwriter's true instincts favoured a jazzier style. According to 'Bones' Howe, whom he approached as a possible new producer, Geffen thought 'Waits had a lot of jazz and beat influences that didn't come out on his first album.'[14] Geffen believed Howe would be a good fit for Waits since 'Bones had a background in jazz. I thought that he was a perfect mix of jazz and pop for Tom.'[15] When Geffen played Howe early demo tapes of Waits, the veteran producer thought 'This is a really interesting songwriter, great images and all that and just a hint of a jazz influence in it. I also heard traces of Jack Kerouac in there.'[16] When Howe first met Waits, they sat down together, and

> in ten minutes we bonded. He asked me about Jack Kerouac. When I was working as an engineer at Radio Recorders [Verve founder] Norman Granz once sent me a box of tapes

– recorded in a hotel room in Miami – of Jack Kerouac reading his material. It was wandering and meandering . . . So, I went through this whole thing and made an album out of it and I told Tom about it. I said, 'There are great things, great little short bits of poetry and long meanderings of wanderings.' He said: 'Did you know that he once made a record with Steve Allen?' I said, 'No . . . He said "I'll make you a tape of it." I knew, when we were going to trade tapes, that I'd made a friend.'[17]

Waits also liked Howe's story of the way he had been forced to record Ornette Coleman's *The Shape of Jazz to Come* at night since the great jazz musician was working as an elevator man in a Hollywood department store during the day.

The relationship Waits formed with Howe was to become one of the most central during his entire Los Angeles decade. The older man would produce the next seven albums for Waits; he also became a mentor for the young singer. 'I guess I was a father figure in a way. Tom was a lonely man at times. We had a real friendship as well as a working relationship. He'd talk to me about all kinds of stuff. I was a lot older than him, more experienced in the business, so I could help suggest things.'[18] When Howe discussed with Waits the sound for his new album, 'we decided what we wanted to do was to have a little band – horns and a rhythm section and stuff, not just do it guitar orientated. He thought that was great.'[19]

The recording sessions of *The Heart of Saturday Night* at Wally Heider Studios on Cahuenga Boulevard featured musicians whom Howe selected for their ability 'to improvise and play in different genres, particularly in jazz'.[20] For the pianist and arranger, Howe suggested Michael Melvoin, who had played with Sinatra and Peggy Lee, as well on the Beach Boys' iconic *Pet Sounds*. Back in the 1950s, Melvoin had accompanied the Beat poet Kenneth Rexroth, which impressed Waits. Howe knew Melvoin 'could take Tom's general instructions about the kind of sound he wanted and put it into musical form. We were working with a poet. Tom didn't care about the technical level of musical ability, he just wanted songs to have a certain feeling or colour-palate. This was a challenge for musicians who have that advanced technique.'[21] Melvoin knew he was dealing with an extraordinary talent. 'I'd describe [the lyrics] as top-rank American poetry . . . I was in the presence of one of the great Beat poets. I was amazed by the richness of Tom's work. The musical settings he was using reminded me of certain roots jazz experiences. I felt great affection for him personally and professionally. My enthusiasm was full blown right away.'[22]

Some musicians were confused by the young songwriter's 'Beat' appearance. Waits 'didn't look like the usual people you ran into, with his Salvation Army clothes, scruffy beard and kind of a beat-up hat and talking in a voice that you could barely understand,' thought Jim Hughart, the bassist. 'It took me a while to realize it wasn't costume, but just the way he was. I figured he couldn't be broke, and had, at least, a father who was in academia. He seemed to be living in self-imposed poverty.'[23] Waits stayed in his 'Beat' character throughout to hide his insecurity in front of such veteran musicians, but also because he was continuing to develop his persona during the album's recording, as Melvoin realized: 'I thought of Tom as a professional poet who was in character. He needed to be thought of as the character. It's where you and your body and your personal experience are the artifact.'

The Heart of Saturday Night is the album where Waits starts to find his distinctive Los Angeles voice, which deepens and growls; assorted characters and narrators begin to strut across the urban stage that he has given them. The album immediately differentiates itself from *Closing Time* with the opening track, 'New Coat of Paint'. Matching a sassy, New Orleans-style jazz piano, Waits adopts a 'Blacker' sound; Howe noted the way Waits absorbed some of the qualities of African American musicians. The song introduces the album's basic narrative of a long night's journey into loneliness. We start with the singer and his woman getting ready to go out; if she will wear a dress, he'll put on a tie. The evening seems ripe with bucolic promise; the couple will be able to laugh at their traditional lovers' symbol – a bloodshot moon resting in a sky the colour of Burgundy wine. However, as the album sinks deeper into the nightscape with each song, the drink will take hold. The listener, like the lovers, will end up chasing melancholy ghosts as dawn beckons.

Waits, although now ensconced in his Los Angeles world, glances back to his past. In 'San Diego Serenade' he declares that he never saw his hometown until he had stayed away too long. As a world-weary narrator, he has become a nocturnal figure, never seeing morning until he'd stayed up all night. The track 'Shiver Me Timbers' also harks back to San Diego days with a sailor about to leave port, abandoning the domesticity of friends and family. Waits invokes Jack London's novel *Martin Eden* (1909), as well as Captain Ahab from Melville's *Moby Dick* (1851) to give an epic, kaleidoscopic sweep. But the song's thrust of a young man setting out for adventure is very much a Beat sensibility. The image of clouds looming up as if they are newspaper headlines is straight out of Kerouac. Waits uses historical and literary references to underpin his song's evocation of the restless transience that defines the American soul. Originally a land of Eastern Seaboard communities, Waits infuses the idea of American seafaring with an awareness of the settlement of the virgin landmass; the Americans have colonized their subcontinent as if it were an inland ocean.

This period sea shanty is juxtaposed with the contemporary 'Diamonds on My Windshield', another song about capturing the sense of movement. This time Waits recalls his endless shuttling between LA and San Diego; how his regime of late nights and constant freeway driving makes him want to sing. The driver has to battle his way through hard rain falling along the I-5 interstate to Los Angeles. He visualizes Southern California's rolling hills and fields of concrete as the interstate signs appear and disappear overhead and he searches for the 101 – Hollywood's freeway. 'Diamonds on My Windshields' uses a staccato rhythm to mimic its highway odyssey. With glimpses of Californian place names and landscapes flashing past, the song feels the closest to the Kerouac-inspired jazz recitals that Waits wanted to emulate. In a radio interview, he told how he'd been freed up as a songwriter by being able to 'throw down some color and not worry about any sort of meter at all. Lately I seem to be more concerned with that than writing real songs.'[24] Effective in its simplicity, Waits's spoken-word delivery is accompanied by Hughart's taut bass and a light brush on drums, mimicking the looped shuffle of windscreen wipers. 'Diamonds on My Windshields' fits in with the album's sequence of songs about nightlife, but its semi-improvised style foreshadows the jazzier scat direction Waits would use on his next record, *Nighthawks at the Diner*.

The album's title track, '(Looking for) The Heart of Saturday Night', balances these loose, jazz elements with a gentler lyricism. Waits was a fan of Mose Allison, a blues pianist and singer. He thought Allison's taut songwriting was 'so damn stylized that you can't help but love him to death – he's like honey poured all over you'.[25] '(Looking for) The Heart of Saturday Night' has exactly that kind of honeyed softness in its lilting melody. Saturday night, Waits sings, carries a longed-for hope, the anticipation of romance. It'll be like nothing else in the person's life. Dedicated to pleasure, it's the reward for the weekly slog, an attempt to erase the rest of the week. It's another momentary celebration of the freedom to step into your car, take off into the neon-lit night to see what a sprawling city like LA can offer (echoing the earlier celebrations of 'Another Saturday Night' from Sam Cooke or 'Saturday Night at the Movies' by The Drifters).

Waits grounds the track with sound effects recorded from traffic on Cahuenga Boulevard (he and Howe had set up a tape recorder outside the studio to capture car horns during rush hour).

Waits's imagination is drawn to the topographical: his songs feature locations or sounds with a geographical exactitude. The edited street noises add immediacy and authenticity. Waits contrasts this urgency with lyrics that become insecure or doubtful. The tear in the eye is one of melancholy. The song muses on whether it's really possible to turn it all around by combing one's hair or washing one's face. The simple repetition of stumbling suggests not. The heart of Saturday night is only a momentary release.

The album has a pleasing thematic unity; nearly all the songs are closely observed vignettes or imagistic fragments centred on Saturday night. The title track closes both sides of the record, returning as a refrain, 'The Ghosts of Saturday Night'. Like Kerouac, Waits aims to capture a mythic, poetic quality in the common urban life of Americans, despite knowing it to be insubstantial and elusive. He locates it through tiny auditory traces; he can hear pool balls crack or neon buzz. But Waits also knows such ghost-like epiphanies will escape him, just as they do for his song's characters.

The song 'Depot, Depot' has a liminal, shadowy feel. Hanging out at the Greyhound Bus terminal in Downtown LA, Waits is in complete limbo: he isn't coming or going. The city nightscape is imbued with an exactitude. The wind at midnight blows down Sixth Avenue, turning Waits blue with loneliness and the cold. The authorities had long neglected Downtown Los Angeles, letting the old centre become rundown and eerily deserted at night. Compared to the shiny photo-spots of Beverly Hills and Westside, whose air-brushed images the media loved to present to the tourists, Waits felt an affinity with Downtown, which was lost and broken. During a radio interview, he explained its appeal. 'Not many people go to DTLA. The *Free Press* did a big article called "Downtown LA; Who Needs It?" I live in Silverlake so I'm about ten minutes from Downtown. I go down there just to hang out. Not too many people live down there, they go there to work and hang out that's all.'[26] Waits also claimed the bus terminal was 'a great place to take a

People watching individual coin-operated television sets at the Greyhound Bus terminal, Downtown LA, 1969, referred to in the song 'Depot, Depot' from *The Heart of Saturday Night* (1974).

date', so long as you remembered to bring 'plenty of quarters for the TV chairs'.[27] There were fifty coin-operated Tel-a-Chairs at the Greyhound Terminal on Sixth Avenue, right next to Downtown's Skid Row. In the song, Waits namechecks himself as a peeping Tom, a voyeur in need of a peephole. It's another of Waits's typical paradoxes; he can't make any romantic connection at a place that exists solely for connections; he goes to a terminus but finds only immobility and stasis; he sings about a destination, which is no place to go.

The songs on *The Heart of Saturday Night* are supple enough to contrast and blend into each other. Mike Melvoin recalled how 'material from one song could appear magically in another so that the barriers even between songs were transgressed.'[28] Compared to the lonely protagonist of 'Depot, Depot', the mouthy narrator of 'Fumblin' with the Blues' is a voracious sexual braggart: he describes himself as a 'shimmy-shyster', who shoots pool while shaking his head. Such a boast has the swaggering essence of the whole song; full of innuendo ('head shaking' is a phallic reference), male unreliability and sexual desire as a game in which men and women circle each other ('shimmy' is a dance move mimicking intercourse). But this hard-drinking stock character, who boasts how all the bartenders know his name, is just as insecure as the loner at the bus terminal. Waits emphasizes how the misogynist's time is mainly spent with other men in darkened dives or pool halls, lamenting being forsaken by women, who are labelled as savage and cruel. With its New Orleans, R&B electric piano and delirious, scatting vocals, 'Fumblin' with the Blues' puts real musical distance between Waits and his Laurel Canyon country-rock contemporaries.

The Heart of Saturday Night, as a whole, lays out the terrain of Waits's alternative LA with its lowlife inhabitants: waitresses, drunks, truck drivers, street sweepers and gas-station attendants. The closing track, 'The Ghosts of Saturday Night (After Hours at Napoleone's Pizza House)', may seem a backward glance, a snapshot of his

Front cover of *The Heart of Saturday Night* (1974).

National City days. However, like the song's street sweeper, who clears up the debris of the night's revelry, Waits uses the track to round up his nocturnal vision of LA in an album filled with the lonely, the desperate and the hungover. Susan Michelson, a girlfriend of Waits who worked in a San Fernando Valley diner, may have been a model for Irene, the waitress who serves up a sobering cup of coffee to the bleary-eyed sailor, full of lust for her marmalade thighs. Namechecking Napoleone's Pizza Place anchors the closing track as if it is a memoir or personal reflection, and shows Waits turning autobiography into myth. 'I knew I was working with a genius. I knew this was of serious, real value. It wasn't ephemeral. Tom's work is intrinsically timeless,'[29] Melvoin declared. Some of the song's poetic observations are so concrete and particular that Sal Crivello, Napoleone's owner, swore he could authenticate them. But other images, like a town crier with nickels in his hands, or the used-car lot with its carpet of diamond flags fluttering in the breeze, have a timeless opacity. Waits ends with simple, universal images. The final edition of the newspaper reaches the stand as dawn breaks.

The back cover of *Heart of Saturday Night* portrays a drunk-looking Waits leaning on a newspaper stand. The grainy black-and-white photographs on the back have a realistic quality – in marked contrast to the full-colour painted artwork on the front. Here a dazed-looking Waits stands smoking in front of a neon-lit cocktail lounge at closing time. We're still in Los Angeles, but now it's also noir-land, as the lurid light spills out over the sidewalk. A blonde hooker eyes Waits up; he plays with his ear and looks down to his feet. It's unclear whether he's responding to the lady of the night or feigning indifference. The image captures his bashfulness in the presence of women. Whereas the stark naturalism of the photographic images grounds the album in everyday contemporary experience, the cover painting, with its retro-jazz-style, reflects Waits's enduring fondness for the 1950s and pays direct homage to Frank Sinatra's classic recording 'In the Wee Small Hours of the Morning' (1959). When *The Heart of Saturday Night* came out in 1974, the fashion was for cheese-cloth shirts. An 'old' Tom is pictured in a peaked hat, tie and pointed shoes, like a man out of time. When asked about *The Heart of Saturday Night* thirty years later, Waits responded with his trademark self-deprecation: 'It was very ill-formed, but I was trying. In those days I think I really wanted to see my head on somebody else's body.'[30]

The question of Waits's 1970s image is central to how he was channelling his diverse musical, cultural and personal influences. He began to create a composite identity or amalgam out of Beat writings, jazz and blues tradition, 1940s American film noir and pulp fiction, which he combined with his family background. Carey Driscoll, a friend from San Diego, saw Waits perform shortly before he recorded *The Heart of Saturday Night*. He understood the process by which Waits had gradually reinvented himself.

> He created a character for himself and then became that character. I wouldn't even say it was a conscious creation of a character; more that every day you become a little further to the left of dead center and before you know it you have become the Tom Waits character that the public knows rather than one his classmates knew.[31]

Waits's compulsive need to create and inhabit a character drew polarized reactions from those who knew him. Two friends, whom Waits would hang out with at the Troubadour club, couldn't be more opposed in their opinions. Paul Body, the doorman at the time, liked the way Waits's appearance was different. 'I thought he looked very hip. He looked like he'd stepped out of a Chandler novel. Everybody else was doing the sensitive singer-songwriter thing and he was more like the big city.'[32] Robert Marchese, the club manager in 1974, felt the scruffy lounge-singer act was inauthentic. 'I just thought Waits was fulla shit, which I would always tell him. You know the whole mystique of this funky dude and all that Charles Bukowski crap. Because nobody was really like that. He was basically a middle-class San Diego mom and pop schoolteacher kid. And it was his impression of how funky poor folk really are.'[33] Although Marchese is right about Waits's Whittier origins being middle-class, he misses the point of how the singer was creating an identity to define his version of LA. By becoming 'Tom Waits', the character who sought out Hollywood's grungy intersections or Downtown's desultory bus-terminals, and 'Tom Waits', a lounge-singer versed in the city's jazz and literary traditions, he wasn't patronizing down-and-outs or the poor. He was laying artistic claim to his own vision of Los Angeles, a very different one to the 1960s Beach Boys surf culture or the 1970s country-rock aesthetic of Laurel Canyon.

Mike Melvoin had a better sense of what Waits was attempting in his music and persona: 'I found it a lot easier to relate to Waits's view of LA than I did to the Eagles. The Eagles milieu was the milieu of the record industry itself.'[34] Waits had reason to be grateful to the Eagles – their cover of 'Ol' '55' had earned him much-needed royalties. But the depth of his hostility to their music ('The Eagles were about as exciting as watching paint dry. They don't have horse shit on their boots, just dogshit from Laurel Canyon'[35]) reveals the extent to which he wanted to head off in the opposite direction to their self-congratulatory comfort zone. Waits didn't want it to be easy. Following a Beat aesthetic, he believed the type of music he was exploring demanded that it should be difficult: artists needed to be tested against the harsh grain of experience in order to bring back insights from the frontline. 'I think I wanted some resistance. So that I could be genuinely committed to what I do. I didn't want it to be too easy. It wasn't.'[36]

Waits found more than enough of the hardship or resistance he felt he needed as a young musician on the road, touring the USA. Herb Cohen often booked him as an opening act for artists whose musical style was so different that their fans would boo him off stage. 'It was the old case of one-size-fits-all industry push on a new songwriter,' he told *Rolling Stone*. 'Throw you out there and see what you can do.'[37] Waits's time touring as support act for Frank Zappa and the Mothers of Invention was his most scarring experience. It should have been obvious to see that his jazz- and blues-based piano style wouldn't go down well with Zappa's acid-head audience. But Waits could be supplied cheaply since Cohen was also Zappa's manager. Zappa was once described as 'a confirmed misanthrope, who treated the outside world with extreme cynicism and scorn and restricted his human relations to as few people as possible'.[38] So, as Waits put it, Zappa had no compunctions about deploying him as a 'rectal thermometer' to gauge the audience. He 'was using me to take the temperature, sticking me up the butt of the cow and pulling me out'.[39] Unsurprisingly, Waits found performing his poetic ballads in front of thousands of people 'united together chanting "You suck" full volume in a hockey arena' deeply disturbing.[40] Some 25 years later he remained haunted by his experiences; 'the constant foot stomping and hand clapping, "We! Want! Frank!" It was like Frankenstein, with the torches, the whole thing.'[41] 'I still have nightmares about it. Frank shows up in my dreams, asking me how the crowd was . . . I've dreams where the piano is catching fire and the audience is coming at me with torches, dragging me away and beating me with sticks.'[42]

One way of dealing with potential hostility is to create a mask or a protective persona to act as a deflective shield. To some extent this is what Waits was doing with his marriage of Beatnik poet and drunken lounge singer. But such a dense mechanism could also alienate a less sophisticated public. What was unusual yet still comprehensible within an LA context could potentially baffle audiences elsewhere in the States. 'In cities like Minneapolis, Philadelphia, Boston and Denver I'm a very bizarre cultural phenomenon.'[43] Although Waits spent much of the 1970s on the road, his experience of touring points to how much he was part of Los Angeles. It was LA that gave Waits his cultural purchase, this unique blend of Beat and noir, jazz and blues, spoken word and guttural growl, urban poetry and cinematic image description. That's not to say Waits didn't make a big impression on audiences elsewhere. The best description of his early stage show was given by TV producer Don Roy King, who witnessed his performance in New York:

> Waits started his set, in character . . . a half-buzzed derelict with the voice of a bulldozer, slurring his way through a metaphor-rich stream of consciousness. I couldn't wait for him to drop the act, to see what he was really like, to hear how he sounded. Song after song went by. Each one rich and gutsy. Each with its own syncopated rich stutter-step of images and

dark-side tales. The moods swung and flipped and flayed. But Tom never changed. He played the role straight through, never looked at us, never smoothed out the gravel. The whole set was that derelict. A gutsy, shrewd act.[44]

Occasionally Waits was paired with artists who understood and related to his music and worldview. Fellow blues lover Bonnie Raitt found touring with him 'enriching . . . a portal to the world you didn't usually get to visit. He's a real original. He's a window on a scene we never got close to. He's able to make all the double-knits both tragic and romantic at the same time.'[45] Waits returned the favour by singing backing vocals for 'Sweet and Shiny Eyes', a track on Raitt's *Home Plate* album.

Waits wanted to use the restless impersonality of touring as part of his creative process. To be a good songwriter, he claimed it was necessary to be something of a private investigator, 'keeping your anonymity . . . so that you can go anywhere, any part of town, [and] sit in a corner', like a professional eavesdropper.[46] From his earliest days, he'd written down snatches of overheard conversations from bars, diners and pizza joints. Touring exposed him to the worn, lived-in textures of American lives. If one was to write with any depth, Waits felt, one needed to know whether there was gum under the table or how many cigarettes were in the ashtray. The drab, soiled locations he stayed in during his early tours fed directly into the world he was constructing. 'I would wind up in these very strange places – these rooms with stains on the wallpaper, foggy voices down the hall, sharing a bathroom with a guy with a hernia. I'd watch TV with old men in the lobby. I knew there was music in those places and stories. That's what I was lookin' for.'[47]

Twenty years earlier the photographer Robert Frank had also criss-crossed the USA, using his lens to capture the peculiar and the banal, the everyday tawdry appearance and essence of ordinary American lives. His photo essay *The Americans* punctured the glossy, upbeat images of the age of Eisenhower to reveal deep currents of anxiety and loneliness. In his introduction to the book, Jack Kerouac wrote how Frank had 'sucked a sad poem out of America and onto film. That crazy feeling in America when the sun is hot on the streets and the music comes out of the juke box or from a nearby funeral . . . that's what Robert Frank has captured.'[48] Waits, who was later photographed by Frank, loved *The Americans* and tried, in his writing, to emulate something of the book's approach. However, he was on the road not as a mute observer but an active performer. His conception of what went into the act of performance deepened through his experiences: 'I try to take myself up onstage and reach some level of spontaneity and just be as colorful and entertaining as I can without having to memorize it all. I want to avoid the unnaturalness of performing.'[49] He knew it was important to make an audience feel at ease but 'you can't get too loose. It's just kind of like sitting around in your living room but people don't have to pay in their living room and they want a spectacle.'[50] Patrick Humphries saw an early performance in which Waits was trying to balance a sense of natural presence with the need for entertaining spectacle:

> Onstage, Waits writhed, like the songs inside him were struggling to get out. And as he sang, those long white hands wrapped around the microphone stand, like they were sending out semaphore signals. Sometimes, Waits seemed in mid-seizure as he spasmed through a song. His stage wear was hat, black suit and a tie as thin as the sole of a hobo's boot. At times, Waits looked like a bookie, doing the tic-tac, with his arms flailing.[51]

Slapping down aggressive hecklers with his wit ('your opinions are like assholes, buddy, everybody's got one'[52]), the once shy songwriter had to work out how to project his inner confidence in his art. At times Waits drank heavily to deal with his anxiety at appearing in front of threatening audiences. Humphries believed that the regime of poor diet, chain-smoking and too much booze turned Waits from a 'sweet-voiced troubadour' into 'a gnarled and grizzled old soak'.[53] Waits acknowledged it had taken its toll: 'It was starting to wear on me, all the touring. I'd been travelling quite a bit, living in hotels, eating bad food, drinking a lot. Too much. There's a lifestyle that's there before you arrive, and you're introduced to it.'[54]

Relieved to be back in LA after extensive touring, Waits moved to 1309 North Coronado Street in Echo Park, a larger apartment than his tiny Silverlake cave. He described his new neighbourhood as 'Mexican Oriental', claiming he spent his free time at 'the Food House and the Casino club, the Mohawk . . . I play a lot of craps'.[55] Los Angeles was the city in which Waits felt completely at home, able to cruise its endless streets in his battered vintage car or hold court in one of its cheap diners. Drummer Bill Goodwin recalled how, after rehearsing, 'Tom and I would get into his Caddy – an old 55 Fleetwood four-door with fast food wrappers and newspapers on the back seat and just cruise around. I'd grown up in LA and we did what I'd done as a kid, which was cruise the Sunset Strip.'[56] Waits liked to visit the Paradise Motel on Sunset ('nice in summer when there's a carnival across the street') or Duke's, a coffee shop that lurked right under the Tropicana Motel on Santa Monica Boulevard.[57] Everyone went to Duke's, it was the place where LA musicians liked to hang out. Appropriately enough, Waits chose to be interviewed there by *Los Angeles Free Press* in 1974.

Tom Waits slouches on the corner stool, a shamble of news-papers at his feet. His place at the counter cluttered with utensils, ashtrays, and a package of bound volumes; a kind of spontaneous collage, he is, mirror to three months on the road, then home again on Santa Monica Boulevard, here underneath the Tropicana Motel, this bright, clattery, bustling, public dining room, his cap, vest and crumpled shirt, his eyes a little bleary, weary, wary – a sly grin rising from an empty coffee cup.[58]

As an image of Americana, the idea of the diner appealed to Waits as a cohering device for his next album. A confirmed night owl, he also wanted to continue his investigation into the allure and loneliness of the American night. 'The moon sure beats the hell out of the sun,' he told *Rolling Stone*. 'There's something illusionary about the night . . . your imagination is working over-time . . . there's food for thought at our finger-tips and it begs to be dealt with.'[59] His first shot at a title was 'Nighthawks on Easy Street'. Putting his two themes together he settled on *Nighthawks at the Diner*. It would be the most self-consciously 'Angeleno' of all his LA recordings.

Herb Cohen had first proposed a live album to capture the improvisational quality of Waits's Beat-inspired spoken-word performances. But producer 'Bones' Howe advocated the safety of a studio recording with 'an invited audience and a nightclub atmosphere'.[60] He felt it would create a better sounding record. Thus the 'hybrid' *Nighthawks at the Diner* was devised: a 'live' double album recorded over two nights but performed at a studio in Beverly Hills. Howe put the *Heart of Saturday Night* musicians back together; bassist Jim Hughart liked how the studio was transformed into 'a nightclub with checkerboard tablecloths and peanuts and pretzels and wine and beer . . . We did four shows each night and we changed the audience after each show.'[61] *Nighthawks*' studio audience was mainly music industry associates and friends, including a full contingent from the Troubadour. On the record, Waits is quick to acknowledge the local make-up of his public: 'Looks like a bona fide, high voltage, decked out in full regalia Angelino audience.'[62]

Cohen had also suggested using a stripper to open the shows and warm up the audience. Dwana, a 'classic old tassels-turner' with a murky Hollywood past, entered, heralded by the *Pink Panther* theme.[63] The old-time burlesque queen, according to Howe, 'put the

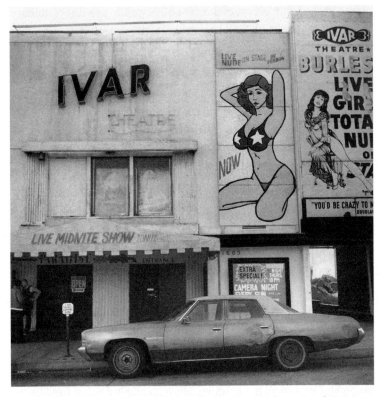

Ivar Theatre, 1987, a sleazy Los Angeles landmark and a favourite of Waits's.

room in exactly the right mood. Waits came out and sang "Emotional Weather Report". Then he turned around to face the band and read the classified section of the paper while they played. It was like Allen Ginsberg with a really, really good band.'[64] Mike Melvoin agreed: the live 'ambience was great and interaction between Tom and the band sensational'.[65]

The live recording allowed Waits to intersperse his 'recitals' with bawdy anecdotes about experiences in lowlife Hollywood haunts. He uses a stand-up or vaudeville-style delivery with risqué asides about his pent-up sexual frustration. The opening track, 'Emotional Weather Report', sets the tone as a portrait of shabby loneliness and a mood-picture of one of the sleaziest LA neighbourhoods. Waits picks out the intersection of Sunset and Alvarado as a direct homage to Charles Bukowski, who lived and wrote about the whores, junkies and alcoholics in his part of Downtown LA (a mile from the Dodgers' stadium). These crossroads also featured a celebrated open-all-hours corner-stand, linking it to the album's late-night diner theme. Waits's reference to a ticket-taker's frozen smile at the Ivar Theatre pays homage to his performing heroes Lenny Bruce and Lord Buckley, associated with this burlesque theatre. Many of the self-conscious local references are lost on anyone unfamiliar with East LA or old Hollywood haunts. The parochialism is intentional and, in one sense, the point. To create a diagnostic map of what he calls his interior emotional state, precarious and messed-up, Waits super-imposes himself onto the external topography of LA. He intertwines himself with the city in extended meteorological metaphors. Acting as a prologue for the album, 'Emotional Weather Report' reveals the extent to which Waits is attempting to weave his personal, musical life into the wider rhythms of the city. He tells his 'Nighthawk' audi-ence that he's a lonely nighthawk too. Staying out until the early hours or on the road for months at a time, Waits has nothing to come home to. Least of all in his fridge. His appetite for either food or sex remains distinctly unsatisfied. He resorts to flirting with divorced, middle-aged waitresses in late-night Los Angeles diners.

In 'On a Foggy Night', Waits uses a bare acoustic guitar to accompany his half-sung, half-scat vocals. The first in a series of film-noir songs, it explores Hollywood's use of LA as a site of betrayal, corruption and loneliness. Waits pretended it was a soundtrack to a 1940s thriller for which he'd just managed to finish the score a few weeks ago: 'One of those "triangle" films.' George Raft fights Fred MacMurray to win the heart of Rosalind Russell. The film ends with MacMurray driving a big old Plymouth along a foggy road with Raft stowed in the trunk 'with a little piece of his lapel sticking out ... and this song comes on the radio'.[66] The non-existent 'plot' of this song noir is the act of getting lost on an abandoned LA road.

From that point onwards, everything can unravel. In his introduction to the track, Waits riffs about getting into one of his much-cherished vintage autos, a '58 Buick Super, in the small hours of the morning. He mixes up precise Los Angeles street locations (Fifth and Vermont, Santa Monica Freeway, La Cienega turn-off) with an imaginary film scenario (a driver putting on the radio, lighting a cigarette and running into a fog bank) to create a journey to nowhere.

The song 'On a Foggy Night' turns this dark, imaginary journey into a metaphor for being out of one's depth in love. Waits name-checks Old Gold, a cigarette brand whose surreal commercials featured female models as life-size packets. The 'Dancing Butts'

Poster for *They Drive by Night* (1940, dir. Raoul Walsh). Waits's love of Hollywood noir is strongly present in his songs. 'On a Foggy Night', he claimed, was the soundtrack to an imaginary George Raft movie.

performed during ad breaks with their heads and bodies hidden, but their 'alluring' legs exposed. The song explores the connection between sexual insecurity and treachery in noir: the lover's abandonment meshes with that of constant criminal double-crossing. It's a world where the lone male figure is essentially lost. He is misinformed or misdirected. The interchange where he was heading

'Dancing Butts' advert for Old Gold cigarettes, cited by Waits in his introduction to 'On a Foggy Night', on *Nighthawks at the Diner* (1975).

Ed Ruscha, *Norm's, La Cienega, on Fire*, 1964, oil and pencil on canvas.
Waits was attracted to LA's diners as iconic emblems of Americana:
'I've had strange-looking pattie-melts at Norms,' introduction to
'Eggs and Sausage', *Nighthawks at the Diner*.

never intersected. Waits underscores the language of noir with its imagery of urban confusion. The protagonist, under a dense fog of uncertainty, cannot even tell whether he has arrived at a motel or not. Waits combines this existential unease with lush clichés of popular romantic desire. The narrator is marooned under an ominously bloodshot moon. Billy Wilder and Raymond Chandler's screenplay for *Double Indemnity* (based on James Cain's novel), which blends betrayal and erotic longing, was a favourite of Waits's. He knew the script by heart and, according to 'Chip' White, a drummer who toured with Waits, made sure 'the whole band knew it. One of us would take Fred MacMurray's character, another Barbara Stanwyck's. It's like learning the lines to a song.'[67]

The last song on side one, 'Eggs and Sausage (in a Cadillac with Susan Michelson)', quotes the album's title: 'Nighthawks at the Diner'. Waits describes a composite diner, whose late-night customers are seen as strangers who meet around the coffee urn. He addresses the live audience, who sit around chequered-cloth tables set up in the recording studio, as though they are the song's own cast of insomniacs or gypsy hacks. This blurring of artifice and

Edward Hopper, *Nighthawks*, 1942, oil on canvas. Waits references Hopper's painting of urban isolation in both the title and image for the album *Nighthawks at the Diner*.

reality is heightened by the way Waits deliberately namedrops local references to Los Angeles diners such as the Copper Penny and Norm's in his introductory spoken-word tour. Norm's restaurant on La Cienega Boulevard had been the subject of a painting by LA-based artist Ed Ruscha. Like Waits, Ruscha portrays Norm's as an icon of Americana, picturing it with the flat, graphic style he used for images of the Hollywood sign. Ruscha's *Norm's, La Cienega, on Fire* (1964) gives the building a surreal edge; it burns with a comic-book enthusiasm. Waits shares Ruscha's sense of bizarre and the comedic when he describes one particular dish as a strange-looking pattie-melt, but he also imbues his evocation of the diner with the aching loneliness of anonymity. Waits told local radio in 1975: 'After you hang around enough diners, it seems a place you always go when you're feeling like a refugee from a disconcerted love affair – you end up at a 24-hour place. In LA we got a place called Norms. All the losers are there, and the waitresses are all good looking.'[68]

Another iconic image which influenced the album is Edward Hopper's *Nighthawks* (1942), one of the most celebrated twentieth-century American paintings. Based on a restaurant in Greenwich

Village, *Nighthawks* has a universal urban quality that Waits appropriates. There's something melancholic and sinister about the distance between the figures in the painting. The hunched man in the foreground, who sits mysteriously with his back turned, gives the image a noir-like atmosphere (*The Killers*, a 1940s film noir based on a short story by Ernest Hemingway, begins and ends in a diner with the murder of its protagonist). The positions of the man and the woman who sits beside him indicate separation rather than companionship, dislocation not comfort. The painting's form is shaped by the movies; its widescreen frame is highly cinematic. The window, with its translucent glow, acts as a screen within a screen. The viewer is on the outside, looking in (Hopper provides no

Front cover of *Nighthawks at the Diner* (1975).

entrances to the diner); the voyeuristic act of watching the lives of others is foregrounded, as it is in cinema.

In a naturalistic photograph for *Nighthawks at the Diner*, Waits reworks Hopper's image. The singer is the focus; he sits at a table within the diner but looks directly at the camera outside. Waits includes himself within the scene and meets our gaze. The diner's interior texture and his insouciant stare make Waits customer and commentator. The photo, unlike the painting, shifts the focus back to us, the audience. But Hopper and Waits have the same central theme: the paradox of loneliness and isolation within the crowded 'modernist' city.

'Nighthawk Postcards (from Easy Street)' is the album's centre-piece, a spoken-word Beat poem lasting an epic 11 minutes – the type of lyrical riffing that Waits called 'an improvisational adventure into the bowels of the metropolitan region'.[69] Waits populates his night-world with con-men and cabbies, hustlers and suckers. He piles up image after image to flesh out his nocturnal urban rhapsody with exactitude. As in 'The Heart of Saturday Night' there's an extraordinary attention to auditory detail: the sound of rain-soaked tyres is compared to whispering brushes. But unlike 'Heart of Saturday Night', the lyrics become clotted and too rich; the moon, a standby in Waits's writing, is seen as both a cue-ball and a biscuit; it's yellow and buttery in a sky whose inky darkness is compared to obsidian. The rumbling of evening trains recalls the ghost of a recently departed jazz-drummer.

In 'Nighthawk Postcards' Waits tries to emulate Kerouac's Benzedrine-fuelled prose with its loose, looping lines. For both writers the night is pure music, an occasion to weave slang terminology and popular cultural allusions into their inspired riffing. Waits refers to Earl Scheib, the world's largest car-body-repair shop, and Texas Guinan, an actress who owned gin mills and whose trademark greeting was 'Hello Suckers'. The same woman is namechecked by Kerouac on his *Poetry for the Beat Generation* album. In 'Nighthawk

Postcards' Waits shares his literary father's failing: he overwrites. The track's excessive length and lack of musical development mean that the focus of the poetic imagery becomes blurred and lost. Other songs feel slight or generic, such as the blues lament 'Warm Beer and Cold Women'; Waits runs the risk of self-parody by playing another self-pitying boozer, listening to country and western music in a last-ditch saloon and claiming he doesn't fit in.

Nighthawks' studio audience, lubricated by drink, responds with beery enthusiasm. Waits knew he could always please his father, Frank, when he assumed the character of the lachrymose drinker: 'my old man likes me a lot. He sits right up front & tosses down some Scotch on the rocks and gets snookered and enjoys himself thoroughly. He says, "That's my son up there."'[70] 'Better Off without a Wife' also celebrates a sad male life with a list of reasons for staying single. This bachelor doesn't have to ask permission if he wants to go fishing. The self-mocking humour, present in the introduction and the song, allows the narrator to resemble a version of Waits himself. At this stage in his career, the amusing, half-drunk but literate loner was an image that he seemed content with: 'I've got a personality the audience likes. I'm like the guy they knew – someone raggedy and irresponsible – who never really amounted to much but was always good for a few laughs. A victim, just a victim. But I don't mind the image.'[71]

In a press release at the time, Waits gives a snapshot of his LA existence. The partial 'mask', which he had adopted, was still in its infancy, and hadn't yet started to harden or restrict him: 'I drink heavily on occasion and shoot a decent game of pool and my idea of a good time is a Tuesday evening at the Manhattan Club in Tijuana.' The City of Angels, real and imagined, fed his creativity: 'I am a dedicated Angeleno and have absolutely no intention of moving to a cabin in Colorado. I like smog, traffic, kinky people, car trouble, noisy neighbors, crowded bars, and spend most of my time in my car going to the movies.'[72]

3

Everything's Broken

All of a sudden it becomes your image and it's hard to tell
where the image stops, and you begin, or where you stop,
and the image begins.

– Tom Waits, 1976[1]

At first 'Spare Parts I (a Nocturnal Emission)' on *Nighthawks at the Diner* seems a familiar Waits portrait of nocturnal LA street-life; the Ivar Theatre features with its live shows, the dawn sky displaying the colour of Pepto-Bismol to the customary drunken tramps. But the track is also a departure. For once, Waits shared the songwriting credit with another musician – Chuck E. Weiss. The two men had become firm friends after an inauspicious first meeting outside a club in Denver. Weiss was wearing 'some platform shoes and a chinchilla coat, slipping on the ice in the street'. Waits, according to Weiss, 'looked at me like I was from outer space, man'.[2] At the time Weiss thought that the younger man 'was just some bum folk singer'.[3]

More grifter and good-time boy than dedicated musician, Weiss had hung out in Colorado's clubs since he was a teenager. He claimed he'd played drums with Lightnin' Hopkins and boasted to Waits he knew Muddy Waters, Howlin' Wolf and Willie Dixon; in fact, he'd tried to corner every blues legend who had passed through the Rocky Mountains state. When Weiss moved to Los Angeles, ostensibly with ambitions to make it as a singer, he crashed at Waits's East LA place. He quickly made himself an integral part of Waits's life, to the point of even collaborating on songs. Old friend Bobi Thomas found herself replaced by Weiss. 'When Chuck came into Tom's life, he and I stopped hanging out so exclusively together. Little by little they became inseparable.'[4] Paul Body knew Weiss from the Troubadour: 'Chuckie was sort of Tom's hanger-on . . . they were buddies, confidantes. Chuckie was the wilder of the two because Waits was still a kid. Weiss was a little older. He was a mentor for all of us in a way. He was the really street-smart guy . . . he knew all these guys and we didn't.'[5] Since first headlining at the Troubadour in August 1975, the club had become the musical home for Waits. He and Weiss formed the nucleus of a regular 'Troubadour gang', which included Paul Body, Robert Marchese, lighting engineer Artie Leichter and Louie Lista, a blues *aficionado*. Art Fein, a publicist for the Asylum label, recalled Waits's quick drunken wit. 'It was like having a standup comedian on call. I was having a drink with him one night and we saw some Beverly Hills girl with this rich guy. Tom lent over to me and said what he imagined the girl was saying to the guy: "Put your stiff throbbing C-note into my juicy bank account."'[6]

Herb Cohen had set up a few European shows for Waits in 1976, including appearances at Ronnie Scott's. In front of new foreign

Waits 'sharing a curbstone' with his Troubadour Crew (Paul Body, Robert Marchese and Chuck E. Weiss), named on 'Jitterbug Boy' from *Small Change*.

audiences, Waits was free to self-mythologize and tell tall tales about his exploits with the colourful characters he hung out with back in LA, like Chuck E. Weiss, who'd 'sell you a rat's asshole for an engagement ring'.[7] Eager, receptive British critics were regaled with 'stories of cruising LA in a big old honker of a car, equipped with a six pack of Miller High Life singing along to Ray Charles's "What'd I say?" Or James Brown begging "Please, please, please."'[8] Mick Brown, who saw Waits in London, wrote that he was 'the most delightful, original, outrageous, and courageous manipulator of musical mesmerization, you are likely to come across in a long time'.[9]

But Brown's colleagues in the music press were more divided in their opinion about Waits's authenticity. Some felt his refusal to comply with the expected standard-issue, denim-and-cowboy-shirt look and his adoption of a battered-suit and a down-and-out exterior meant he couldn't be genuine. For Brown, the question was irrelevant. 'The whole of rock and roll is a matter of self-invention anyway, so it never worried me or preoccupied me. What excited me was that he had immersed himself in this character to the point where it wasn't an act and had become an identity.'[10]

The year 1976 marked a turning point in the development of Waits's persona. Having created the character of drunken but witty songwriter on his *Nighthawks* album, Waits was expected to live up to it, on and offstage (which, in his roistering Troubadour circle, he could do). The 'stewed-bum' image had to be maintained and the role performed continuously. Waits's shambolic appearance on the *Mike Douglas Chat Show* in 1976 gives a flavour of how good he was at staying within character at all times. TV producer Don Roy King was a witness:

Mike was asking simple 'How did you get started' kinds of pre-written questions. But Tom was answering in this other-worldly or rather underworldly way. He was sputtering and wheezing and barely intelligible but genuinely poetic. Street poetic. His answers sounded like quotes from some Clifford Odets Depression era play. Mike was getting nervous. I was holding my breath. Tom was mesmerizing.[11]

However, in other interviews, Waits started to display the tell-tale signs of an inveterate boozer (repeating the same joke about curry three times to one journalist). Life on the road was made bearable by alcohol and he was touring heavily. 'When you're on the road doing clubs, it's hard to stay out of the bars in the afternoons,' he told *Downbeat* in June 1976. 'Then you hang around the club all night and you're up until dawn, so you hang around coffee shops. It stops being something you do – it becomes something you are.'[12] Waits deliberately chose to make life on tour difficult for himself by staying in dingy flophouses while putting the rest of the band up in decent hotels. When Ry Cooder asked him why he did that, Waits replied 'Well, nobody can complain.'[13] It was also part of his 'commitment' to a sense of vocation; the artist as 'doomed' romantic. He had always venerated the idea of the jazz musician as a heroic but wasted figure, playing until he dropped, sleeping in his clothes, rooming in dives and fuelled solely by drugs or alcohol. Waits risked becoming the victim of his own myth-making. Paul Body noticed how touring had changed Waits's voice when he returned to LA. 'When he went to Europe, something happened. When he came back it was different. He caught a cold or something and after that the voice was forever gravelly. The sweet voice that's on *Closing Time* and *Heart of Saturday Night* was gone.'[14]

The gentle, melodic tones of 'Ol' '55' may have disappeared, but Waits's gruffer voice, one which he often uses as an index of character, grew in power and presence as it deepened. In his notes to *Tom Waits: Used Songs, 1973–1980*, a collection of early Waits material, Hal Willner observed how Waits could make this huge sound, which issued forth from his small frame, seem literally terrifying. His voice was like 'something out of a Tex Avery/Max Fleischer cartoon. He seemed in pain, as if his body couldn't contain the sound.'[15] Journalist and friend David McGee, with whom Waits would hang out in New York, noticed his outlook started to darken at this time; he no longer seemed the 'bashful charmer' of earlier encounters. McGee believed that Waits was ambivalent about *Nighthawks at the Diner*, regarding it as 'a holding pattern and not the forward movement he felt his career needed'.[16] The seamless flow and integration of Los Angeles stories and anecdotes into his stage show had seemed like a departure, but Waits sensed the album lacked the quality songs to support what *Rolling Stone* described as his 'jive-talking, finger-popping . . . twitching mannerisms'.[17] Ideas about a new album had been forming; *Music to Seduce a Divorced Waitress By* was one putative title; *Pasties and a G-String, a Beer and a Cheap Shot* another, more salacious, suggestion. But it was the raw experience of witnessing a fresh murder scene that gave him the title and defining mood. Waits was out with David McGee when they stopped by a pizza parlour to find it blocked off with police tape. On the floor inside was the corpse of a Black teenager, dark blood pooling outwards, with his head beside a gumball machine. At the time Waits speculated as to whether the dead youth had got 'rained on' by the pizza man's .38. Later he admitted that 'I was scared shitless . . . Some guy had just shot him. He was sprawled right there against the wall.'[18] It became the genesis for 'Small Change (Got Rained on by His Own .38)', the brooding title track on the new album.

From the outset, there's a greater depth and darkness to the songs on *Small Change*; the lyrics have more immediacy or bite. Waits's newly ravaged voice on the opening track, 'Tom Traubert's Blues (Four Sheets to the Wind in Copenhagen)', growls out in suffering as though he bears an open wound. The pain and despair of urban isolation is self-inflicted – something the singer knows he has to pay for. Waits's drunken tramp feels abandoned in a place where everything seems broken. He is stranded, lost even to himself and knows there can never be a way back home – wherever

Morrison Hotel, 1969, a Downtown LA hostel right next to where Waits drank and talked with down-and-outs, inspiring the track 'Tom Traubert's Blues' from *Small Change* (1976).

that might be. Although it's subtitled 'Four Sheets to the Wind in Copenhagen' and references the sleazy side of that city, the song is deeply imbued with the desolation of Los Angeles. Its origin lies in the Skid Row area of Downtown LA, between Fifth and Main (near a low-rent hostel for transients that The Doors used as the cover photograph for their album *Morrison Hotel*). Waits deliberately chose to hang out there because he knew that 'every-one of the down-and-outs had their own story', as he recounted to Bones Howe. He took a bus downtown, 'found a liquor store, bought a pint of rye, squatted down in the street and talked to everybody that came by'.[19] Afterwards Waits returned home, threw up and immediately wrote 'Tom Traubert's Blues'.

Avoiding sentimentality in his treatment of the plight of the homeless drunk, Waits conveys the weight of human suffering through sharp, concrete images; the tramps wear shirts stained with whisky and blood; they've lost everything, even their St Christopher medals. Waits wants to make the listener understand what these old men in wheelchairs know: namely how the world for the homeless can shrink to the size of a battered old suitcase. The psychological wounds, which have brought them so low, will never heal. Waits's unsparing portrait of men clinging to the last vestiges of their dignity emphasizes their continuing humanity. He achieves this balance by contrasting his vocal harshness with the soft lilt of a classic melody, borrowed from the Australian anthem 'Waltzing Matilda'.

Waits probably first heard the song on Harry Belafonte's *Streets I Have Walked* (1963), an album owned by his father (that other 'lost' drinker). 'Waltzing Matilda' is the story of a tramp with a sack on his back who stops by a waterhole and waits for his kettle to boil. He steals a sheep, stuffs it in his knapsack and evades the law by drowning himself. Although the song narrates the tale of a suicide, the jaunty waltzing tune makes it feel celebratory.

Waits uses the theme to transpose and universalize LA's Skid Row experience: 'When you're "waltzing Matilda", you're on the road. You're not with your girlfriend, you're on the bum.'[20] In other words, a place where everything's broken is somewhere that anyone can end up.

The next track, 'Step Right Up', demonstrates a huge shift in vocal register. Waits is now transformed into a loquacious, hustling conman, selling a miracle product, a universal panacea. He presents himself as a classic American archetype, the snake-oil salesman whose success rests on the persuasive inflections of his voice. Drawing on deep-throated DJs, family preachers and the fairground barkers of his adolescence, Waits creates his own rhythmic patter, showing how adept he is at making language its own musical instrument. He switches his previous command of Beat jive-talk into an indictment of advertising. The United States was such a 'product-oriented society', Waits once stated, that even music can become another commodity. 'All that jargon we hear in the music industry is just like what you hear in restaurant or casket business. Instead of spouting my views in *Scientific American* to our product-oriented society, I wrote "Step Right Up."'[21] The product Waits is selling is left deliberately vague. It can fillet or chop, dice or slice. It will even mow the lawn or pick the kids up from school. This ultimate miracle commodity is so all-encompassing that no one can work out exactly what's being sold. Yet, ironically, it's still a must-have item.

The subject of 'Jitterbug Boy' is another American archetype, the buttonholing drunk with a never-ending supply of tall tales. The song's extended subtitle is a roll call: 'Sharing a Curbstone with Chuck E. Weiss, Robert Marchese, Paul Body and the Mug and Artie.' Waits pays an affectionate, inebriated tribute to his Troubadour gang with their wild antics and 'wilder' stories. Although he includes himself in the group portrait, Waits revealed that the garrulous 'Jitterbug Boy' was based on 'a buddy-wuddy of mine, his name is Chuck E. Weiss . . . the kind of guy who would steal his own car . . . One of those guys who has been everywhere, knows everything, done everything, you know.'[22] In the song, the arch-boaster has slept with Marilyn Monroe, boxed with Rocky Marciano and taught Louis Armstrong and Minnesota Fats everything they knew. The title refers to a jitterbug dance from the swing era, which Waits acknowledges with a piano homage to George Gershwin's 'I Got Plenty of Nothin'' and vocal scatting in honour of Satchmo. The song is another light-hearted commentary on the effects of drinking. The juddering 1930s dance movements were said to resemble alcoholic 'jitters', as Cab Calloway's 'Call of the Jitterbug' makes clear:

If you'd like to be a jitterbug
First thing you must do is get a jug
Put whisky, wine and gin within,
And shake it all up and then begin.
Grab a cup and start to toss
You are drinking jitter sauce!
Don't you worry, you just mug,
Then you'll become a jitterbug.[23]

'The Piano Has Been Drinking (Not Me)' is a further comic exploration of the archetypal drunken crooner. Waits parodies his own laconic bar-room-philosopher act, getting ever more soused in joints so dark one can't locate a waitress with a Geiger counter, and the spotlight is so harsh that it resembles a prison breakout. But another track on *Small Change*, 'Bad Liver and a Broken Heart (in Lowell)', shows Waits trying to change his music and thinking.

> I put a lot into that: I tried to resolve this cocktail-lounge, maudlin, crying-into-your-beer image that I have. I was really starting to believe there was something amusing and wonderfully American about being a drunk. There ain't nothing funny about a drunk. I ended up telling myself to cut that shit out. On top of everything else, talking about boozing substantiates the rumours that people hear about you and people hear that I'm a drunk.[24]

Waits, the hard-drinking son of a hard-drinking father, knew all there was to know about the attraction of alcohol; how it could bring both a heightened awareness and an increasing self-pity with its alluring mixture of romanticism and cynicism. He opens 'Bad Liver and a Broken Heart' with a snatch of 'As Time Goes By' from *Casablanca*, a homage to Humphrey Bogart's iconic portrayal of Rick, the bar owner slumped in front of a piano with his heart broken by Ingrid Bergman. Bogart (who was also the definitive Philip Marlowe, Raymond Chandler's hard-boiled private eye) imbues Rick's character with a drinker's trademark cynical exterior (disappointment at the world's failure to measure up) and a sentimental interior (believing that he was once 'truly' loved). The subtitle '(in Lowell)' is a clue to how Waits uses the song as a personal reality check; the pressing need to avoid romanticizing drinking in his own work. Lowell was the family home of the booze-ravaged Jack Kerouac, Waits's literary father figure. Alcohol not only killed the older writer but led to the disintegration of Kerouac's literary ability during the last decade of his life.

There is a subtle link to that other alcoholic writer, F. Scott Fitzgerald, in Waits's first full tribute to Hollywood noir, 'Invitation to the Blues'. The song features a waitress, who might work at Schwab's Pharmacy, a popular Hollywood soda fountain parlour on Sunset Boulevard. This was where Fitzgerald suffered his first heart attack while buying cigarettes. Schwab's advertised itself as the place where movie stars like Lana Turner were discovered. The song's female figure resembles glamorous 1940s actress Rita Hayworth, known for playing both *femmes fatales* and waitresses. Abandoned by her sugar daddy for a socialite, the young woman is hanging on, determined to make it somehow. Perhaps she'll be spotted. Billy Wilder created a replica of Schwab's on the Paramount lot for *Sunset Boulevard* (1950), his satiric attack on Hollywood's values. The disillusioned writer, played by William Holden, goes there after he is rejected by the studio: 'Schwab's was kind of a combination office,

Schwab's drugstore in Hollywood, c. 1980, cited in 'An Invitation to the Blues', from *Foreign Affairs* (1977).

coffee klatch and waiting room. Waiting, waiting, waiting for the gravy train.'[25] Waits also imbues his song with a sense of limbo, as the man tries to puzzle out the intentions of the waitress (who is also the *femme fatale*): whether she is single and for real. The sense of inevitability in the melody is underlined by use of the title as a refrain. The man will accept her offer or 'invitation', which, of course, will prove to be a one-way ticket to misery.

The *femme fatale* is one of the most stereotypical elements of film noir. In the work of writers such as Mickey Spillane, women are always to be feared for their ability to seduce and control the men under their spell, and, inevitably, deceive them. Waits, who had read his fair share of pulp fiction, has a fascination with this dubious side of the genre, its obsession with loose or devious women. In the song 'Pasties and a G-String (at the Two O'Clock Club)' he pays tribute to the sleazy atmosphere of American strip clubs. The Two O'Clock Club was an old-style Burlesque club owned by an actress called Bella Fleming. Known by her stage name, Blaze Star, she had gained notoriety for her affair with corrupt Louisiana governor Earl Long (played by Paul Newman in a studio biopic in 1989 called *Blaze*). Waits also mentions Chesty Morgan, a 1960s striptease artist who had an acting career. His witty lyrics describe and embody the lascivious desperation of guys who watch in the dark and get erections, which, Waits suggests, are harder than Chinese algebra. The song revels in its own hot-under-the-collar verbal evocation of sleaze, with a heightened use of poetic alliteration and repetition: the word nape is put with neck, lips are made to rhyme with hips. There's a deliberate mimicking of 'girlie' magazine vocabulary, mixing up sexual innuendoes with automobile slang; the description of baby moons refers to breasts or buttocks as well as the shiny hubcaps of cars. The woman is objectified to the point of resembling a sticky bun or confectionary, all creamy and sugared. The jazz backbeat, to which strippers would twirl their tassels, is mirrored by solo accompaniment from bebop drummer Shelly Manne. Waits's evocation of

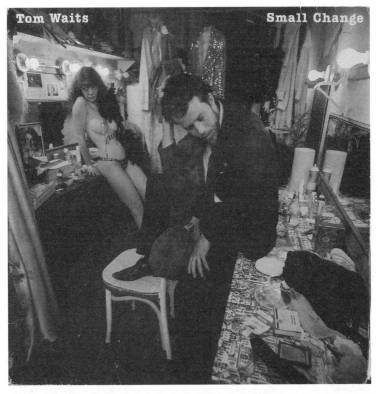

Front cover of *Small Change* (1976).

an American strip club is also enhanced by the album's seedy cover image. A crumpled Waits is holed up backstage in a striptease artist's dressing room, littered with make-up, pill bottles and dildos. The photograph's soiled quality has a greater naturalism than the *Nighthawks* cover image. A bored and disinterested stripper, scantily clad in pasties and a G-string, looks away from Waits. He resembles a seedy private eye, a dishevelled 1970s Philip Marlowe, Raymond Chandler's white knight who moves through a 1940s Los Angeles, awash with political and sexual corruption. Martin Scorsese's film *Taxi Driver*, which reworks a version of the alienated male adrift in a sea of vice, was released in 1976 (the same year as *Small Change*). Scorsese's protagonist, like one of Waits's disillusioned male loners, is also viewed via a classic film noir perspective, highlighting his deeply problematic relationship with women.

An animated short, made to accompany the track 'The One That Got Away', also plays with another 'fantasy' image of a stripper. It's a cartoon noir where, this time, a woman of the night pursues a bashful Waits down neon-bathed streets, eager to wrap herself around him. Once more, like 'Invitation to the Blues', we're in Holly-wood noir-land, full of broken dreams and guilty menace. 'The One That Got Away' features a litany of colourful characters, losers sunk in self-pity for missing the one chance that would have put them on 'Easy Street': Costello, once champion at St Moritz Hotel (a Sunset Strip drinking hole patronized by Waits and Bukowski), pianist Andre, who should've got Dooley Wilson's role in *Casablanca*, and a louche character in a snakeskin shirt, who looks like Vincent Price (the bisexual horror-movie actor known for his role in the 1960 screen version of Edgar Allan Poe's *The Fall of the House of Usher*). The song's narrator loses everything: his car keys, pride and sense of equilibrium. 'The One That Got Away' is another embittered post-card to LA from Waits, with allusions to favourite landmarks: Ben Franks, a coffee shop and gathering spot for the bohemian set in the 1950s; the Ivar Theatre, a Hollywood theatre that had become a strip joint full of transgender people; the Sewers of Paris, a shady night-club with a clientele of 'ageing closet cases, servicemen, runaways fresh from the Greyhound Bus Station who had come to Hollywood to become famous, thugs fresh out of jail and drag queens of any race'.[26] Waits brilliantly introduces semi-obscure slang vocabulary to give the track the real feel of a slice of crime-scene noir. A coffin is described as a wooden kimono and the grave as a deep-six holiday. To escape is to do a Houdini and to become enraged is jumping salty. Best of all, midnight on Friday becomes the far more ominous and poetic time of 'half-past the unlucky'.

The first of Waits's albums to create a complete amalgam, *Small Change* is made up of characters whose dreams have been shattered, references to movies from Hollywood's golden age, pulp-fiction phrases lifted from the pages of Raymond Chandler or Dashiell Hammett, Damon Runyon or Nelson Algren, and sordid images of lowlife 1970s LA. Waits's dark re-imagining of Los Angeles draws on its self-image as the city of dreams, where the movies act as a lure and a projection of the American dreamscape. The album is filled with a parade of dreamers, who left their home in the Midwest or the Deep South to take a Greyhound straight for LA. After experiencing the City of Angels, they face the growing realization that 'this is it.' No matter how desperate these failed musicians, actors, waitresses and strippers become, they'll never amount to anything more than *Small Change*. Eavesdropping like a private eye, Waits had observed and listened to the stories of his city. 'The girls come in from Nebraska, wanna be in motion pictures, Where I live I hear a lot of them stories. They end up on their backs in one of the rooms. There's a lot of sadness. I see a lot from where I'm living. I don't see much hope. Can't go any further West.'[27]

The title track, 'Small Change (Got Rained on with His Own .38)', is the darkest and most intense song on the album; a miniature pulp fiction in its own right. It tells of the death of a small-time gangster named Small Change, who, as he leaves a diner in a quiet part of the city, on his way to the racetrack, is shot with his own gun. Waits draws on his experience of witnessing the murder scene of a young Black man. He was struck by the blasé reaction of the police, for whom such killing was a mundane, daily reality. 'The cops were sitting around saying "Hey Charlie, where you goin' on your vacation?" And there's this little cat oozin' life, lyin' in his own blood.'[28] In the song the police talk among themselves, making dirty jokes about Seattle whorehouses while the witnesses are too fearful to speak. In such a climate, even the fire hydrants will plead the fifth amendment.

By being elliptical with the narrative, filtering it through the other characters' reactions, Waits creates depth through his visual precision; he makes all the details count. The whores' mouths resemble razor blades and their eyes, stiletto heels; naked mannequins stand like silent witnesses with Cheshire-cat grins in the bargain store across the street; a newsboy steals Small Change's pork-pie hat; no one bothers to close the dead man's eyes as his blood seeps over the linoleum floor towards a jukebox. The scene's cinematic quality is enhanced by the use of extreme close-ups; a racing form sticks out from his pocket, marked for 'Blue Boots'; his fist is still closed tight round a $5 bill. Waits never directly refers to the real victim but picks up on how his head lay next to a gumball machine. There'll be no more chewing gum or baseball cards for Small Change: the machine becomes an epitaph.

'Small Change' marks a real advance in Waits's songwriting. He claimed that he didn't feel completely confident in his craft until after he had composed this song. Invoking the period fiction of Chandler or Hammett, he is able to deepen his portrait of contemporary violence and sleaze. Paradoxically, the noir framing helps Waits to both distance the real killing and bring it into sharp focus. Like the hyper-reality of a crime scene in Wegee's high-contrast flash photographs, Waits forces us to see the blood-soaked sidewalk before it is hosed down.

Musically, Waits also deepens his persona on the album. The wounded voice he described as 'oiled with paint stripper straight from a broken bottle and caressed by the fumes of uncut Turkish rolled in sandpaper' gives greater texture to his vocals.[29] He chose to play piano himself on the recordings, dropping the accomplished Mike Melvoin, who sensed that Waits had felt cramped in some way. 'Tom liked the way he played for himself. It was easier and more satisfying too, not to have some jazz pianist with a character of his own on board.'[30] Bones Howe set up the recording sessions at Wally Heider Studios on Cahuenga Boulevard in the way he used to make jazz records in the 1950s: more about getting a great single take than having a lot of tracks to mix. The result was what Waits considered the best of his early albums. 'I'd say there's probably more songs off

Small Change that I continued to play on the road and that endured. Some songs you may write and record, but you may never sing them again. Others you sing every night and try and figure out what they mean.'[31] *Small Change* was a rare commercial as well as critical success for Waits. He could now afford to put together a regular band, whom he called The Nocturnal Emissions (a nod to the track he co-wrote with Chuck E. Weiss), for extensive touring. He chose Fitz Jenkins on upright bass, Frank Vicari on tenor sax and Chip White on drums; 'I got a Black bass player, a Sicilian tenor and a Cherokee and African drummer. We can go into any neighbourhood in the world and hang out.'[32] At a Nocturnal Emissions gig in Pittsburgh, they were supported by none other than Bukowski, whom Waits viewed as a kind of mentor. 'He was like a big bear. He had this enormous head, as big as Frankenstein. He had a big presence and huge shoulders, and that face that looks like a mask, a scary mask. I was fascinated with him.'[33] Despite the importance of Bukowski's influence on his songwriting, Waits held back in his presence, refraining from grilling the grizzled writer, who was old enough to be his father. 'I didn't want to be too cloying or inquisitive. He had his own world, his own life.'[34] Chip White, the drummer, recalled how, at the gig, Bukowski had brought his beer cooler onto the stage and downed one can after another without saying a word. 'Finally, someone yelled out, "Hey man, say something!" Bukowski burped in response and began reading.'[35]

There's a sense of Waits raising the stakes with *Small Change*, seeing it as a turning point in his musical and personal life. He told his friend David McGee, who was writing about him for *Rolling Stone*: 'I've got to clinch something before we get out of the Seventies. I've got a lot invested in this whole thing . . . in my development as a writer. I don't want to be a has-been before I have even arrived.'[36] Waits's anxiety about his future can be detected in his remarks about the treatment of fellow singer-songwriter Mose Allison, one of his icons. Allison, despite his songwriting talent and previous musical achievements, had been dropped by his record label, Waits told the *New York Times*, 'because people couldn't put an easy tag on him. Well, he's not exactly a blues singer. And he's not really progressive jazz, exactly, and he's not pop. So, they get nervous and drop him.'[37] Waits committed himself to intensifying his approach, going deeper into his self-appointed role as bard of the streets. Another important measure of success, he told McGee, was whether 'my old man thinks what I'm doing is good'.[38] Waits was still seeking the approval of Frank, the father who had abandoned his family; his creativity was still driven in part by a need for respect from an alcoholic father whose self-inflicted damage he could both chronicle and copy. In 'Tom Traubert's Blues', Waits makes the narrator (called Tom) ask a character named Frank whether he can borrow a couple of bucks from him. Waits defined his creative ambitions as personal and modest. 'For me it's more of an internal thing. I'm just trying to do something that I can be proud of, trying to create something that wasn't there before. My wants and needs are small and limited. I'm not going into real estate or buying oil wells or becoming a slumlord.'[39] Eschewing the options of becoming a slumlord or oil baron, Waits chose to intensify his experience of the lowlife that he wanted to explore in his writing; living in 'self-imposed poverty', he moved into the Tropicana Motel. 'You could imagine you were living like the Orwell book *Down and Out in Paris and London*. You could imagine you were in some place that was constantly sweating and heaving and offering up ideas. I was trying to have a genuine authentic artistic experience. That was what I wanted.'[40]

Owned by Sandy Koufax, a pitcher for the LA Dodgers in the early 1960s, the Tropicana had been a favoured location for musicians, actors and assorted characters before Waits moved in. Paul Morrissey had shot his 'trash' movie, *Andy Warhol's Heat* (1972), a pastiche of Billy Wilder's *Sunset Boulevard*, at the Tropicana. In the film the sexually predatory motel manager, played by Pat Ast, declares: 'I have a lot of show folks staying here – you know, musicians and stuff. But don't get the wrong idea, you know, I run a respectable place.'[41]

Chuck E. Weiss had become a resident in 1975 purely on the grounds that the motel was right next to Duke's, his favourite coffee shop and hangout: 'I was driving from Silverlake to Dukes every day to eat. So, I thought "I'll just move there."'[42] The Tropicana had attracted a varied bohemian clientele back in the 1960s. Jim Morrison liked to crash at the 'Top Trop', as it was known, during the writing and recording of his song noir, 'LA Woman'. At different times the motel had housed Van Morrison, Bob Marley and the Wailers, Sly and the Family Stone, Sam Shepard and Alice Cooper. It was where Stevie Nicks and Lindsay Buckingham had holed up on arriving in Hollywood. The name 'Tropicana' evoked images of well-being with freshly squeezed citrus fruit. In reality it was 'a Motel 6 with shag carpeting. Barely a working TV – old cigarette butt-holes burned into different things,' as a veteran resident put it. The main attraction lay in how 'you could mingle with the famous and infamous'.[43] The Top Trop's rundown gutter-chic made it a West Coast equivalent of New York's Chelsea Hotel.

Waits was less interested in the music industry types than the fact it had 'started out as a nine-dollar-a-night motel for Fuller Brush salesmen. It wasn't really very musical first time I came there, and it slowly got a reputation for bands.'[44] He liked the motel's unhealthy banality; the 'nice little cigarette machine in the lobby and the swimming pool that was painted black'.[45] Waits claimed the darkened kidney-bean-shaped pool, which resembled a diseased lung, matched his mood most of the time. It was unclear whether the pool had been painted black to avoid cleaning or to hide the stains created by bands throwing in the rusty patio furniture. The Tropicana was the ideal stage and laboratory at this point in his LA life. To live in a motel was a statement of anti-domesticity; to make your home in a place that could never be home, whose identity was one of transience and restlessness. As a 'non-restful' resting

The New York Dolls at the Tropicana Motel, 1973, photograph by Bob Gruen.

place, the Top Trop perfectly embodied his shifting, treacherous noir (in 'On a Foggy Night' the narrator cannot tell whether it really is a road motel); it's a place where everything, the location and all relationships, seems provisional and unreliable.

According to Rick Dubov, who knew them both, Waits and Weiss had 'become like twins, totally inseparable';[46] Waits took a bungalow, which adjoined Weiss's at the rear of the motel.

Paul Body recalled the state of Waits's bungalow. 'You'd enter from the back, and it was like a little house. You couldn't see anything because it was filled up with junk that you could barely maneuver through.'[47] Squeezing a Steinway upright piano into his apartment by sawing off a draining board and demolishing a broom cupboard, Waits made the two rooms a space of creative chaos; emblematic of his state of mind and assumed identity. Charles Schwab, in his notes for *Used Songs*, recalled opening the fridge for a beer only to find 'a claw hammer, a small jar of artichoke hearts, an old parking ticket, and a can of roof cement'.[48] Director John Lamb navigated the albums and ashtrays, books and beer cans:

> He had two adjoining rooms with the common wall removed to make the joint bigger. Newspapers, manuscripts, ash trays and empties cluttered up the digs about waist to shoulder high throughout. A path literally led from the fridge to the piano – the piano to the couch . . . couch to the bedroom and so on. If it was foliage, you would have to hack your way through . . . the path was just wide enough to maneuver your torso through, sometimes having to turn sideways to navigate a right turn.[49]

Waits had started an unlikely on-and-off affair with Bette Midler, the singer and actress. Seeing him perform for the first time at a New York club, she 'fell in love with him on the spot' and headed straight for his dressing room to offer her congratulations and advice: 'You need some feathers, girls, hula skirts, and beaded curtains. Then you might have something.'[50] Midler revealed to journalist Grover Lewis how Waits had been too embarrassed to invite her back to his bungalow: 'Tom lives knee-deep in grunge. I grew up in lots of clutter, and delicate I ain't, so I kept after him until he finally invited me over.'[51]

The Tropicana offered Waits the opposite of a refuge; it was a highly public place, where he could live out his persona as the chronicler of LA's lowlife. His residency was part of a decision to push deeper into his role, rejecting the pastoral privacy of the Laurel Canyon 'cabin' lifestyle. Waits asserted different criteria for success; for him 'life in the streets was more fascinating.'[52] He told the *Los Angeles Times* that 'you almost have to create situations in order to write about them. So, I live in a state of self-imposed poverty.'[53] Waits's famed Tropicana tenure was part of a 24-hour performance-art act on a stage, which spilled out onto the street, to Duke's and Santa Monica Boulevard. Tom Nolan watched him 'outside Duke's one morning about eleven o'clock. He had this long black car parked next to the curb and he's got the hood up and his sleeves rolled up and he's taking the carburetor apart. He was in his own movie and you wanted to buy a ticket.' It was as if he'd extended the fellowship of 'sharing a curb' with his Troubadour roisterers to all aspects of his life. Michael Hacker saw him 'sitting on the sidewalk like a wino. He was full-on in his persona and I thought "Here's this minor rock figure and he's literally sitting on the curb, just hanging out."'[54]

Waits's days and nights hanging out in West Hollywood can be seen as a refreshing refusal to put distance between himself and his audience. But it also derives from a romantic conception of the artist's sensibility, an attempt to create an organic connection between the work and the lived experience. His vintage cars were like accessories; their state as legendary as his apartment, their back seats stuffed with books, newspapers and Styrofoam cups. Jerry Yester remembers helping Waits find a pristine 1952 Buick. Within two weeks he had reduced it to a trash mobile. 'Every wrapper was still in the car and he kind of revelled in that. He said, "A car is like a suit. It's gotta' fit real well."'[55]

Although it's often claimed that Waits avoided narcotics, much preferring alcohol, Chuck E. Weiss certainly used the Tropicana as part of his drug-fuelled lifestyle. 'Chuckie was doing a lot of drugs then. Chuckie didn't drink but he did anything else he could get his hands on,'[56] according to Robert Marchese, the Troubadour manager. Given how intertwined the two men's lives had become, how Waits and Weiss, living cheek-by-jowl, liked to party together, it's reasonable to assume they weren't averse to sharing drugs at times. But Weiss was a hanger, as Howe put it, pure and simple, while Waits wanted 'somebody to hang-out with'.[57] Marchese saw how, behind the mask of a street guy, Waits was a highly focused workaholic. 'Tom wrote constantly. He practiced a lot. He was on the scene and all that, but he knew when it was time to work. Tom wanted to be a star. Chuckie was the farthest thing from that. He had no organizational skills and no direction.'[58]

The 'workaholic' Waits pressed on, presenting Howe with demo tracks for a new album. When Howe listened to the material, he immediately saw it as 'a black-and-white movie'.[59] On tour Waits had been spending a lot of time watching Hollywood thrillers. One late-night movie viewing on his hotel TV was interrupted when an unknown couple entered the room and refused to leave; it felt like the noir had spilled out of the film and into his life (Waits had to give the grifters money for another room before he could return to his movie). To deepen the noir approach witnessed in *Small Change*, Waits decided to create more cinematic settings or soundscapes for his songs. Howe brought in Bob Alcivar (who had worked with Lord Buckley) to score the tracks as if they were mini movies. Alcivar found collaborating with Waits 'a joy'.[60] His jazz arrangement of 'Potter's Field', a nine-minute spoken-word piece, translates Wait's film-noir obsessions perfectly. The scene-setting orchestral introduction pays homage to Gershwin's 'Rhapsody in Blue' with a solo clarinet, drawing us into a menacing, monochromatic world. Waits acknowledged that the song was partly inspired by a film image: 'Widmark on the prow of a barge, bringing Thelma Ritter's body back from the pauper's burial ground in Potter's Field in a grey dawn.'[61] Sam Fuller's violent noir *Pickup on South Street* (1953) starred Richard Widmark as a small-time thief and Thelma Ritter as an informer. What motivated her, she confesses, is a desperate attempt to avoid a pauper's grave. 'If I were to be buried in Potter's Field,' she protests, 'it would just about kill me. I've almost got enough to buy the stone and the plot.'[62] Potter's Field is a public burial place for the poor, the unclaimed or the criminal:

When someone is found dead on the street with no identification, they freeze them and if no one claims them and they aren't identified, they just throw them into a pine box with all their personal belongings and effects. They put them on a barge . . . that leaves at midnight . . . and send them out to Potter's Field. They throw 'em in the mud ditch . . . stack them twelve high in the excavation.[63]

Waits also drew on knowledge of New York's East River, whose treacherous eddies swept bodies into its backwater. Joseph Mitchell's *The Bottom of the Harbor* (1959) tells how people who'd drowned in winter would stay there until spring. A dozen bodies could show up in April, found by Harbor Police: 'suicides, bastard babies, old barge captains that lost their balance on a sleety night out attending tow ropes, now and then some gangster or other'.[64]

To narrate the track Waits created the figure of blind Nickels, an alcoholic stool pigeon. An informer, like Thelma Ritter's character, Nickels tries to score some whisky in exchange for information on a possible gangland hit. But this is noir; Nickels offers cryptic clues, surreal images gleaned from a maniac's dream. He teases us with

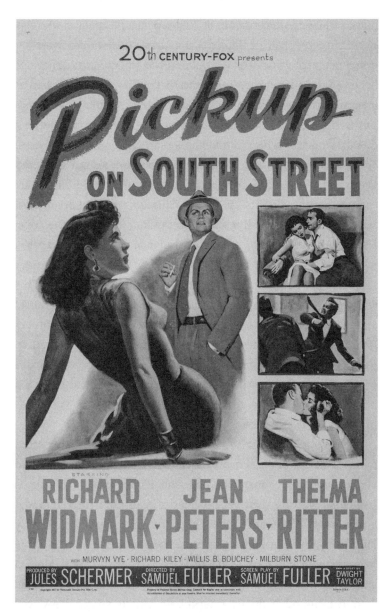

Poster for *Pickup on South Street* (1953, dir. Samuel Fuller), a film Waits drew inspiration from for his epic song 'Potter's Field', on *Foreign Affairs* (1977).

hints about the whereabouts of Nightstick, a pickpocket who has stumbled across half a million dollars. Alcivar uses waves of swirling horns and strings to help Waits build the sinister atmosphere of his layered, allusive narrative. 'Potter's Field' is an infernal web of images and lies, with blind Nickels at its centre, spinning the thread. At the song's end, Nickels hints, Nightstick is to be found in Potter's Field, a cemetery where all the corpses are unknown. In his lyrics, Waits relishes the chance to imitate Runyonesque slang. He savours words and names, which transport us into an underworld; Nightstick is a black-painted police club; High Chicago, a type of seven-card stud poker; Dragnet's Eye and Bloodhound, names for the cops; Ham and Egger, a name for an ordinary Joe or worker. Waits weaves in classical allusions: the steamer's captain in the grey dawn merges into Charon, the ferryman carrying the dead over the Styx. This shadowy world, which Waits obsessively revisits, consists of punks and whores, lowlife hoods and alcoholics who'd sell their mothers for a shot of whiskey. Double-crossing rogues, they are betrayed in turn. Gamblers, who mark the cards they deal, will become scarecrows, hollow figures whose bleeding hearts will be cut out if it's discovered that they squealed. The only certainty is the constant proximity of death: the edge of Potter's Field.

The song 'Muriel' also deals with the ghosts of the departed and violent death. Waits bases the underlying story on a celebrated Hollywood figure, a man who had it all. Ernie Kovacs was a 1950s comedian with his own TV show and a beautiful wife, the model and actress Edie Adams. One night, driving home after a Beverly Hills party where he had consumed a few too many cocktails, Ernie 'wrapped himself around a telephone pole there on Santa Monica and La Cienega and', as Waits told his audience, 'he's history'.[65] Aside from her husband's fatal accident, Edie was known for her Muriel Cigar commercials, in which she parodied Marilyn Monroe, accompanied by Stan Getz's lush saxophone and ending with a riff on Mae West's catchphrase: 'Hey why don't you pick one up and smoke it

Edie Adams and Ernie Kovacs in a promotional photograph for the ABC TV Show *Take a Good Look*, November 1960. They are the famous and ill-fated Hollywood couple behind the song 'Muriel' on *Foreign Affairs* (1977).

sometime?'[66] 'Muriel' shows Waits's knowing sophistication; how he can create a commodified pastiche of noir. The new album, which he called *Foreign Affairs*, from the outset deals with self-referential parodies of the noir genre. The *New York Times*'s obituary of Edie Adams noted that her work 'both embodied and winked at the stereo-types of fetching chanteuse and sexpot blonde'.[67] Waits amalgamates different strands of American popular culture, playing with the movie tropes of the femme fatale, the masculine cigar and the fatal car crash. What holds it all together is the need to sell. Waits directly uses the language of advertising. His lyrics are commodified (there are instructions to buy another cheap cigar) and hackneyed (he describes a diamond twinkle in one's eye). The language may be deliberately cliched but it's subtle in its allusions. Edie Adams, it turns out, was famously given an expensive diamond engagement ring by Ernie, who was also a celebrated cigar smoker.

The Hollywood movie sensibility of *Foreign Affairs* also infuses 'I Never Talk to Strangers'. Its cinematic quality was seized upon by Francis Ford Coppola, who would use the song's treatment of the male/female relationship as inspiration for his *One from the Heart*. The song arose from a date between Waits and Midler at Musso & Frank Grill, a celebrated Hollywood restaurant. She had declared her idea of a good time in LA was 'to go to the Fat-Burger with Tom Waits'.[68] He responded by citing her as the only girl he knew 'who'll come over and sit in my kitchen and not make fun of me'.[69] Waits decided he wanted to do a duet with Midler and structured the song like a dialogue scene; he regales Midler with what she labels as his 'sad' repartee. The influence of hard-boiled noir flirtation, as in the scene from *Double Indemnity* between Fred MacMurray and Barbara Stanwyck, is palpable.

> Stanwyck: 'There's a speed limit in this state, Mr Neff. 45 miles an hour.'
> MacMurray: 'How fast was I going officer?'
> Stanwyck: 'Around ninety miles an hour.'
> MacMurray: 'Suppose you get down off your motorcycle and give me a ticket.'
> Stanwyck: 'Suppose I let you off with a warning this time.'
> MacMurray: 'Suppose it doesn't take.'
> Stanwyck: 'Suppose I have to whack you over the knuckles.'

MacMurray: 'Suppose I burst out crying and put my head on
   your shoulder.'
Stanwyck: 'Suppose you put it on my husband's shoulder.'
MacMurray: 'That tears it. 8.30 tomorrow evening then.'[70]

In Waits's duet, the male and female voices are similarly wary,
scarred from the endless war of the sexes. When Waits tries to sweet-
talk her, Midler fends him off, displaying as much contempt and
disdain as Stanwyk shows to MacMurray. She tells him his life
resembles a dime-store novel and his type of guy is ten-a-penny.
Neither figure wants to be made to seem a fool since only 'suckers'
fall in love with total strangers. But Waits, for once, allows the song
to end on a slightly hopeful note. There's an unexpected move away
from cynicism when Midler adds that, maybe, Waits doesn't appear
to be a complete chump.

In 'Jack and Neal/California, Here I Come', Waits looks backwards with a final and most direct tribute to his literary father figure,
Jack Kerouac. What had changed from his earlier, Kerouac-inspired
Beat prosodies on *The Heart of Saturday Night* and *Nighthawks at the
Diner* was the impact of his friendship with Weiss. The reckless,
hard-living Weiss fulfilled a role for Waits similar to the one Neal
Cassady performed for Kerouac. In *Visions of Cody*, the book that
focuses most intensely on his relationship with Cassady, Kerouac
states how 'he had become the great idiot of us all, entirely irresponsible to the point of wild example and purgation, for us to learn and
not to have to go through.'[71] Neal Cassady (the model for Sal Paradise
in *On the Road*) wanted to be a serious writer like Kerouac. Chuck
E. Weiss wanted to be a singer-songwriter like Waits. But neither
had enough self-control to become real artists (Cassady had to be
locked inside a room in order to write). Their role was to act as
muse, subject and sidekick; to represent the wild pleasure-principle.
Barney Hoskyns has pointed out how 'they functioned as Ids to the
Egos of the men who observed them and had the discipline to make

art of their observations.'[72] Waits was very much aware of how, compared to the damaged Cassady, Kerouac was far less crazed and out of control.

'Jack and Neal' re-imagines a cross-country road trip to California undertaken by Kerouac and Cassady, full of drugs, drink and sexual adventure as they pick up a red-headed nurse. Waits's images of lonely landscapes mirror the melancholy beneath *On the Road*'s embrace of breathless abandon and existential freedom. The track segues into 'California Here I Come', a 1920s song by Al Jolson, celebrating the idea of the West as a dreamland of opportunity and fulfilment. Waits merges his evocation of Kerouac and Cassady's haphazard careering across the continent, full of drunken poetry and lustful girls, with this seemingly very different idea of Californian adventure. But the suburban dreams of the 1920s act as an ironic parallel to *On the Road*'s bohemian freewheeling. Kerouac was seeking after epiphanies or some kind of enlightenment. Although the promise of 'the road' offers a far more transient vision than the conventional settler dreams serenaded by Jolson, both paths are quintessentially American in their search for a happiness of 'the soul'.

Waits employs jazz rhythms in 'Jack and Neal' to replicate the looping flow of Kerouac's prose. The track and the trip are lubricated by constant references to drink and drugs: Benzedrine pills, MD 20/20 (an alcoholic beverage resembling a fizzy drink) and cheap kosher wine called Manischewitz. The song is full to bursting with musical allusions and sexual incidents; Neal dreams of Charlie Parker, Wilson Pickett plays on the radio, someone croons 'Underneath a Harlem Moon' to the nurse, who exposes herself, mooning at the traffic. Even the landscape is sexualized; moonlit foothills appear like breasts in the car mirror.

'Jack and Neal' is a further instalment in Waits's series of 'songs of the road', which began with 'Ol' '55'. But it's a farewell of sorts to Kerouac. Waits moves on from the literary influence that had helped form his late-adolescent self. He never idealized Kerouac like so many of the writer's followers, who saw the father of the Beats as a kind of secular saint. 'He wasn't a hero who could do no wrong. He saw a lot, got around. He wasn't nearly as mad and impetuous as Cassady.'[73] Waits knew about Neal Cassady's sad demise down in Mexico in 1968. He'd fallen into a coma after sleeping rough one cold, rainy night, having passed out from another hard-partying session. Drink also took Jack Kerouac a year later. 'He had a great stool at the bar and nobody sat there but Jack,' Waits remarked, understanding how alcoholism can be a kind of long, drawn-out suicide: 'He was writing his own obituary from the moment he began, and I think he was tragically seduced by his own destiny.'[74]

The finest song on *Foreign Affairs* is 'Burma-Shave'. It's Waits's most successful attempt to interweave images drawn from film noir with impressions or tales taken from his own past and contemporary Californian social life. At 6 minutes 30 seconds long, 'Burma-Shave' is an epic song of the road, recording a futile attempt at flight and escape. Waits loosely based the song on a Nicholas Ray-directed noir, *They Live by Night* (1948). Over the movie's opening, Ray had superimposed a bold summary of his theme: 'This boy and this girl, were never properly introduced to the world we live in.' In his song Waits namechecked the film's leading man, Farley Granger, who, with co-star Cathy O'Donnell, plays a Bonnie-and-Clyde-type couple on the run from the law. He is wounded; she tries to keep him alive. Waits admired Farley, the 'baby-faced hood', for the way he conveyed innocence as well as criminality. In the movie, Granger and O'Donnell are naive fugitives, creating their own fantasy world as the police close in on them. Ray's portrait of young misfits, who are literally and symbolically trapped, prefigured his classic *Rebel without a Cause* (1952). Waits exploits this underlying noir narrative to give the song a doom-laden sense, a dark, inevitable fate, which he contrasts with that bright, archetypal American dream of there always being somewhere better just down the road. Waits sings of

Farley Granger and Cathy O'Donnell in *They Live by Night* (1948, dir. Nicholas Ray). Waits drew inspiration from this for his song 'Burma-Shave', on *Foreign Affairs* (1977).

escaping a place that is no more than a wide spot in the road and names it Marysville, a tiny Californian town. He merges Granger's movie girlfriend with an autobiographical account of his own cousin. 'I have a lot of relatives in this little town called Marysville and a cousin . . . Corinne Johnson, she was always, "Christ man, I gotta get out of this fuckin' town". . . She finally did. She hitchhiked out, stood by this Foster Freeze on Prom Night . . . got in a car with some guy who was a junior delinquent and he took her all the way to LA.'[75]

The girl in the song knows she'll go crazy if she stays in Marysville, where folk are half-dead. Hitching a ride in a car, the road ahead appears like a ribbon to her – the moon like a bone. Her Farley Granger lookalike is different from anyone she's known. The heavy rhyme of 'bone' with 'known' creates an ominous foreshadowing. The couple head for Burma-Shave, an imaginary destination; they're literally on the road to nowhere. 'In the song I used Burma-Shave as a dream, a mythical community, a place two people are trying to get to. They don't make it.'[76] The real Burma-Shave was a billboard advertising shaving cream. Waits recalled how the hoardings interspersed the highway he travelled on during childhood trips out of LA with his father: 'I remember seeing Burma-Shave signs all the way across the country along Route 66.'[77] From the back of his father's Chevrolet station wagon, he'd view the billboard flash past and assume it was a town's name. The signs even spelled out personal messages:

> They have these limericks, broken up into different signs like pieces of a fortune cookie. You drive for miles before you get the full message. 'PLEASE DON'T' five miles 'STICK OUT YOUR ARM SO FAR' another five miles 'IT MIGHT GO HOME' five more miles 'IN ANOTHER MAN'S CAR – BURMA-SHAVE.' They reel you in.[78]

Vivid, concrete images convey the girl's edgy restlessness; her hair spills out like root beer, grain elevators disappear in the car's rearview mirror. She's so exhilarated at her escape that she feels like a criminal jumping parole. The repetition of 'Burma-Shave' at each stanza's end works like an incantation; the words intoxicate, summoning up a dreamland. The male fugitive calls himself 'Presley', aspiring to young Elvis's rebellious image. (Visiting Graceland, Waits relished seeing 'the bullet holes in the swing set' as uniformed usherettes delivered a memorized text, 'gesturing at the rusted play structure: "Elvis and the boys were having a little too much fun one night and came out for some target practice."'[79])

Death is the destination for the nameless girl from Nowhere-ville. The fatal crash is staged minimally, like a scene from a Godard film; images of a twisted machine and smoking tyres. Waits infuses his narrative with feelings of inevitability, desperation and regret. A shadow falls over the shotgun side of the car; the image gathers up the phrase's original sense of riding beside the driver, while holding a gun and looking for trouble. 'Burma-Shave' shares several associations with other songs on *Foreign Affairs*. It echoes 'Jack and Neal' with their wild road trip into the Golden State; it mirrors 'Potter's Field's' dark intimations of mortality; it uses stylized dialogue-form like 'I Never Talk to Strangers', when the wannabe Bonnie and Clyde flirt with each other; and, just as with 'Muriel', which also ends with a fatal car crash, the song is named after a commercial brand, using American advertising slogans.[80] Waits makes his voice lighter and floating. In contrast to 'Potter's Field's' layered cinematic soundtrack, he pares back all accompaniment to the narrative for 'Burma-Shave' save for piano and a short trumpet solo to close the track.

Compared to the tour-de-force of 'Burma-Shave', the album's title track, 'Foreign Affair', has an amused, even flippant tone. Waits's lyrics feel like they've been lifted from a slightly dated, conventional 1940s novel (more Daphne Du Maurier than Raymond Chandler). The theme is betrayal and infidelity; sexual attraction resembles a criminal investigation where the pleasure lies in the pursuit not the arrest. Although Waits revisits familiar noir territory, his treatment of the subject is light and his language abstract and vague.

Foreign Affairs as an entire album demonstrates just how sophisticated and self-conscious Waits's use of genre and character had become. To shoot the cover images, he picked George Hurrell, who had photographed many Hollywood golden age icons (Greta Garbo, Joan Crawford, Norman Shearer and Marilyn Monroe), an ideal choice to capture the monochromatic noir atmosphere of *Foreign Affairs*. In deep shadow, Waits is portrayed embracing a mysterious woman, shrouded in darkness. Only her ring-encrusted right hand, holding a passport across his chest, is visible. The image adorns an album that presents sexual relationships as fraught, provisional and unreliable. The female model for the photo was Marsheila Cockrell, who worked at the Troubadour. According to Paul Body, Marsheila

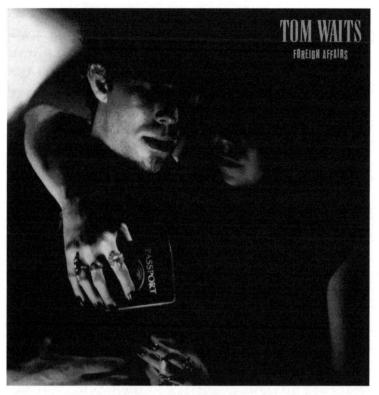

Front cover of *Foreign Affairs* (1977).

wasn't officially a girlfriend of Waits, 'but thought she was'.[81] An album exploring the treacherous ground between men and woman features a couple who may, or may not, be together; art reflecting life reflecting art reflecting life. The back cover image adds to the album's representation of noir: Waits resembles a 1940s hoodlum with slicked-back hair; an image poised between a Hollywood headshot and the portrait of a potential psychopath.

In *City of Quartz*, his seminal social history of Los Angeles, Mike Davis notes how the crime novel, in the hands of writers like Chandler, Hammett or West, exposed 'the parasitical nature of Southern California', portraying the amorality of 'the depraved or ruined middle classes'.[82] Davis points out how the 1940s film noir adaptations further developed the genre as the hardboiled American novel is filtered through the perspectives of exiled German expressionist filmmakers such as Fritz Lang, Billy Wilder, Edward Dmytryk, Robert Siodmak and Otto Preminger. The marriage of American pulp fiction with German modernist cinema reworked the image of LA. 'Geographically it shifted from the bungalows and suburbs to the epic dereliction of Downtown's Bunker Hill, which symbolized the rot in the heart of the expanding metropolis.'[83] Noir didn't limit its view of corruption to the personal or individual level; it boldly asserted that the entire system was rotten. For Waits, who was exploring the legacy and insights of the genre in the 1970s, noir's portrayal of Los Angeles as being permeated with betrayal, depravity and violence wasn't just a creative perspective. It made perfect sense in the context of what he could witness in the everyday street-life of the city. The late 1970s was a heavy, violent period in LA. Shootings of unarmed civilians, choke-hold deaths and racial profiling by the LAPD had created widespread public disaffection with the police. Assaults, gang violence, drive-by shootings and homicides were an increasing part of the city's fabric as the drug culture took hold of many neighbourhoods. Waits's musical home, the Troubadour club, was no exception. It had become overrun with dealers and drugs, according to Robert Marchese. 'The bar tenders were all fucked up on pills and coke. It became an ugly scene and Doug Weston was fading.'[84]

In his Tropicana apartment, Waits was living next door to pimps and witness to violent altercations. While the motel provided him with strong material for his songwriting, the prevalence of guns and people with heavy drug problems meant his attempt to blend autobiographical elements with 'the low-side of the road' was becoming problematic. He had blurred the line between the real and the imagined to the point that it disappeared. Taking on a boho-drinker persona had been a way of deferring questions of identity. The act was a self-protective device, a screen to deflect attention. 'The fact is everybody, who starts doing this, to a certain extent develops some kind of persona or image in order to survive. It's much safer to approach this with some kind of persona, because if it's not a ventriloquist act, then it's really scary.'[85] But life at the 'Top Trop' dissolved distinctions between Tom Waits and 'Tom Waits' to the extent that he was losing himself. 'When I moved into that place it was like nine dollars a night. But it became a stage, because I became associated with it . . . I think I really wanted to kind of get lost in it all . . . so I did.'[86]

Waits had advertised the fact that he lived at the Tropicana Motel in the liner notes to *Small Change* (a decision that he later admitted was unwise). As a result, he would get constant calls at all times of day and night from people with clinical problems. All kinds of stalkers, drawn like moths to his motel bungalow, pestered him. 'Waits fans were worshippers, girls and boys who would camp out on his lawn and wait for their prophet to speak. When he did speak, he would say something like, "Get the fuck OUT of here and don't come back."'[87] One woman travelled from Japan to confront him, arriving just as a car smashed into a telegraph pole and blacked out an entire block of Sunset Boulevard. Another girl escaped from an Illinois mental hospital and hitchhiked all the way to LA to meet Waits. Dressed in black, she sat on his porch like an avenging dark angel, waiting for him to return in the early hours. When rebuffed, the girl repeatedly phoned Waits threatening to kill him. With pimps on one side, Waits's other next-door neighbour was an unemployed, mentally ill actor who liked to break into Waits's apartment whenever he was away. One time Chuck E. Weiss discovered the actor, high as a kite, playing Waits's piano at three in the morning.

Even Duke's, Waits and Weiss's cherished coffee shop next to the Tropicana, witnessed a scene of violent unpredictability. On the morning of 27 May 1977, Waits was eating there with Bobi Thomas and Chuck E. Weiss when plainclothes police officers started arguing with one of Duke's regulars. Seeing the deputies become physically aggressive with the man, Waits and Weiss leapt to his defence. Waits was indignant at the way the cops had 'taken over the tables of some people that we knew at the restaurant. They had bullied their way into a table. We let 'em know we didn't think it was the kind of thing we do around here, and they didn't like that.'[88] Bobi Thomas recalled Waits shouting that she should go and call his manager, Herb Cohen. When Waits and Weiss followed her out to the phone box, the cops pursued them. Cohen described the scene: 'the cops came running out, pulled their guns, threw Tom and Chuck to the ground and handcuffed them. They told Chuck they were arresting them for homosexual soliciting and being drunk and disorderly.'[89]

The trial lasted three days. Waits's lawyer, Terry Steinhart, presented eight eyewitnesses who all confirmed the police report was fabricated and testified that Waits and Weiss had suffered extreme abuse. Mike Ruiz, a rock 'n' roll drummer, told the jury how the police

Waits outside Duke's Coffee Shop with Tommy Ramone, 1977.
The phone box was a key feature of the trial at which Waits was
acquitted of assaulting LAPD officers.

put Waits in a headlock, ramming and pounding his head into the side of a phone booth. The District Attorney asked Ruiz to help him re-enact this scene; Ruiz could be Waits and the DA would act as the cop. Ruiz was quick to retort: 'No, you be Waits, and I'll be the cop.'[90]

At the trial Waits was described as 'uncharacteristically well groomed'.[91] Asked whether he'd sworn at the police during the show-down, Waits replied that he'd 'growled a little under my breath. It was somewhere between a harrumph and a Bronx cheer.' The cops testified that Waits had 'assumed a combative stance with clenched fists', taunting them and challenging them with 'You want to fight, come on.' Waits told the *Rolling Stone* reporter assigned to the trial that 'those guys must have got their dialogue from Dragnet.'[92]

Much later Waits confided to Jim Jarmusch about how he'd feared the cops taking them to a lonely place to be shot. They were thrown into the back of a pickup truck at gunpoint: 'Guy says, "Do you know what one of these things does to your head when you fire it at close range?" He said: "Your head will explode like a canta-loupe." I thought about that. I was very still.'[93] Found not guilty of disturbing the peace, Waits and Weiss then sued LA County for false arrest, imprisonment, assault and battery, malicious prosecution and defamation of character. The case 'dragged on for five years before I got my day in court'. Waits won: 'It was insulting and embarrassing, so I felt it was my duty to make sure the record reflected the truth of the matter.'[94]

4

I'm Never Going Home

I've got a lot of miles under my belt, and I can't go back.
– Tom Waits, 1977[1]

The impact of punk rock on the late 1970s music scene was embraced by Waits. Its discordant, confrontational sound was a welcome antidote to the blandness of the faux country rock that had held sway for much of his time in Los Angeles. 'I'd rather listen to some young kid in a leather jacket singing "I want to eat out my mother" than hear some of those insipid guys with their cowboy boots and embroidered shirts doing "Six Days on the Road".'[2] On a personal level, Waits was coming face to face with an influx of new wave bands frequenting the Tropicana. Attracted by its dystopian chic, the New York Dolls, Blondie, the Ramones and The Clash were just a few of the bands to stay there. Chuck E. Weiss claimed that, after Waits had moved in, 'the place started to get an international reputation.'[3] Waits's 'open' residency had become a thing of myth; stories, true and invented, about the motel's wild goings-on multiplied. And the confusion or crossover between Waits's life and his art intensified. The arrival of a real 'femme fatale' in the shape of young chanteuse Rickie Lee Jones aided and abetted that process of self-mythologizing.

Waits declared that the first time he saw Rickie Lee Jones she reminded him of the 1950s film star Jayne Mansfield: 'I thought she was extremely attractive . . . my first reactions were rather primitive, primeval even.'[4] It's significant that Waits's first sighting of Rickie Lee was through the 'gauze' of the movies. Jayne Mansfield was marketed by Hollywood as a sultry blonde bombshell, a poor man's Marilyn Monroe. The studios refused to take her seriously as an actress and she was reduced to minor, trashy roles. A semi-tragic figure, she was killed in a car crash at the age of 34. However, many of the male and female characters who populate Waits's songs would idealize a woman like Mansfield: his drunken, self-deluding male loners would perceive her as a projection of their ultimate dream lover; his strippers and whores would view her moment as a Hollywood sex-bomb as an inspirational story.

Chuck E. Weiss was the first to meet 23-year-old Rickie Lee Jones in 1977. Just as Waits had done five years before, Jones was attending 'Hoot' nights at the Troubadour in the hope of being spotted. Weiss heard her perform a couple of songs, including 'Easy Money', which she'd written herself, and was very impressed. He thought she 'appeared to be a real free-form spirit that wasn't interested in any of the hoopla that went on around Hollywood'.[5] Jones vividly remembers her first encounter with Weiss and Waits outside the Troubadour: Waits 'wore a hat and held his cigarette like it was a wand. He was speaking to Chuck but what I heard was his body. He leaned on his car, but he was looking at me.' These three figures, who would be 'forever linked in the public's mind, initially became linked as they sang Stephen Sondeim's "Jet Song" on the sidewalk of Santa Monica Boulevard one summer night in 1977'.[6] Soon afterwards, the three began to create their own West Side story.

Rickie Lee was an archetypal wild-child of the late 1960s. She defined her wandering, vaudeville family as 'lower-middle-class-hillbilly-hipster' but, even then, she felt the pressing need to rebel. 'My family were outlaws, to an extent. The atmosphere at home was not one of "Father Knows Best", which is how I saw the rest of the world. My parents were pretty wild – they passed the misfit thing on to us.'[7]

After her parents split up, she became a runaway at fourteen, stealing a car for kicks in her hometown of Phoenix in Arizona, and heading out for California. 'A friend and I had been walking around all night . . . just having fun, and we decided we wanted to go somewhere – to San Diego. I got in a car and my friend drove. We neglected to tell the owner that we were taking it.'[8] By the time she turned eighteen, she had escaped to Los Angeles, drawn, like so many young American dreamers, by the promise or possibility of West Coast reinvention. Jones barely scraped a living. One story has her being fired as a waitress at a low-rent Italian restaurant in Echo Park, returning home only to find her musician boyfriend had taken off, leaving her 'with a bounced rent check and no car'.[9] Her early tough tales reveal an ability to self-mythologize as much as her attraction to the jazz side of life. When Waits met Jones, she was starting to perform her own songs and living as a waitress in Venice Beach. A hangout for Beatniks and Hippies in the 1960s, Venice had become extremely rundown a decade later. Its 'bikers, degenerates, drunken men and toothless women' provided Jones with material similar to Waits's, although, as she admitted, 'I never did hang out. I just wrote about it.'[10] What attracted her to Waits was the way he lived 'like one of his characters. I was intrigued by a man who needed access to the seedy side of life to write. I liked those types of people.'[11]

Waits was supportive of Rickie Lee's pursuit of a singing and songwriting career, impressed by the strength and sex appeal of her live performances. He found her style highly arousing, describing Jones as coming across like 'a sexy white spade'.[12] Sharing a love of jazz, the Beats and the dark recesses of LA night life, their friendship had turned into an affair within a few months of meeting:

> It was autumn now. I came to the Troubadour around 9 o'clock and sat at the bar, Waits was there. We both knew why we were there at the same time. Tom invited me home with him. We made love amid his dirty sheets and the clothes in

piles everywhere . . . the path to Tom's bedroom was scrawled through a living room of miniature skyscrapers of record covers and piles of newspapers and old magazines that had gone to seed where they landed. The bed was the only refuge. There I was safe, worshipped. He was a lion, so much more than his persona could ever contain.[13]

Waits tested his theory on alcohol and women during their relationship, which was founded on a mutual appreciation for the bottle. 'She was drinking a lot, and I was too, so we drank together. You can learn a lot about a woman by getting smashed with her.'[14] Careering around West Hollywood hangouts (the Tropicana, the Troubadour, Canters) in search of parties to gatecrash or drugs to score, Rickie Lee became one of the boys. 'I remember her . . . coming by one night to holler in my window to take her out celebrating. There she was, walking down Santa Monica Boulevard, drunk and falling off her shoes.'[15] She formed an intimate 'Gang of Three' with Waits and Weiss; an echo of the famous hard-drinking *ménage-à-trois* that Neal and Carolyn Cassady created with Jack Kerouac. 'Sometimes we were three. I don't know, when we were three, whether I loved one more than the other,' Jones later confessed, recalling how they would drive together: 'the three of us, me riding in the middle, were the last Neanderthals, the Holdouts of the Tropicana Motel.'[16] Like the complicated, dissolute lives of the Beat figures they venerated, Jones, Waits and Weiss were all aware of the self-mythologizing element. For Rickie Lee, they were 'real romantic dreamers who got stuck in the wrong time zone, so we cling, we love each other very much'.[17]

Whether highlighting the racist statues on the manicured lawns of Beverly Hills mansions or poking fun at stiff music industry executives, the three dreamers were, for a short, intense period, very close. Rickie Lee seemed, if anything, more streetwise than Waits, having had to fend for herself from an early age. Weiss was also

Bande à part: Tom Waits, Chuck E. Weiss and Ricky Lee Jones, Shangri-La, Zuma Beach, June 1979.

besotted, describing Rickie Lee as playful and nurturing, tough and soft. She could more than match his appetite for drugs. For Jones, Weiss and Waits were comrades-in-arms, or even a surrogate family. Cocooned in their bubble, they appeared like a gang of three outsiders, a *bande à part*, like the trio of young misfits joined in love and rebellion in Jean-Luc Godard's film of the same title (1964). Waits, Jones and Weiss created their own parallel, nocturnal world; an amalgam of Bukowski and the Beats, vintage movies and twelve-bar blues, rejecting the perceived phoniness of LA's music scene and the 'straightness' of the city's daytime existence. 'All the people come out at night. It's a world that isn't available during the day. To be a part of other people's lives, you have to go to where they are at night. Those people weren't the types to be at Denny's at ten in the morning.'[18] Like Waits, Rickie Lee preferred LA as a night city. She liked it 'very quiet and empty at night' since it was easier to 'fill in the darkness' with her imagination.[19] It was at night that she liked to visit Waits at his Tropicana haunt and swim in the dark pool. 'I'd look up at the moon and imagine, "So this is what it's like to be a movie star, to own the moon and have the whole history of the beauty of your life still approaching."'[20]

Over forty years later, in her autobiography *Last Chance Texaco*, Jones could still evoke the intense physicality of her relationship with Waits: 'We'd cruise along Highway 1 in his new 1963 Thunderbird. With my blonde hair flying out the window and both of us sweating in the summer sun, the alcohol seeped from our pores and the sex smell still soaked [in] our clothes and our hair.'[21] The closeness of the two singer-songwriters, the way they were exchanging not only song ideas but 'each other' became, for Jones, self-consuming at times: 'Tom and I were beautiful beyond compare, and so nourished (and inspired) by each other's hearts, that for a short time we nearly consumed each other.'[22] This romanticized, self-conscious and cinematic quality marked and defined their affair. 'We liked to stay in motels, which became our own little home, our private fiction, so we could drive around Los Angeles and land in some motel, where we could continue our film noir together.'[23]

For Waits, the affair with Rickie Lee could stimulate a new kind of mythmaking. Rather than look back through the prism of Hollywood noir and celluloid fantasies, as he'd done in *Foreign Affairs*, he could create his own myth of a contemporary LA romance. There were current movie echoes as well. With *A Star Is Born* in 1976, Hollywood had recently re-made its story of a fraught love affair between an established artist and his new, talented lover (Kris Kristofferson and Barbra Streisand playing the updated versions of 1954's James Mason and Judy Garland). Waits was doubtlessly aware of how the aspiring Jones was emulating his way of writing about street life in songs like 'Easy Money'. Rickie Lee later acknowledged how she had used Waits's 1970s persona as camouflage. 'I took on his swaggering masculinity. It was a good coat to wear, a good thing to hide behind; myself being so very vulnerable, that big persona seemed safe.'[24] One of Waits's key collaborators, pianist and arranger Mike Melvoin, was convinced that Jones had 'cadged her entire characterization from Waits whole'.[25] But, as Barney Hoskyns points out, given how much of Waits's own boho-jazz persona had been borrowed from references to other musicians and writers (Ray Charles, Frank Sinatra, Bob Dylan, Jack Kerouac), Jones's admiration for Waits hardly mattered. All new artists are partially formed by influences; the crucial point is what he or she does with such borrowings. Jones didn't simply copy and project a fantasy of living on the jazz side of life with a man she loved. The relationship was rich enough to inspire both to create new songs:

> We were religions, we converted to each other, we inspired each other, and we spoke in tongues. He growled, I cooed. He softened, I growled. Our natures similar, both of us apparently lacked the ability to hang onto our core identity. We wanted to be parts of stories because without a story, who were we?[26]

Waits named his new album *Blue Valentine*; it is a valentine of sorts, a coded message of love and affection to Rickie Lee, who claimed she had been 'playing one of Tom's sexiest characters. His entire record ... seemed to be inspired by his relationship with me.'[27] It's the start of Waits moving away from the jazz-piano-based musical texture that had defined his previous five albums and performances to date. He described his new sound as 'contemporary urban blues, sort of like the music of Ray Charles, of Jimmy Witherspoon'.[28] He wanted to find a much harsher edge to his music as an appropriate response to the times he was living in and the unpredictable feel of LA's sprawling street life:

> I'm playing the electric guitar for the first time and shit, I know three chords just like every other guitar player. There's more blood in this record, more detective stories. It just comes from living in Los Angeles, hanging out where I hang out. I feel like a private eye sometimes. I'm just trying to give some dignity to the things I see without being patronizing or maudlin about it.[29]

The album's new song titles clearly indicate the heightened atmosphere and violent landscape Waits sets out to explore: 'A Sweet Little Bullet from a Pretty Blue Gun', 'Red Shoes by the Drugstore' and 'Romeo Is Bleeding'. His disaffection with the goldfish-bowl-style quality of his Tropicana life can be seen in his need to rent a room on Sunset and Van Ness away from the motel's ambit in order to compose: 'I live in a neighborhood that far from insulates me from life out there. I feed off it. But at some point, you have to go away and sit down and recollect all of the things you have been through. You have to let your imagination work along with your memory.'[30] Instead of using the old upright encased within his 'Top Trop' den, Waits chose to compose on guitar, weaning himself away from piano-based jazz melodies. 'I wrote [in the past] primarily on piano and you write a certain type of song on the piano.'[31] Waits was drawing on his early passion for the Delta blues and funk – he wanted a more soulful, 'Blacker' feel to the music. Bones Howe grasped how the origins of *Blue Valentine*'s sound lay in Waits's fascination with New Orleans' R&B and helped him find ex-funk bassists, a great saxophonist called Herb Hardesty from Fats Domino's band and a drummer, Earl Palmer, who'd played on Little Richard's 'Tutti Frutti'. Hardesty was struck by Waits's openness to musical collaboration. 'I didn't know Tom until Earl Palmer called me to LA. He specializes in musical freedom. If you feel like jazz you put it in, if you want to get a little bluesy you put that in too. There's complete freedom, it's one of the most interesting groups I've ever worked with.'[32] Waits cut his ties with his band, Nocturnal Emissions, during *Blue Valentine*, and put together a new group made up of Herb Hardesty, another New Orleans veteran, Big John Thomassie (percussionist with Dr John) and the guitarist Arthur Richards.

Given how Waits's fresh creative energy was being fuelled by his LA-based relationship with Rickie Lee, he underlined this by his choice of artwork for *Blue Valentine*. Instead of the earlier anonymous females, typified by the fantasy woman of *The Heart of Saturday Night*, or the hired stripper on *Small Change*, Waits featured his actual girlfriend as the enigmatic blonde alongside him. When Waits and Weiss invited Jones to the cover shoot, she was 'excited to be there' knowing she 'was to be a romantic lead in this movie'.[33] Although Rickie Lee has her back to camera, the photo presents her lying against a car parked at an all-night gas station. It's a self-conscious movie scene, bathed in neon and fluorescent light, theatrically 'staged' by Waits as he pins Jones up against the bonnet, his amorous intentions evident. The autobiographical element is further emphasized by use of Waits's own customized 1964 Thunderbird car and Weiss popping up as a voyeur on the inside sleeve photo. Weiss looks away as Jones clings tightly to Waits's body.

Back cover photograph for *Blue Valentine* (1978), by Elliot Gilbert,
featuring Rickie Lee Jones.

According to Jones, whose sexy, encouraging whispers had 'kind
of turned [Waits] on', the photographer had spotted what was hap-
pening and asked her to be in the shot. 'Tom said, "Come closer." I
leaned myself against him, I slid down his body and he raised his
arms. There is the enigma of our very private love and passion caught
in that photo.'[34]

Waits chose to open *Blue Valentine* with a rare cover version,
Stephen Sondheim's famous 'Somewhere', which Maria sings to her
lover as he lies, bleeding to death from a gunshot wound in *West Side
Story*. In contrast to the abrasive blues tracks 'Red Shoes by the
Drugstore' or 'Romeo Is Bleeding', which define the album, Waits

Inside sleeve photograph for *Blue Valentine* (1978),
by Elliot Gilbert. Rickie Lee Jones is seen clinging
to Waits as Chuck E. Weiss looks away.

gives a full string orchestration to this musical tribute to Rickie Lee (she had sung lines from her favourite musical the night they met outside the Troubadour, before they'd ever spoken). Waits had asked Jones to come to the recording of 'Somewhere'. 'He wanted me to know it was for me, my *West Side Story* influence and my gentle nudging him to sing with his own voice,' she said.[35]

The sweeping romantic escapism of the track yearns for a time and place far from the urban violence and squalor explored elsewhere in the album. Waits asserts both the lyrical promise and the impossibility of his relationship with Jones. His vocal delivery also maintains this duality; he splits or subdivides himself between a lighter, wistful tenor and his darker, growling inner blues voice.

Blue Valentine is filled by Waits with characters who meet violent deaths. It was his take on how dark and murderous parts of Los Angeles had become. 'Small Change', the earlier track based on a homicide, had been an isolated example. But now the crazed violence of LA streets became an unavoidable subject. Waits spoke about how he'd drawn inspiration from reports in local newspapers: 'most of the stories in *Blue Valentine* took place in LA over the last few months.'[36] The young women in the city, whose lives are portrayed, were highly vulnerable. 'I'm not optimistic about things. I knew this girl who had her arms cut off. It's getting very sick out there.'[37]

'A Sweet Little Bullet from a Pretty Blue Gun' and '$29.00' record the fate of girls who had come to LA with the usual hopes of movie stardom only to be forced into prostitution by pimps. 'Sweet Little Bullet', set on Hollywood Boulevard, tells of a fifteen-year-old girl's suicide. In the song, the gun's sweet bullet puts scarlet ribbons in her hair; the blood imagery part of *Blue Valentine*'s recurrent use of red as a symbolic motif. In real life, the girl had leapt to her death from a seventeenth-storey window. Waits based '$29.00' on another real incident. Around 3 a.m. one night, he was disturbed by his Tropicana neighbours. The pimp was being harangued by one of his girls: 'She had her dress ripped by a trick and she wanted him to reimburse her for the dress and the dress cost $29 dollars.'[38] The resulting track was a raucous, edgy eight-minute blues track, ending with the cops arriving too late to save the little Black girl in a red dress; the police sirens wail uselessly as an ironic epilogue.

The album's harsh urban sensibility is perfectly set out by 'Red Shoes by the Drugstore'. A forceful electric bass, shrieking lead guitar and skittish electric piano give the song a jittery, driven quality, appropriate for its frustrated narrator. A gangster's moll waits for her man at the soda counter, unaware that he's already dead, having been killed in a failed heist. Waits moves back and forth in time, with references to *Little Caesar*, a popular Edward G. Robinson gangster flick from the 1930s, notorious in its day for its sleazy amorality. There's also a nod to the present day with the description of a little blue jay who wears a red dress. Waits connects Rickie Lee with red (her jacket is deep scarlet in the album cover photographs) and alludes to a Christmas escapade when she came by 'one night to holler in my window to take her out celebrating getting her first pair of high heels. There she was walking down Santa Monica Boulevard, drunk and falling off her shoes.'[39] Waits refers to the Skybar, a darkened lounge on Sunset, where he, Jones and Weiss liked to hang out. The song showcases his confident, intense lyricism; it evokes the noir genre with cinematic images and another *femme fatale*, but also with real urgency and a sharp, personal focus.

'Romeo Is Bleeding' echoes 'Somewhere' and 'Red Shoes by the Drugstore'; the former's Romeo-and-Juliet theme is reflected in the protagonist being shot in the chest after stabbing a sheriff to revenge his brother's death; the latter's strong red symbolism is repeated when Romeo feels the blood seeping through his shoes. Again, Waits uses a true story, this time concerning the shooting of a Latino gang member who bled to death in an East LA movie theatre. Waits flavours his narrative with strong Mexican slang: flamboyant young gang members are *pachucos* and the song ends with Spanish expletives, *hijo de la chingadre madre* (which translates as 'you son of a fucking whore'). As a first foray into Hispanic Los Angeles, it's a late response, given his childhood trips south of the border with Frank, and the Latino presence in his Silverlake haunts. He draws on another classic Hollywood gangster movie, this time *Angels with Dirty Faces* (1938) with James Cagney (whom he'd cited in *Small Change*'s 'Invitation to the Blues'). Like Cagney, whom he watches on the screen from his movie theatre balcony seat, Romeo must die like an angel with a bullet. Waits varies the album's driven blues sound with a Jimmy Smith jazz-style electric organ; despite the darkness of the subject, its jauntiness seems appropriate.

One of *Blue Valentine*'s most original tracks is 'Christmas Card from a Hooker in Minneapolis'; the title alone resembles a Raymond Carver short story. On an album where his music becomes more fused with real or personal elements, Waits also deepens his ability to inhabit alternative personas. This protean quality will prove to be his way forward as an artist. The song has the form of a spoken note from a prostitute to an ex-boyfriend called Charlie. She tells him her life is coming together; she's expecting a baby, has a good place to live above a dirty bookstore and has met a musician who'll take care of her and the baby, even though it isn't his. She insists she's finally off the drink and drugs. Waits brilliantly conveys the fragile interiority and self-destructive impulses of this lost figure. Initially, the song's greetings-card form seems open as the narrator addresses her old flame, starting each stanza with an affectionate 'Hey Charlie'. But Waits deploys an ironic reversal to undermine everything that's gone before. The hooker's final call-out to Charlie is followed by her admission that the entire song, everything she has declared, is a complete falsehood. There's no husband or jazz musician and her attempt to reach out to Charlie is a sad ruse; she's actually back in jail, ineligible for parole until Valentine's Day and desperately needs money for a lawyer. The device of an unreliable narrator turns the song on its head and allows Waits to highlight the layers of his character's self-deception. The song seems a sentimental address, but the narrator's wilful self-destruction turns it into a statement of bitter futility. The hooker is yet another Waits figure destroyed by time; everyone she used to know is dead or in prison. The lyrics foreground a musical detail, mentioning a record by Little Anthony and the Imperials. In concert, when Waits performed 'Christmas Card from a Hooker in Minneapolis', he would segue from Little Anthony's hit 'Going Out of My Head' to the festive 'Silent Night'. By framing his track with snatches of a song about a distraught mental state and an ironic version of a seasonal hymn, Waits makes clear 'Christmas Card's' painful duality. While 'all is calm, all is bright' around her, the hooker's mind is unravelling,

New Orleans R&B, the defining sound of *Blue Valentine*, fuels both 'Wrong Side of the Road' and 'Whistlin' Past the Graveyard'. The first is an exhilarating statement of adolescent rebellion; the singer flatly proposes telling Mama and Papa to go and kiss your ass. It's a celebration of naughtiness and nonconformity (Christmas carols need to be strangled and prayers scratched out), which recalls the high jinks Waits got up to with Rickie Lee and Weiss. The track 'Whistlin' Past the Graveyard' is an even jauntier blues; its fast rhythm matching the quick-fire boasts of a braggart who, since he has never told the truth, can never tell a lie. This 'rude boy' stumbles into town on a freight car, sticks around long enough to get into a fight and then leaves. Waits pushes beyond the narrator's stereotypical persona. He sets up his character's bombastic self-promotion to puncture it. Underneath is a lonely and lost existence. When he boasts he was born in a taxicab and so he's never going home, the claim has a personal feel, echoing Waits's tall story about his restless entry to the world.

In contrast to the rest of the album, the title track, 'Blue Valentines', has more of Waits's earlier jazz mode. Its sparse 'Blue Note' sensibility matches the subdued confession of a criminal, who has left behind his past and his lover. He receives a card from his girlfriend, whom he cannot contact. If he does, it will be the end of him. It's a pitch-perfect song noir or what Waits called a movie for the ear: an auditory evocation of a lonely man, who sits and drinks, haunted by bad dreams and guilt, trying to obliterate the memory of what he has lost. Every night he feels his bleeding heart cut open. Each Valentine's Day he'll die a little more. The song's surface seems maudlin but, underneath, its portrait of a lover mired in self-pity is clear-sighted.

To flesh out his 'movies for the ears' in performance, Waits began to make his stage show more overtly theatrical or cinematic.[40] He combined sets, props and lighting to heighten the audio-visual experience of his music and complement the persona he was projecting. Waits had already used as an onstage prop an old streetlamp to croon under or cling to, playing with the clichéd image of a lovelorn suitor from a classic movie like *Singing in the Rain*. Now, for his *Blue Valentine* tour, Waits had an entire gas-station frontage constructed, complete with gas pumps and spare tyres, to echo the album's cover image. The 'Super '76' gas-station stage-set referenced such images as *Standard Station* (1966) by Ed Ruscha or *Gas* (1940) by Edward Hopper, two American painters whose influence is felt on *Nighthawks at the Diner*. Los Angeles-based Pop artist Ed Ruscha has specialized in detailing commodified emblems of Californian life: gas stations and sidewalks, shop fronts and neon signs. Ruscha revels in the way LA's architecture resembles the flat two-dimensionality of film and stage-sets. In his series of wide-screen photos *Every Building on the Sunset Strip by Ed Ruscha* (1966), Ruscha obsessively collects and maps out entire LA districts. Such immersion into the surface texture of the city matches the 'urban' sensibility of Waits, who often names 'real' locations within which he places or stages his lyrical narratives. Waits and Ruscha seize upon gas stations and diners as iconic images precisely because they embody the city's mobility, restlessness and transience. By incorporating such detailed sets in his live concerts Waits wasn't simply trying to inject more of a sense of theatre. It shows how he was aiming to create a whole

Ed Ruscha, *Standard Station*, 1966, oil on canvas. Waits shared Ruscha's interest in LA's car culture. On the *Blue Valentine* tour, Waits used a set with gas pumps and tyres.

world just as much as a persona: 'kind of making a fiction in a nonfiction world. Taking the real world and then getting rid of certain things I didn't want to be there and adding certain things that I hoped would have been there.'[41]

Waits had long been frustrated at how his image had frozen into the wino man. This typecasting had been a blessing and a curse. In his early days it had helped him to establish a strong persona, but, by the time of *Blue Valentine* (1978), he desperately needed to be more three-dimensional. He told Louis Lista, a Troubadour *habitué*, he felt like 'an old prizefighter who's just going through the motions. I keep doing this character – the down-and-out but amusing and interesting Bowery character. And it's the same routine I've been going through for so long as a live performer.'[42] One way of escaping the curse of the wino man was to turn his concerts into miniature Broadway shows, anticipating *One from the Heart* (1982) and *Franks Wild Years* (1987). It allowed Waits to impersonate a wider range of styles: for 'Burma-Shave', he would arrogantly slouch between the gas pumps like Marlon Brando in *The Wild One* (1953) or a leather-clad Elvis, as if he'd stopped to pick up his runaway cousin and leave Maryville far behind, delivering the lyrics in hushed, complicit tones. Waits became the song: he bent and twisted his body, trying to inhabit different selves. 'His stage act was now a virtual mime show of contorted gestures with one arm raised over his head while the other's long double-jointed fingers crawled on his shoulders like a tarantula. Bent over with his eyes closed, his tousled head lost in a shroud of cigarette smoke. The voice sounded blacker than ever.'[43]

While Waits was putting together *Blue Valentine*, the little blue jay in a red dress had been discovered. 'Easy Money', Rickie Lee Jones's ode to bohemia, had been picked up and covered by Lowell George, the cocaine-addicted lead singer of Little Feat. This led to Warner Records deciding to sign the 24-year-old singer-songwriter. Rickie Lee Jones's eponymous debut album was released in March 1979. Her subtle, soulful blend of jazz and funk had an immediate appeal, a little surprising given punk's presence in the musical context of the late 1970s. The songwriting on *Rickie Lee Jones* is influenced by Waits; 'On Saturday Afternoons in 1963' and 'The Last Chance Texaco' display something of his 'gutter' romanticism and melancholy, but Rickie Lee's sound was very much her own. The opening track, 'Chuck E.'s in Love Again', was based on a remark that Waits had made. Late one night in Denver, Weiss had phoned Waits at the Tropicana to say he'd met a distant cousin whom he 'really liked'. Hanging up, Waits turned to Jones and simply reported 'Chuck E.'s in love.' The song was one of 1979's biggest hits; its overnight success completely changed the dynamic between the three friends. Weiss claimed he initially felt 'honored' that a friend had composed a song about him (Waits had already written 'Nighthawk Postcards' partly about Weiss on *Nighthawks at the Diner* and had namechecked him in two songs on *Small Change*: 'Jitterbug Boy' and 'I Wish I Was in New Orleans'). However, as a chart-topping single, 'Chuck E.'s in Love Again' brought a completely different level of exposure. 'When it became such a huge hit, I wasn't as honored as before,' Weiss admitted. 'It affected all three of us . . . It had to do with her success, and we were all taking drugs and getting high. And that intensified the drama of it, for sure. And we were very young. Things after that were never really normal again.'[44] Over the years, Weiss would become entirely identified with the song – as if his life had been taken away and reduced to one popular hit. For Waits, Rickie Lee's enormous overnight success must have been a little galling. 'Tom didn't have as much recognition as Rickie Lee and he'd been around much longer,' as Weiss pointed out.[45] It was like a replay of A Star Is Born, this time in the West Hollywood of Waits's song 'Wrong Side of the Road'.

Rickie Lee was given the A-list treatment from Warner Records, in marked contrast to how Waits had been sidelined by Asylum/Elektra, which, over the years, had shown little interest in investing in and promoting him as a top artist. For a Rolling Stone cover story to promote her album, Rickie Lee took the journalist on a tour of Duke's (where she was photographed with Chuck E. Weiss by Annie Leibovitz), the Tropicana and even the cluttered interior of Waits's bungalow. She pointed out the piano where he'd let her compose. 'I thought you'd just like to see this nice, crazy little place. Now you've seen just about everything in my world.'[46]

Waits was away on tour while Jones was showing journalists his apartment. It must have been odd to see how easily his world was now being presented as part of Rickie Lee's. Weiss started to re-evaluate his friendship with Jones, harshly reinterpreting her motives and actions as being rather less innocent or spontaneous than he had supposed:

> I found out a lot of the things she did were very planned and contrived. It was quite surprising. It was planned as to whom she would want to meet to get along. As soon as she got some recognition, she knew exactly what to do, what manager . . . what lawyer to approach. She had it all worked out.[47]

Jones's meteoric success and Waits's heavy touring had put strain on their relationship but it had always had its difficulties. Waits hinted at its less-than-perfect nature when he told *Rolling Stone* that their 'relationship wasn't exactly like Elizabeth Taylor and Mike Todd' (a Hollywood 'golden' couple).[48] Jones felt that she always had to 'stay in character' and pretend that she didn't need anyone. 'I loved Tom but he always played a game where I had to act like I didn't need him. That hurt me, I had no ability to not need the thing I loved. Tom felt like he could come and go as he pleased. He did not want to be [in] a couple.'[49] Waits was both attracted and troubled by Rickie Lee's tough act, her wilder side: 'she scares me to death. She is much older than I am in terms of street wisdom. Sometimes she seems as ancient as dirt and yet other times she's like a little girl.'[50]

Ironically, it was Waits's attempt to create a more stable, conventional relationship that precipitated the end of their affair. Accompanying Jones on the last engagements of her first, successful European tour in the summer of 1979, Waits seemed more at ease as part of a public couple than before. 'There is a photo of Tom holding my foot; his affection was constant and very physical. We always needed to touch each other. I cannot remember anyone else holding me so completely that I felt safe to go outward.'[51] Returning to LA, Waits and Jones entertained the possibility of sharing a life together. He took Jones to visit

a humble little house he'd seen for rent in Echo Park, a Hispanic neighbourhood with lots of gang members. We got out and looked in the windows, then sat on the front porch floor. We watched the lights of the city and dreamed about a life together in that house with our kids. I would make the dinner and he would make the lawn. He was laughing and joking about crabgrass and I wished we would never leave, just stay there. Tom and Rickie on the porch.[52]

Tom Waits and Rickie Lee Jones backstage in London, September 1979, shortly before their break-up, photograph by Adrian Boot.

It was a short, ill-fated attempt to play at being a couple. Instead of staying in the Tropicana Motel and recovering from the fatigue of touring, Waits and Jones 'ran ahead' and moved into the house. Although Rickie Lee claimed that she wanted to be 'the character who would be happy living there with Tom', she couldn't play the role strung out on drugs.

Deep down she knew 'we belonged elsewhere. Tom had left the Tropicana and I had left the beach. We may as well have been in the closed quarters of a rocket ship to nowhere.'[53] When Waits abruptly ended the relationship, Jones was distraught and sought consolation in heroin. Holed up in Chateau Marmont, she descended into a drug-fuelled psychosis. On her 'break-up' album, *Pirates* (1981), the song 'A Lucky Guy' voices the bitterness of an abandoned lover whose desperate pleas and passionate declarations only make her look foolish. Her love is unwanted. However, songs such as 'Living It Up' and 'We Belong Together' look back fondly to Jones and Waits's shared times when they were young and had no fear.

Waits has mused on the reasons why their *amour fou* has become mythic over the subsequent forty years; 'Maybe the reason people are so obsessed with this [is that] it wasn't a great love affair, maybe it's mythology, just part of their pop thing.'[54] However, given how both Waits and Jones, self-aware chroniclers of their emotional states, had imbued their time together with a mythic quality, it's not surprising that it still has an iconic status. Rickie Lee sensed that Waits was always the more secure; more at ease with himself than she could ever be. 'He was always, I thought – maybe this is because I was in love with him – much more charming than me. He could charm the socks of you. He seemed to be able to really make friends with big wheels and do it gracefully on their level.'[55]

One Hollywood 'big wheel', Sylvester Stallone, who had enjoyed massive success as the star of *Rocky* (1976), befriended Waits, who was keen to develop his acting. Bones Howe witnessed their unlikely friendship: 'Sly and Tom had got to be friends somehow. Maybe Sly saw him at the Troubadour. He was suddenly there. It wasn't unusual because Tom had a way of accumulating people – people just appeared all of a sudden.'[56] Stallone asked Waits to play a cameo role in his movie *Paradise Alley* (1978). The only catch was the role: a down-at-heel saloon piano player named Mumbles. 'Stallone said "Be a drunken piano player in an Irish bar . . . That should be easy." I'd like to have played an axe-murderer, but this is a start.'[57] Despite the opportunity, such casting merely served to confirm the popular perception of Waits's stereotype.

Waits's break-up with Rickie Lee came at the point when he showed the greatest dissatisfaction with his identity and LA life. Severing his ties with Jones was part of a general desire for change.

Waits was tired of playing 'Tom Waits' for people who didn't appreciate his talent and wanted a comic stand-up routine from a semi-drunk pianist. 'Wino man' identity had created space for Waits to differentiate himself from other LA singer-songwriters, and his jazz-bohemian persona had facilitated his ability to absorb and rework a wide range of cinematic and literary references. But he'd set a trap for himself by becoming like a 'character' within one of his song noirs. The life and outlook of a drinker alternates between lush sentimentality and hard-boiled cynicism. Alcohol inflates the senses, leading to a 'heightened', romantic sense of the world (which is why it is often used by writers), but it also assails and depresses the ego with its accompanying waves of self-disgust and self-pity. The bitter declarations of cynical indifference to the world mask the person's wounds; like Humphrey Bogart playing 'hard-boiled' Rick in *Casablanca*, drunk and slumped across his table, demanding the pianist play 'As Time Goes By'. This was the risk Waits was running, aware (given his father's example) of how drink can hollow out an individual, reducing human complexity to a two-dimensional stereotype.

On chat shows Waits could keep banal TV hosts guessing as to whether his drunken act was real or not. But play a part long enough and the mask hardens into the face. Waits later acknowledged how drinking and drugs had caught up with him: 'When you begin, it's a man takes a drink. When you end up, it's a drink takes a man. Keeping my balance during that period was tricky. When I was in my twenties, I thought I was invincible, made out of rubber. You skate along the straight razor and flirt with it all the time.'[58] One of the main reasons behind Waits's break-up with Jones and his increased distance from Weiss was their heavy narcotic use. During their time as romantic dreamers, Waits, Weiss and Jones had shared pretty much everything. But 'that whole side of jazz-junkie life', according to Paul Brody, wasn't 'his thing'.[59] Follow the jazz-junkie life, as Waits knew, and you'll end up in dark and heavy situations.

'I found myself in some places I can't believe I made it out alive. People with guns. People with gunshot wounds. People with heavy drug problems. People who carried guns everywhere they went . . . You live like that you attract lower company.'[60] So, when Rickie Lee Jones made a full confession of the extent of her drug habit, revealing that she had been using heroin for much of their time together, Waits used it as the pretext to end the relationship. According to Jones, 'Tom replaced his love with contempt, the pat reaction of strangers to heroin addicts. Not what I might expect from a friend or family. He saw me as a stereotype, just another junkie.'[61] Just before finishing with Jones, Waits had also ended his fabled residence at the 'Top Trop'. The Tropicana had become an amusement park for rock stars; when its dyspeptic pool was repainted black, Waits saw it as a sign of the pressing need for radical change. 'That's when I said this has gone too far. It was a pretty heavy place at times. I had a good seat at the bar and I could see everyone in the room, but I think there are other things to write about.'[62]

The decision to move out of his bungalow wasn't a simple relocation or even a doomed attempt to set up house with Jones. Waits knew he had to try and reach a new stage in his development as an artist; the Tropicana was bound up with everything negative in his life, including creative stagnation. The year 1979 was the first time since starting his recording career that he hadn't put out a new album. The rhythms that had defined his life, home and away, recording and touring, felt like an endless dysfunctional cycle. 'The whole *modus operandi* of sitting down and writing and making an album, going out on the road with a band . . . Away for three months, come back with high blood pressure, a drinking problem, tuberculosis, a warped sense of humour. It just became predictable.'[63] When Waits finally parted company with his West Hollywood haunts, he didn't tell many people where he was going, choosing to be more reclusive. He moved to the quieter East LA, near where his father lived. The small house on Crenshaw Boulevard was chosen, Waits claimed, because it was such a long street that no one would find him.

Waits had stayed in his motel bungalow for years because, paradoxically, he had wanted a home that wasn't a home. To feed his early creative process, he needed rootlessness. Waits had embraced Kerouac's Beat paradox that a constant sense of movement could provide its own destination; that in order to find oneself, it was necessary to get lost. But, instead of transience or restlessness, the Tropicana had begun to represent stasis.

> When you can't go back and live in the world you come from and you can't live in the world you're in, you get in your little sports car and drive ninety miles an hour down a dead-end street. There was always the danger of getting sucked down . . . I felt I'd painted myself into a corner. I'd fallen in with a bad crowd and needed a new landscape, a new story.[64]

Following *Blue Valentine*, Waits was poised on the threshold of a new direction, but yet unable to progress further. 'I'm kind of obsessed . . . not in the sense of being psychotic, it's just that I've got a lot of miles under my belt and I can't go back . . . it's very difficult for me to go home.'[65]

This deepening sense of frustration and limbo, of exhaustion with his chaotic LA life and sadness at the break-up of his 'Gang of Three', fed directly into Waits's last album to be fully centred on Los Angeles, *Heartattack and Vine* (1980). His musical response was to push *Blue Valentine*'s electric R&B towards an even harsher sound and make his 'wounded' voice more ravaged. Hoskyns has accurately characterized the keynote for the album's unrelenting urban grit as Howlin' Wolf in Hollywood Babylon – a brutal blues that cranked up the guitar and drums and unleashed Waits's voice at its most savage and untamed. Waits turns on his own city; by renaming Hollywood as 'Heartattack', he signals his disgust, making the place bear the sign of its amoral heartlessness. *Heartattack and Vine* embodies the full madness of LA, its junkies strung out and its whores battered, their desperate lives played out to the screaming of police sirens.

In *Small Change* and *Foreign Affairs* Waits had explored the nature of Los Angeles through its literary and film associations. He filtered his contemporary experience of the city through earlier aesthetic representations. But in *Heartattack and Vine* Waits eschews much of this technique, as if his use of genre had put too much distance between himself and the city's seething insanity. Waits was no longer content to mimic the perspectives of Chandler's private eye, Philip Marlowe, who, as a white knight, can still steer an honourable course through the venality and corruption surrounding him. Waits spurned any Beat-inspired quest for consoling epiphanies amidst neon-drenched late-night sidewalks. Instead, he responds to LA's dark, death-obsessed heart with the snarl of a semi-psychotic street predator, spitting lyrics out like verbal daggers, driven on by the savagery of his heavy percussion.

The idea of the title track came to Waits while he was sitting at a bar on Hollywood Boulevard near Vine Street. A middle-aged woman, who had been sleeping rough, staggered in. Sweating and red in her heavily made-up face, she collapsed on the floor, crying out that she 'was having a heart attack. The bar tender took one look and said, "Yeah, right, you can have it outside."'[66] For the narrator, Waits affects a street predator's cheap, jeering sarcasm. He eyes up a girl from out of town who wears a see-through top. He might be willing to bet that she's still a virgin, but it's not even 9 a.m. There's still plenty of time for her to lose whatever's left of her innocence. She should stay in the Midwest rather than visit the junkie streets of Hollywood. Otherwise, she'll end up crawling down Cahuenga Boulevard on a pair of broken legs. Waits repeats quotations from children's skipping rhymes ('Liar, liar, pants on fire' or 'Rich man, poor man, beggar man, thief') to give an infectious but mocking tone. This narrator could be a pimp or a pusher. Want to get high on heroin? Want to do stuff that'll kill you? Then why not do another line? *Heartattack and Vine* is a long way away from *The Heart of Saturday Night.* No alluring *femmes fatales* smile at coy musicians on sidewalks bathed in neon here. The lyrics are spat out in caustic aphorisms: don't you know there's no Devil? It's only God when he's drunk. Waits evokes a hellish urban vision, expressing its savagery with Howlin' Wolf-style snarling and violent electric guitar. It's an attempt to push beyond his previous musical boundaries and intimates the far greater change that lies ahead:

> It wasn't 100 percent successful, but it's usually the small breakthroughs that give you a tunnel to laterally make some kind of transition. The title track was a breakthrough for me, using that kind of Yardbirds fuzz guitar, having the drummer using sticks rather than brushes, small things like that. More or less putting on a costume.[67]

Heartattack and Vine is poised between his past (a farewell to Tom's LA wild years) and his future (the radical personal and musical break to come). Waits created the album by living and working in a studio only a few yards from its titular address. He'd chosen to use the legendary RCA building at Sunset Boulevard and Ivar Avenue in Hollywood, partly because Ray Charles and the Rolling Stones (who had recorded '19th Nervous Breakdown' in 1965) were among the artists to have worked there. He wanted to discipline himself to write fast, sleeping at times on a couch in the studio. 'I was writing each night and every day so that when the band got there, I'd have something new for everyone.'[68] Pushing poetic images, disparate lines and verbal fragments into some kind of coherence, he'd hand a song to Howe in the morning, record it during a session that would begin at 2 p.m. and then start working on the next composition. Waits claimed he enjoyed this way of working so much that next time he'd cage the band up with him. Larry Taylor on bass, 'Big John' Thomassie on drums and Ronnie Baron on an electric Hammond organ gave the record its driven, edgy blues. 'The subject-matter I was dealing with was caustic enough to require an ensemble that perhaps sounded a little more jagged.'[69] The pleasure Waits derived from playing with this band can been felt in the instrumental track 'In Shades' (initially called 'Breakfast in Jail'), which has a great retro R&B swing to it. This intense way of working (the album was recorded in one month) ensured the gritty R&B numbers have a compositional and thematic overlap. To balance and contrast with these slices of urban noir, Waits included several softer ballads ('On the Nickel', 'Saving All My Love for You' and 'Ruby's Arms'), which received string arrangements.

Echoing the title track's LA topology, 'Downtown' drags the listener to experience Temple Street in Downtown Los Angeles, with addicts on 'crank' (methamphetamines), cross-dressers clad in Pierre Cardin and wearing lipstick, small-time fencers of stolen goods and sexual predators. Waits counterbalances the sleazy lounge-blues feel of the electric organ with a voice that's almost a scream. Another swirling, impressionistic collage of lowlife escapades and sordid liaisons, the narrator can't decide if he wants to embrace the girl or push her around. Waits includes a sly self-reference when he quotes Montclair de Havelin, an absurd name he used as an alias while on tour. His strung-out alter ego shakes as though he's got St Vitus' dance and looks to score drugs. It's as if Waits revisits 'Depot, Depot', his earlier ode to Downtown social life, and replaces its wistful loneliness with a far more manic desperation.

This mood of barely suppressed hysteria and craziness is amplified in 'Til the Money Runs Out'. The song is doused in blood and alcohol; the narrator sells a quart of blood and buys half a pint of Scotch. Waits places us in an urban pit of pimps driving Eldorado Cadillacs, junkies whose heads are split open and drunks downing green Chartreuse by the pint. Into a world where nothing seems right, Waits puts another personal reference with an image of a 'pointed man' in the final stanza. Paul Body had given this nickname to Waits, who loved to wear sharp, chiselled shoes. In the song the pointed man complains that he can't go back to his hotel room since all they do is shout. He responds to this hellish state of affairs by using his brand-new tie to hang himself from the rafters.

Heartattack and Vine's cover has a sweaty, ill-looking Waits photographed in a necktie. Scrawled at the top of this image is a false phone number of a David 'Doc' Feuer, a real psychiatrist who Waits had been visiting around this time. The cover design is a facsimile of a soiled, sensationalist LA local newspaper; the kind of throwaway Sunday paper bought on Saturday night as 'Til the

Front cover of *Heartattack and Vine* (1980). Waits is pictured wearing a thin tie and the phone number of his psychiatrist is scrawled on the cover.

Money Runs Out' suggests. Waits, by imagining his own suicide, not only hints at his own unsettled state of being but kills off his 'wino man' persona. 'Til the Money Runs Out' is an epitaph of sorts, part of his need to bid farewell to the Tropicana years. The song underlines this with its repeated, ironic quoting of 'bye-bye baby, baby, bye-bye', the inane chorus from a Four Seasons song that was a big hit back in 1965. 'Mr Siegal' promises another brutal rupture with the past. The song's narrator pledges to burn this hotel down, if he can locate the matches. Its title is a nod to Bugsy Siegel, the notorious gangster who helped turn Las Vegas into the mob's playground. But this song is one of exhaustion and entropy; its last line desperately asks a direct but unanswered question: how is it possible to get out of here?

'On the Nickel' was composed separately from the rest of the album, but it returns to his former haunts. The song was commissioned for a documentary on Skid Row at Fifth Street in Downtown LA. In the song Waits revisits his past – the place where four years earlier he'd squatted down to drink and talk with the homeless, and which resulted in 'Tom Traubert's Blues' on *Small Change*. 'On the Nickel', the finest song on *Heartattack and Vine*, is a melancholic and tender counterpoint to the raucous cynicism that defines most of the album. Waits risks sentimentality with a self-conscious kind of nursery rhyme (he opens with the playground chant 'Sticks and stones may break my bones'). The rough-sleeping down-and-outs are an alternative version of J. M. Barrie's lost boys, those who never comb their hair. The song is a lullaby for hobos. Waits asserts that, no matter how far down these tramps have fallen, every one of them began as some mother's son. Waits opens the song out to include anyone who has felt the world get bigger once they were on their own. Balancing a piano accompaniment with Bob Alcivar's sensitive string orchestration, 'On the Nickel' shows his hoarse, croaking delivery still able to convey deep wells of feeling. In fact, the song's emotionality and elegiac tone is held in check by Waits's jagged voice. The UK music press noted how *Heartattack and Vine* pushed his trademark growl into ever more broken territory. 'Waits's voice no longer sounds like it's simply been lived in – more like it's been squatted in by 13 separate Puerto Rican junkie families with tubercular in-laws,' according to NME, while *Melody Maker* saw it as a 'deformed instrument, happiest with words like "bitch", and resembling the hacking up of stubborn phlegm'.[70] Waits's favourite description of his own sound was that of 'Louis Armstrong and Ethel Merman meeting in Hell'.[71]

The rasping, painful quality of Waits's voice, haunted by a memory of its former sweetness, gives his ballads extra layers of regret and inevitability. 'Ruby's Arms', the final track on *Heartattack and Vine*, is a farewell address to a lover who remains asleep as her man disappears for good. Waits's 'persona' steals out into the dawn, grabbing his jacket and boots (like 'Ol' '55', the first track on *Closing Time*). As he leaves, he tells his sleeping lover, Ruby, that the scarf from her clothesline is all he's taking. It's a single, cinematic scene of departure. He pledges never to kiss her again. Or to break her heart. Given how Rickie Lee was linked with red in Waits's imagination, 'Ruby's Arms' summons up their affair for the last time. The tender final line, with its repetition of goodbye, makes it an elegy. Waits says farewell to his 'scarlet' woman, whose heart he'd broken, and also to his persona and lifestyle of the previous decade.

Waits's wild years were catching up with him. Turning thirty, he confessed he was concerned about his physical well-being. 'I felt like I was caving in inside. I couldn't walk two blocks without coughing and wheezing. So, I said "What am I doing killing myself? I don't want to live hard, die young and have a beautiful corpse. I really don't."'[72] Waits gave up his cherished Lucky Strikes, no small sacrifice given how integral smoking had become to his onstage presence when he'd cloak himself in wreaths of cigarette smoke. His health fears were symptoms of a wider malaise, caused by the confusion between his work, public persona and private life. Retreating from the Tropicana to a hideaway on Crenshaw Boulevard wasn't a large enough change to break the sense of stasis and repetition: 'You're like a wound-up toy car who's hit a wall and you just keep hitting it.'[73] Increasingly, Waits felt he needed to move away from Los Angeles and his musical identity. In 1980 he tried to relocate to Manhattan: 'I was disenchanted with the music business. I moved to New York and was seriously considering other possible career alternatives.'[74] Waits moved into the Chelsea Hotel, ironically citing the range of new bars the city offered as a good reason for the change. He attempted to work with a different producer from Bones Howe, his old Hollywood father figure. But New York didn't provide any answers. The city merely exacerbated his sense of being lost:

> It was 30 below. I was paying $600 a month for a miserable little apartment, and I spent $300 on locks for my doors, because I was constantly worried about burglars. One of my neighbors was this Yugoslavian lady, who wore black pajamas and sticks on her back . . . I was rescued from this situation by Francis.[75]

5
In the Neighborhood

I realized that a guy who writes murder mysteries doesn't
have to be a murderer, which is not to say that I have turned
into Perry Como – although I still look up to Perry a lot.

– Tom Waits, 1981[1]

T he white knight rescuing Waits from his New York malaise
was none other than director Francis Ford Coppola. He had
been much taken with 'I Never Talk to Strangers', a rare
duet which Waits had recorded with Bette Midler for his *Foreign
Affairs* three years previously. Coppola had been trying to imagine
a movie about a troubled romance, one which might point to a new
type of musical film. After hearing Waits's song, he saw a way forward: 'That's a concept! I can have the male & female voice and
they can be involved in dialogue, working out issues in song . . .
paralleling the male and female protagonists in the film.'[2] Coppola
was responding to the structure of 'I Never Talk to Strangers'; the
way Waits had dramatized a conversation between a man and a
woman in a bar in lyric form so that it worked like a movie scene,
complete with tension, disagreement and resolution. According to
Waits, Francis 'liked the relationship between the singers. That was
the impetus for him contacting me and asking me if I was interested
in writing music for his film.'[3] Ironically for Waits, who'd moved to
New York to jump-start a new phase of his life and work, Coppola's
interest meant returning to LA and revisiting the jazz-based music
aesthetic from which he had already moved away. But the chance
to create an entire soundtrack for a director at the height of his
prestige (Coppola had been awarded the Palme d'Or at Cannes for
Apocalypse Now in 1979) was a huge professional leap forward.

By the time Francis called and asked me to write those songs, I had really decided I was gonna move away from that whole lounge thing. He said he wanted a 'lounge operetta', and I was thinking, well you are about a couple of years too late. All that was coming to a close for me, so I had to kind of go and bring it all back. It was like growing up and hitting the roof.[4]

Getting Waits to create the soundtrack for *One from the Heart* was an inspired decision. Coppola wanted to rework Hollywood's Golden Age musical, infusing it with contemporary sensibility and more nuanced characterization. Waits, who had always drawn on mid-twentieth-century musical and cultural references to create his own hybrid forms, was ideal to work on a project that paid homage to Gershwin or Kern. Coppola planned to exploit the potential of the new video-playback system to make a 'retro' movie, which could resuscitate a genre that felt exhausted by the 1980s. Who better to reanimate the spirit of the musical, to create an aural equivalent of *One From the Heart*'s neon-drenched cinematography and production design, than Waits, who'd spent nearly a decade composing his own song noirs?

The call from Coppola to return to LA and work at Zoetrope's production offices on a Hollywood studio lot was a turning point for Waits. Writing a soundtrack was not only a creative leap forward; it meant that he would no longer be viewed just as a cult artist catering to minority tastes. *One from the Heart* let Waits become a mainstream songwriter, who could work at the heart of a Hollywood movie and keep his integrity intact. Zoetrope was an enlightened, re-imagined take on the old studio system. Governed by Coppola's whims and dictates, it was a brave and risky attempt to create a higher-quality Hollywood cinema. Creative figures, whose priorities seemed to be more about a film's artistic success than its purely commercial prospects, were, for once, placed in overall charge.

Returning to Los Angeles a few months after his departure, Waits was boyishly delighted to be given a real office as part of the Zoetrope studio lot. He had always liked the thought of being a songwriter in the Brill Building's tradition, churning out a constant supply of new songs. This was his chance to pretend that composing was a job just like any other. 'I put on a suit and tie, shaved and read the paper, had a cup of coffee and went to work along with millions of other Americans. It was good for me, it disciplined me . . . I had to sit in a little room and they'd ring me up on the phone and put memos under the door. It was like working in an office.'[5] Installed in a mahogany-panelled room, complete with a Yamaha grand piano and coffee table, Waits soon turned his 'David Niven' suite into a smarter version of his old Tropicana bungalow by adding a battered couch and the usual clutter of books, beer cans and ashtrays. Photographer Henry Diltz, who took pictures of Waits's Zoetrope room 'with papers strewn all over the floor and cigarette butts', thought 'it felt like the guy was locked in there week after week.'[6] In effect, Waits was chained to his desk, since the movie would occupy him for two years. *One from the Heart*, he stated, was 'the most rewarding experience I've had since I started working'.[7] But he also 'wasn't used to concentrating on one project so long to the point where you start eating your own flesh'.[8] When Waits worked on a new album in the past, he'd only write twenty songs, selecting the best twelve to fill up both sides of a forty-minute LP. Composing a film soundtrack called for a completely different technique. Waits turned back to the experience of Bones Howe, who had the office next door. 'I had no idea I would be capable of writing an entire score for a major motion picture,' Waits admitted. Howe gave him the confidence to develop a new method.[9]

Waits immediately grasped that film-composing 'was like trying to be an actor and having to try on different gloves'.[10] Writing a soundtrack for a movie forced him to move away from a conception of creativity derived from the romantic tradition, one based

Waits's first film soundtrack, for *One from the Heart* (1982, dir. Francis Ford Coppola), was nominated for an Oscar.

on the idea of the unique, authentic inspiration of an individual, an outpouring of sensibility from the well of imagination. Instead Waits embraced a more modernist, Brechtian idea of the artist as craftsman, foregrounding artistic technique in self-conscious acts of collaboration:

> Film scoring is like writing songs for someone else's dream. Up till then writing songs was something I did when I'd been drinking, and I wasn't absolutely sure I was capable of doing it in terms of being a craftsman. Being part of something very large you have to discuss openly what it is you do and how it relates to a carpenter, a lighting guy and an actor. So, it made me more responsible and disciplined.[11]

However, working with Francis would also have its drawbacks. Although he gave Waits direction, Coppola avoided telling Waits what to do. Instead, he exhorted him to be as prolific as possible so that he could pick and choose from a large pool of ideas. Howe sensed Waits's frustration, mentioning how he 'would come back from a meeting with Francis and say he didn't think Francis really knew what he wanted for the movie'.[12] Coppola's original intention had been to construct dramatic scenes with the specific tracks Waits composed, so that the music would be completely integral to the film. Male and female singers could then act as commentators on the characters' shifting moods and actions. However, in the course of the film's production, scenes were always being reworked. Waits realized he had to surrender to the process of filmmaking, which, in the hands of the notoriously indecisive Coppola, could be chaotic. 'Francis is always changing his mind when he gets inside a film, then he eats his way out.'[13] To cope with such creative fluidity, Waits wrote about twelve different themes to be used wherever Coppola wanted them and then strung them together like a musical's overture. Lyrically, Waits used a version of stream of consciousness, taping or taking note of everything that came to mind. He would then tinker with the melody, throw out some words and try to splice things together, blending his ideas:

> If one line didn't work in a song, I might stick it in somewhere else. I never threw anything away. Because I never knew, when I was writing, what Francis might end up using. What a year and a half ago might have been a scratch track, could have conceivably been used in the final cut of the film.[14]

Waits easily adapted to the more collaborative process of film-making because he had always imagined his songs as mini movies for the ear. Even though his more recent aesthetic was the gnarled intensity and attack of *Heartattack and Vine*, Waits could still serve Coppola's film vision, which needed a 'lounge operetta'.[15] Far from being an auteur who insisted on the strict primacy of his composition, Waits was an ideal collaborator, relishing the alchemy of movie-making, where his contribution was just one among many: 'What do they say? A camel is a horse designed by committee. It's a very involved process. It's like a city. Film staff, crew, cast; it's like you are all building this thing. Everything has to fit. So, whatever you are doing has to be designed in with the overall fabric of the piece.'[16] It was not, perhaps, entirely accidental that while Waits was working so intensely on a film about the nature of romantic love, he met someone who would radically transform his life. Waits immediately told Howe about his 'brief encounter': 'The most amazing thing happened last night. I was sitting here playing the piano and there was a knock on the door and I opened it and there was this beautiful girl standing there. And she said, "What are you doing?" And I said, "I'm writing songs for *One From The Heart*. Who are you?"'[17] It was one of those mythic Waits 'moments', when his art and life were so completely interlaced that each seemed to inhere in the other. The beautiful girl turned out to be Kathleen Brennan, who was working as a script editor for Zoetrope. As chance (or the plot of a romantic movie) would have it, Brennan was the same attractive blonde, dressed in black, whom Waits had glimpsed at a New Year's Eve party in Los Angeles while saying farewell to old Troubadour mates Paul Body and Art Fein, and preparing for a new start in New York city: 'It was love at first sight, no question of it. It was New Year's Eve in LA. We met. I was leaving town the next day going to New York, never to return. But never say never . . . I opened the door and there she was and that was it. That was it for me. Love at first sight. Love at second sight.'[18] Waits and Brennan embarked on a whirlwind romance, driving around LA at all hours, as if the process of falling in love had to be accompanied by the loss of any sense of direction.

> We used to play a game called 'Let's Get Lost'. We'd drive, and I would say 'But baby – I know this place like the back of my hand. I can't get lost.' And she'd say, 'Oh, hell you can't. Turn here, now turn here. Now go back, now turn left, now go right again.' And we'd do that all night until we got lost. And she'd say, 'See I thought you knew this town? Now you're getting somewhere. Now you're lost.'[19]

Brennan was forcing Waits to look at his city and his life afresh. As a metaphor for the transformative power of love and a sense of making a life together as an adventurous step into the unknown, it could hardly be bettered:

> We'd end up in Indian country out where nobody could believe we were there. Places where you could get shot just for wearing corduroy. We were going into these bars. I don't know what was protecting us, but we were loaded. God protects drunks and little children and fools. And dogs. Jesus, we had so much fun.[20]

Tom Waits married Kathleen Brennan in August 1980, only a few months after she knocked on the door of his office. Following the spirit of their spontaneous nocturnal escapades, they held the ceremony at 'Always Forever Yours' Wedding Chapel, a 24-hour service in Watts, southern Los Angeles. Waits claimed he found the chapel in the yellow pages next to 'massage'. 'The registrar's name was Watermelon and he kept on calling me Mr Watts.'[21] The wedding cost the total sum of $70 (the pastor had a bleeper so that he could be paged for the next couple). Waits admitted he had only twenty bucks on him and his new wife had to cough up the rest: 'She said "this is a hell of a way to start a relationship."'[22] Waits was much taken with their diminutive Always and Forever gift bag, dispensed to all newlyweds. It contained 'a novel called *The Vanishing Bride*, a tampax, a couple of rubbers & some Snowy bleach', he told Jim Jarmusch.[23] The wedding party took place at Molly Malones, an Irish pub on Fairfax Avenue in West Hollywood. Jerry Yester, who'd known Waits since *Closing Time* in 1973, declared that 'Waits was the happiest I'd ever seen him.'[24]

Described by a Zoetrope colleague as the furthest thing imaginable from an LA rock chick, Kathleen Brennan was the polar opposite to Rickie Lee Jones. Secure and well-balanced, she'd grown up in Illinois and New Jersey amid a large, close-knit Irish American family. Her warm, supportive background was also in marked contrast to Waits's. Neither his drunken, dissolute father nor his conventional, churchgoing mother could be described as being emotionally available. Waits was happy to tell the world that his bride was 'my true love'.[25] The song 'Jersey Girl' on *Heartattack and Vine* is a pure avowal of his love for her (Brennan's family had moved to Morristown in New Jersey when she was a teenager). It's a lyrical, straight-ahead shout of joy from a guy walking down the street to see his girl. Waits confessed to his 'first experiment with *sha-la-la*' to give the track 'a kind of Drifters feel'.[26] Jerry Yester, who arranged strings for the song, noticed Waits's transformation: 'Overnight the skid row guy was gone, and he became his new character. It wasn't like he was schizophrenic or multiple personality – he just was *his art* at the time . . . One day he said, "This is going to kill me," so he stopped it on a dime. He was no longer the scruffy guy, he was almost dapper.'[27] Waits firmly believed that Brennan had turned his life around. 'If it wasn't for her, I'd be playing a steakhouse somewhere. No, I'd probably be cleaning the steakhouse.'[28] It was as if Waits had been able to rewrite Billy Wilder's Hollywood noir *Sunset Boulevard*. Instead of ending up floating face-down in the pool like the used-up screenwriter William Holden, he manages to survive and to marry the clever girl from the script department.

Waits and Brennan found their first home together on a part of Union Avenue, which runs between Downtown LA and MacArthur Park. Their apartment was wedged between a convenience store and a Filipino church, which, compared to the whores, pimps and drug-dealing neighbours of Tropicana days, seemed to suit Waits. The area consisted of 'churches, dogs, and children. We live in the upstairs of an old home, and it's quiet. Now I'm feeling more that I want to have a little more privacy. And being married and trying to create somehow a life for myself. I'm trying to build more order in my life in that sense.'[29]

Right from the start of their relationship, Brennan became a valued source of advice and support for Waits's career. She was the one to suggest Crystal Gayle as female vocalist for the double act in *One from the Heart*. Brennan understood how Waits and Gayle, an odd and unlikely combination, could form a striking contrast in image and sound. Gayle was a mainstream country and western singer with a huge, international following. Her voice's pure and light delivery ran counter to the guttural tones of Waits, who appealed to more of a minority audience. The neutrality of Gayle's voice meant that Waits's lived-in texture would register more strongly. Waits confessed he found it difficult composing songs for a woman to sing. In the past he'd projected himself into the mind of a female protagonist ('Christmas Card from a Hooker in Minneapolis'). But it was a real progression for him to create a sound texture that could actually embody the female character:

> I found it was hard writing for a woman. There are certain words they are uncomfortable with. I can get away with a certain vernacular, while a woman singing it would have trouble. I had to change things around, put everything into her words. It was tough. I felt like I was writing lines for an actress.[30]

'Writing lines for an actress' allowed Waits to grow as a singer and songwriter. It helped the move away from his previous 'authentic' persona towards a more Brechtian notion of self-conscious theatricality with a widening range of contrasting voices and guises. 'I think it's important now to be able to separate yourself as a performer and writer from who you actually are.'[31] When it came to recording the tracks, Waits elicited a great performance from Gayle – their duets have a musical theatricality with both playing their parts to the full. 'Gayle sang them exactly the way he wanted. She never changed a word, changed a note, anything.'[32] Waits's songs give the narrative of *One from the Heart* a rich subtext. The interior dialogue of the songs allows the characters to develop through their musical themes rather than unnecessary onscreen exposition.

To create Waits's 'lounge' sound, Howe put together an outstanding West Coast jazz group: Shelly Manne on drums, veteran Jack Sheldon on trumpet, Pete Jolly on piano and the great Teddy Edwards on tenor sax. Old collaborator Bob Alcivar created different arrangements, using a jazz trio at times, but also employing a Count Basie-style big-band sound. What is striking about Waits's soundtrack for *One from the Heart* is how well the songs contrast or parallel with each other. Solo tracks 'Old Boyfriends' (performed by Gayle) and 'Broken Bicycles' (performed by Waits) are paired as mournful elegies for old emotional attachments. A dramatized duet such as 'Picking Up after You' has an angry satiric edge, appropriate to its theme of a mutually recriminating break-up. However, 'Is There Any Way Out of This Dream?' was written specifically for Gayle to pay homage to the torch-song tradition as a classic, female show-stopping lament. 'Little Boy Blue' has a very different up-tempo jazz rhythm with Ronnie Barron on the organ; Waits's playful use of scat vocals and nursery rhyme hark back to songs from his *Small Change* period. The title track is a multi-layered composition. Gayle and Waits sing alternate stanzas; their duality reflected in the way Sheldon's Blue Note trumpet solo seamlessly combines with string orchestration. By contrast 'Take Me Home' has a stripped-down simplicity with Gayle accompanied by solo piano. Although *One from the Heart* was composed in Waits's earlier musical idiom, what Howe called 'this Berthold Brecht quality of his work' also emerged. 'Circus Girl', an instrumental montage, has the feel of a Nino Rota band with wheezing woodwind and jaunty, off-kilter accordion, which Waits would use in *Swordfishtrombones*. 'That dissonant quality got more and more throughout the picture. *One From the Heart* was that magic door opening up. Francis just wanted him to be Tom Waits but Tom was already jumping ahead a generation.'[33]

One from the Heart as a movie was a critical and commercial failure. Coppola's film celebrates its own artificiality with a hyper-real style. It's as much a film about the artifice of moviemaking as a love story, which it treats as an urban fairy tale. Since it's set in a heightened, re-imagined Las Vegas, it follows that it's all surface and glitter, a studio-based dream of a dream. LA critics disliked the film's superficiality, missing the point that it was intentionally so. 'The picture comes from the same artistic impulses that inspire airbrush art, 3-D pop-up cards and the deliberately beautiful neon that illuminates LA shops.'[34]

Less than five hours' drive away, Las Vegas has a close, sibling-like relationship with Los Angeles, acting as though it were the larger city's libidinous shadow. LA's materialism and venality are taken to the limit by its Nevadan facsimile, like a younger playboy brother who exists only for excess. *One from the Heart*, as critics realized, was less about Las Vegas than 'the bungalow courts and neon of Los Angeles'.[35] Waits's lyrics create an atmosphere of impermanence, which haunts the American Southwest, its cities enclosed by desert: 'where I've seen false teeth in a pawnshop window. And prosthetic devices. I've seen a guy sell his glass eye for just one more roll,' Waits commented.[36] The film was such a box-office disaster that it brought on the demise of Zoetrope as a major production company. But its soundtrack was universally praised and nominated for an Oscar. Waits's music has outlived its source. *One from the Heart* can now be seen as a standalone tribute to the mid-century tradition of lyricists and composers like the Gershwins, Cole Porter or Jerome Kern.

One from the Heart's setting of his music brought professional acclaim but Waits felt it was a retrograde step in his aesthetic development. Once it was finished, with Brennan's advice, he examined every aspect and working relationship of his career. She made Waits aware that, by signing over the rights of his songs to Herb Cohen, he had received little income from them and had no control over commercial use. Waits confessed his naivety: 'I thought I was a millionaire. It turned out that I had twenty bucks.'[37] Brennan and Waits took over the business side of his career and they severed ties with Cohen, wresting control away after a number of court cases. Jerry Yester recognized that Brennan

was the one who woke him up to what Herbie was doing. She was very smart and just had a lot of really good input. What was so distressing was that Herbie had always been part of the family. It was like your father or brother doing it to you . . . Waits absolutely trusted Herbie to his core and it devastated him when he found out he had grabbed a lot of the royalties.[38]

Waits decided he needed to make a clean break not only from his ex-manager but from 'a lot of the flesh peddlers and professional vermin I'd thrown in with'.[39] Paul Body saw the dramatic transformation Brennan effected. 'Basically, Kathleen saved Tom. I can't say anything better than that. If he'd kept going the other way, it would have just been sort of a dead end. It would have fizzled out and nobody would have cared. But somehow, he managed to reinvent himself and Kathleen had a lot to do with that.'[40] For Waits, the working relationship with Howe was the most difficult to reconsider. The producer had been a great source of support, acting as a father figure. However, they'd done seven successive albums together; Waits felt that he'd reached the end of a cycle and was repeating himself:

> We ended up putting strings on everything. My voice has this cracked quality, so let's put strings behind it. It was like taking a painting that's made of mud and putting a real expensive frame around it . . . When you're working with the same producer and you're . . . collaborating on the records, it's a little harder to go your own way. You want to take everybody with you. For me, eventually, I just wanted to make a clean break. I was rebelling against this established way of recording that I'd developed with him.[41]

When the two men met for a drink to discuss the future, Waits told Howe that he needed to get away from composing on the piano, because he felt he was 'writing the same song over and over again'.[42] Waits's spell composing on a Yamaha grand in his *One from the Heart* office was a regression to a method he'd already rejected on *Blue Valentine* and *Heartattack and Vine*. Howe understood and told Waits that they were like an old married couple. He didn't want to be the reason an artist couldn't create. 'It was time for him to find another producer. We shook hands and that was it. It was a great ride.'[43]

Waits didn't have another producer in mind. Brennan wanted Waits to take control himself. She told him that he needed to 'be responsible for all facets of conceiving, producing, and putting together the whole package'.[44] Brennan had to convince Waits that when it came to his music, he knew it better than anyone else. Given his later development, this seems obvious. But, at the time, it was Brennan's more adventurous spirit that emboldened Waits to take risks. Waits accepted that his wife was less conservative and 'much more of a pioneer' compared to his 'tendency to go back over familiar ground'.[45] Waits told his old San Diego friend Francis Thumm how Brennan changed what he thought about music and composition:

> You get very linear sometimes in music. You know what makes you safe and you don't want to be unsafe. Kathleen has helped me to feel safe in my uncertainty. That's where the wonder and the discovery are. After a while you realize that music – the writing and the enjoying of it – is not off the coast of anything. It's not sovereign, it's well woven, a fabric of everything else: sunglasses, a great martini, Turkish figs, grand pianos. It's all part of the same thing. And you realize that a Cadillac and the race track, Chinese food and Irish whisky all have musical qualities.[46]

One major influence, which Brennan brought to Waits's attention, was the music of Captain Beefheart. Don Van Vliet was a true South Californian original, who had grown up around Los Angeles like Waits. From 1964 onwards, after adopting his 'Captain Beefheart' persona, he created iconoclastic new music through an eclectic mix of Delta blues, avant-garde jazz, acid rock and even classical music. Irascible and visionary, demanding and enigmatic, Captain Beefheart with his Magic Band produced several groundbreaking albums, including *Safe as Milk* (1967), *Strictly Personal* (1968) and *Trout Mask*

Replica (1969), which brought a Dada-inspired modernist sensibility to popular music. 'Once you've heard Beefheart, it's hard to wash him out of your clothes. It stains like coffee or blood,' Waits claimed.[47] By the 1980s Van Vliet had become bored with the music industry and moved to the Mojave Desert to focus on his painting. Beefheart's uncompromising legacy was exemplary for Waits, who described Van Vliet's work as 'a glimpse into the future; like curatives, recipes for ancient oils'.[48] The new album would see Waits experiment with his blues-based sound to create radical acoustic textures like Beefheart's. But *Swordfishtrombones* would also be his own highly original music. It shows Waits not as a copyist but learning from Beefheart to become a risk-taker; to pursue the singularity of his own vision. The continued importance of Beefheart's example is evident in a note of appreciation Waits and Brennan wrote when Van Vliet died, calling him 'wondrous, secret and profound. He was a diviner of the highest order. He described the indescribable. If he were a horse; he'd be unrideable. Long may all that he has given to the world continue to sprout.'[49] In another tribute to Beefheart, Waits marked the lasting significance of this extraordinary musician for his own work:

> He was like the scout on a wagon train. He was the one who goes ahead and shows the way. He was a demanding bandleader, a transcendental composer (with the emphasis on the dental), up there, with Ornette [Coleman], Sun Ra and Miles [Davis]. He drew in the air with a burnt stick. He described the indescribable. He's an underground stream and a big yellow blimp. I will miss talking to him on the phone. We would describe what we saw out of our windows. He was a rememberer. He was the only one who thought to bring matches. He's the alpha and omega. The high watermark. He's gone and won't be back.[50]

At its best, *Swordfishtrombones* would attempt to describe the 'indescribable'; to go ahead and show the way. Waits started to develop a music that pushed beyond his old vocabulary and take him far from his jazz and Beat roots. The new album would also leave LA behind to head off on its own surreal trajectory, mining all kinds of references from world music. Again, Brennan acted as a catalyst. She was the one who 'started playing bizarre music. She said: "You can take this and this and put all this together. There's a place where all these things overlap. Field recordings and Caruso and tribal music and Lithuanian language records and Lead-belly. You can put that in a pot."'[51] Brennan's more eclectic taste made Waits realize that he had been closed to the wider possibilities of music: 'I was such a one-man show I was very isolated in what I allowed myself to be exposed to.'[52]

In composition, Waits had always written diametrically opposed songs: 'bawlers' and 'brawlers', as he labelled his mournful ballads and hard-hitting tales of urban disquiet. Brennan wanted him to seize on this gap between the tender and the abrasive and increase the contrast between the melodic and discordant elements in his work. If Waits were to deepen his embrace of weirdness and dissonance, as Captain Beefheart had done, then his music could better capture the world's full absurdity, grotesquerie and beauty. For the first time since he started recording, Waits banished the use of the saxophone, thinking it had given his songs too mellow and traditional a vibe. Instead, he used heavy percussion in a way he had never attempted. 'I'd been terrified of drums for some reason. I started becoming a bit more adventuresome . . . trying to bring things up and out . . . that I couldn't reach before. You get to an impasse. You kind of have to take a hammer to it – so I did.'[53] For *Swordfishtrombones* he set about creating bizarre, obscure sounds, using a vast range of instruments: metal aunglongs, marimba, bass drum with rice, bell plate, freedom bell, harmonium, bagpipes, parade drum, glass harmonica, African talking drum. Victor Feldman, who had contributed to *Heartattack and Vine* and *One from the Heart*, introduced Waits to this offbeat percussion. In order to find sounds like the 'noise in his head', Waits had to invent what he labelled 'junkyard orchestral deviation'.[54]

This use of 'found' sounds was pioneered by Harry Partch, another iconoclastic musician who, like Beefheart, lived and died in Southern California; a typical composition is entitled 'Eight Hitchhiker Instructions from a Highway Railing at Barstow'. Partch had dropped out of his musical studies at USC in Los Angeles to pursue an avant-garde career, playing harmonium and exploiting 'found' sounds. During the Depression, when he rode the railways and lived as a hobo, Partch literally 'picked up' the idea of making his own musical instruments. From sources like hub caps, empty bottles and aircraft-shell casings, he built a bizarre range of instruments: the Gourd Tree, the Bloboy, the Chromelodeon, the Kithara, the Zymo-Xyl, Marimba Eroica, Spoils of War, the Cone Gong and Cloud-Chamber bowls (pyrex dishes suspended in a frame). Waits admired Partch as a true American innovator:

> He built all his own instruments . . . from ideas he gathered travelling round the United States in the Thirties and Forties. He used a pump organ and industrial water bottles, created enormous marimbas. He died in the early Seventies, but the Harry Partch Ensemble still performs at festivals . . . I'm very crude but I use things we hear around us all the time, built and found instruments. Things that aren't normally considered instruments: dragging a chair across the floor or hitting the side of the locker real hard with a two-by-four, a freedom bell, a brake drum with a major imperfection, a police bullhorn. It's more interesting. You know I don't like straight lines. The problem is that most instruments are square and music is always round.[55]

Partch's project was nothing less than a total re-evaluation of how music is made and heard. Instead of breaking the octave in its usual twelve semi-tones, Partch's version used a 43-tone scale and invented his exotically named instruments to support his musical theories. Waits had become aware of Partch's revolutionary concept of music and admired how this gay, bohemian Californian composer was such a rebel, proud of his alienation from musical and societal norms: 'Once upon a time there was a little boy who went outside, and that little boy was me – I went outside in music.'[56] Partch also quoted the story of Timotheus, who 'was banished from a city because he added two strings to a three-string lyre . . . My lyre has seventy-two strings and I shudder to think what would happen to me in Ancient Greece.'[57] But Waits mainly responded to the way Partch had used household or junk items to create new audio textures or collages:

> I started wondering what would happen if we deconstructed the whole thing. I like things to sound distressed. I like to imagine what it would sound like if we set fire to a piano on the beach and mike it really close and wait for the strings to pop. Or drop a piano off a building and be down there waiting for it to hit with a microphone. I like melody. But I also like dissonance.[58]

Musicologist Francis Thumm brought Partch's work to his friend's attention (after a concert by the Partch Ensemble, Waits struck his chest and said 'It gets you right here'). Thumm had invented an instrument that he called the Gramolodium and helped arrange several tracks on *Swordfishtrombones*. Partch's concept of corporeality (how sound is grounded in the body) was also embraced by Captain Beefheart, with the vibra-phonic sound of percussive instruments in albums such as *Lick My Decals Off, Baby* and *The Spotlight Kid*. Thumm and Feldman were key participants in Waits's sound experiments, but, in addition to being introduced to new percussive instruments, Waits was determined to be open to any sounds in a search for more discordant musicality. 'Someone was fixing a mic and dragging a chair across the floor. It made the most beautiful sound, like *eeeeehhh*. And I was thinking jeez, that's as musical as anything I heard all day, and I'm here to make music.'[59]

Waits had an oddly inverted sense of his own musical evolution. 'I started out complacent and got more adventurous,' he told *Rolling Stone*.[60] As a teenager in the 1960s, he'd once even applied for a job at a golf club as a Sinatra-style crooner. It was as though he lived his musical life in reverse, starting as a cautious old man before entering a radical middle age:

> For a long time I heard everything with an upright bass and a tenor saxophone. I was very prejudiced and Republican in my opinions. Now I'm starting to hear more. It's very hard to stop doing things you're used to doing. You have to dismantle yourself and scatter it all around and then put on a blindfold and put it back together so that you avoid old habits.[61]

Waits has claimed that he didn't feel confident in his songwriting craft until *Small Change*, his fourth album. The quality of his lyrics for 'Tom Traubert's Blues', 'Small Change' and 'I Wish I Was in New Orleans' gave him the impetus to push on as a writer and composer. Always at ease using his own idiosyncratic approach to studio work, he'd describe audio texture he wanted in terms of colours or metaphors. 'I can say "We want kind of an almond aperitif here" or "industrial hygiene with kind of a refrigeration process on this."'[62] But the risks he undertook composing *Swordfishtrombones* outweigh any earlier attempts at reinvention. There was the real possibility that failure could curtail his career. Using a revealing underground metaphor, Waits compared his creative process to that of 'moles who have had the courage to tunnel beneath great rivers because of the risk involved. One bad move, you bring the whole river back up the tunnel and wipe out a whole community.'[63]

Swordfishtrombones deliberately assaults us with 'Underground', its defiant opening track ushering in the darkness of a nocturnal album, one which shuns daylight. Waits described it as like a group of mutant dwarfs performing a Russian march, stomping on a wooden floor, banging on pipes. His voice becomes a series of strangulated grunts or cries, as he pays tribute to the down-and-outs who live in sewers. Waits came up with this theme after hearing about 'late-night activity in the steam tunnels beneath New York City . . . There are entire communities of ladies and gentlemen, living under difficult communities beneath the subways.'[64] This idea triggered a childhood obsession with secret burrowing: 'When I was a kid I used to stare in the gopher-holes for hours and hours sometimes. I tried to think my way down through the gopher hole and imagine this kind of a journey to the center of the earth kind of thing.'[65] Waits wanted a feeling of 'people banging on steam pipes, a thousand boots coming down on a wood floor at the same time. That chorus of men singing. Kind of a *Dr Zhivago* feel to it.'[66] He achieved the exotic tone with the use of bass marimba from Victor Feldman, as well as Larry Taylor on acoustic bass, Randy Aldcroft on baritone horn and Fred Tackett on guitar. Drummer Stephen Hodge revealed the lengths he had to go in order to achieve the density of sound Waits wanted: 'I broke every stick in my bag trying to do "Underground". Finally, I just went and found these parade drumsticks that were like big old logs, and I shoved cymbal felts on top of them, so they were like a big felt mallet.'[67] There's a strong Brecht and Weill influence with its expressionist, music-theatre quality. The song's deep, underground theme is also echoed and enacted at a micro-level of word choice and vowel sound. There is a dominant use of 'o', present in the continuing rhyme scheme (*bones, zone, groan, road, unfold, roots, boots*), and permeating every line to create a constant series of low guttural growls. The sound is subterranean, as if the vowel had buried itself into each word. The song is about a bizarre world of mutant dwarfs but it's also a metaphor for the subterranean musical realm Waits has discovered, a declaration of his new musical intent.

'Shore Leave' continues the intensity of 'Underground' and shares its ambition. Waits surrounds a straight minor blues with odd sound effects and delivers it in a screeching falsetto. He aimed 'to capture the mood more than anything, of a marching marine walking down the wet street in Hong Kong and missing his wife back home'.[68] In a more visceral summary, he described the song as 'a chief boatswain's mate's nightmare with a bottle of 10 high and a black eye'.[69] Although the theme wasn't new (a lovelorn and homesick sailor pining for his girl), what gives the track its semi-hallucinatory quality is its parallel world of exotic sounds; an expressionistic mood-piece in which the music embodies a distorted state of consciousness. The listener is forced to share what the character hears in a nightmarish Hong Kong. 'I wanted to find music that felt more like the people who were in the songs, rather than everybody being kind of dressed up in the same outfit. The people in my earlier songs might have had unique things to say and have come from diverse backgrounds, but they all looked the same.'[70] Waits added low trombone to give the rumble of a passing bus, Balinese metal aunglongs for the sound of tin cans in the wind and rice on the drums to simulate the sensation of waves hitting the shore; it's a melee of disorientating sounds. Fred Tackett plays the guitar with a car key and the banjo sounds like it is about to fall apart. As in 'Underground', the use of marimbas gives an insistent percussive pulse, like the throbbing inside someone's head. Waits starts with spoken word vocals, which change into a more mournful sing-song tone. By the climax he howls dementedly, as if possessed by a foreign she-devil. Projecting himself into the song's warped vision, Waits reached backwards into memories of his time at Sal's Pizzeria in the 'sailor town' of National City:

It was something I saw every night. It was next to a tattoo parlor and country-and-western dance hall and a Mexican movie theater. I imagined this Chinese pinwheel in a fireworks display spinning, spinning, and turning and then slowing down. As it slowed down, it dislodged into a windmill in Illinois, a home where a woman is sitting in the living room, sleeping on chairs with the television on. When he's having eggs at some joint, you know, thousands of miles away.[71]

The songs on *Swordfishtrombones* form an imaginary soundtrack to a strange film, set in distant places with unsettling characters, whom we perceive like a dream or the return of a repressed memory. This is the atmosphere of 'Dave the Butcher', an instrumental inspired by an abattoir worker, who Waits met when visiting his wife's relations in Ireland:

He had yellow hair, looked completely demented, wore a leopard collar made out of real leopard skin and he had two different kinds of shoes, he wore one boot and one Oxford. He worked at a butchery shop, so I tried to imagine the music going on in his head while he was cutting up little pork loins.[72]

The instrumental is driven by a jaunty, unhinged organ. It could be butcher Dave chopping, but it also resembles *Carnival of Souls*, an eerie 1962 horror film set in an abandoned fairground. Ghostly echoes of Nino Rota, Fellini's composer, increase the disorientation. 'Dave the Butcher' is the first of the album's three instrumental tracks; the other two also create weird, lost-in-time soundtracks. Waits wanted 'Just Another Sucker on the Vine' to have a 'Nino Rota feel . . . like a car running out of gas, you know, just before it makes the crest of the hill and it starts to roll back down'.[73] 'Rainbirds' uses a glass harmonica to create a sense of going back in time. Despite the world-music sensibility, which marks Waits's rupture with LA, these instrumental tracks give *Swordfishtrombones* another vision of Californian noir.

At the time of its release, Waits revealed how much of his sensibility still fed off the dark unease of California; as if his music was the accompaniment to a lost David Lynch movie:

> When you drive from Los Angeles to Northern California . . . Leaving Los Angeles is like you're being put upon and then it gets simpler and simpler, darker and darker and then it's hush, quiet, there's no one around . . . There are these little towns, almost like ghost towns. You come off the main highway and there's a café where you expect to see John Garfield or somebody. It has a sign that says 'EAT', there's a car up on blocks and an old grease monkey, prospectors, screen doors, eggs. You feel like you've just broke out of jail and you're stopping for your first breakfast or something.[74]

Waits creates a teasing, elusive narrative trajectory in *Swordfishtrombones*. The listener searches for a thread to bind the individual cinematic scenes together. 'The songs have a relationship. I tried to get them to knit. It's just one guy who leaves the old neighborhood and joins the merchant marines, gets into a little trouble in Hong Kong, comes home, marries the girl, burns his house down, and takes off on an adventure, that kind of story.'[75] The quality of this elliptical narrative is enhanced by the way Waits uses images rather than characters as starting points for songs. This filmic approach to composition (helped by his work on *One from the Heart* and Brennan's sense of complex story structure) gives the album a new dynamism. 'The whole experience of working with images and music works a muscle somewhere in you. With this stuff I tried to run little things in my head, feed them first . . . trying to arrive at some kind of cathartic epiphany in terms of my bifocals.'[76]

The track '16 Shells from a Thirty-Ought-Six' originated with Waits visualizing an image of a man looking for a crow with a guitar strapped to the side of his mule. 'When he gets the crow, he pulls the strings back and shoves this bird inside the guitar and then the strings make like a jail. Then he bangs on the strings and the bird goes mad, out of his mind, as he is riding off over the hill.'[77] Waits builds up this surreal scene by enhancing a blues track with various thumps and bangs. He wanted to have a sledgehammer coming down on an anvil, to give the idea of the sound of a chain gang working by a railway. 'It was a matter of trying to get that feeling of a train going. Originally, I tried just with organ and bass.'[78] His voice feels red-raw, and the lyrics sound mangled with repetitive, industrial hammering.

The track issues forth from a dark, semi-imaginary past, what Greil Marcus labelled 'the old, weird America': a slice of Southern Gothic from Carson McCullers or Flannery O'Connor with the bizarre image of the fluttering, enraged crow trapped behind a guitar's strings.[79] However, like 'Underground', the song is also about Waits's music with its new, angry and discordant percussion. The image of a crow encased within a musical instrument refers to the surreal title of *Swordfishtrombones*, which re-imagines the trombone's elongated brass form as an 'animalistic being' (an instrument that smells bad or a fish that makes a lot of noise). Waits aims to make music possessed with a trapped life-force, dark and transformative. In this sense he makes the song foreground his method. Waits uses highly elusive imagery but, at the same time, clearly reveals how his new aesthetic is created out of these elements. Years later, '16 Shells from a Thirty-Ought-Six' still vibrates with a disturbing, psychotic energy.

Given Waits's long tenure as wino man, there's a mordant irony to 'Town with No Cheer', which is about a man who can't get any alcohol. Waits had read a newspaper article during a tour of Australia about a small town, whose only saloon was closed down and boarded up. To capture this ghost town's loneliness, Waits uses eclectic instrumentation: the asthmatic wheezy breathing of an accordion, the pathetic, plinky-plonk of a child's toy keyboard and a bagpipe's stifled cries (the musician played it as though he was 'strangling a goose').[80] The song demonstrates amply Waits's expressive use and control of language. Attuned to Australian slang, he uses local phrases like 'hotter than blazes' or 'thirsty jackeroo' (a young hired farmhand), seasons his lyrics with references to Patterson's Curse, a vicious weed that plagues farmers, and references an old Aussie drinking song, 'Pub with No Beer'.

The sense of melancholia accompanying his evocation of abandoned towns and wandering sailors is even more pronounced on 'Soldier's Things'. The subject has a natural simplicity and microfocus. The sailor figure finds a box of war mementos and medals. One man's experience of combat, suffering and sacrifice has been reduced to knick-knacks, put in a box and sold for a dollar apiece. Waits 'imagined a pawnshop and raining outside, a bunch of sailors, all the instruments hanging up, a guy pawning his watch. The song was just there, sitting there.'[81] Waits has an extraordinary ability to imbue everyday objects and clothing with a mournful afterlife, as if these human fragments can yield a sense of the individual behind them. 'Shoes in particular that have walked around with somebody else inside them for a long time seem . . . to be able to almost talk. Instruments are always like that.'[82]

Swordfishtrombones was the first album on which Waits collaborated with Brennan. He acknowledged how her sharp critical eye helped make his lyrics more visceral and physical than anything he'd written before: 'She encouraged me to look at songs through a funhouse mirror and then take a hammer to them.'[83] When asked what new elements Brennan had brought to his songs, Waits was fulsome in his praise. 'A whip and a chair. The Bible. The Book of Revelations. She grew up Catholic you know, blood and liquor and guilt. She pulverizes me so that I don't just write the same song over and over again. Which is what a lot of people do, including myself.'[84] Waits recognized that his wife had pushed him to 'plumb the depths of himself' and considered her the co-producer of *Swordfishtrombones*, although she wasn't formally given that credit.[85] On the album Waits dedicated the track 'Johnsburg, Illinois' to Brennan (her early years were spent in this small town 80 kilometres/50 mi. north of Chicago). A second musical love letter to his wife after 'Jersey Girl', the song stands out on this dark, discordant album as a bright piano ballad: its softly sung, intimate lyrics are unadorned. Waits directly states that his girl is his only true love: she is all that he can think of. He links the track to 'Shore Leave', in which a sailor pines for a girl back in Illinois. A short profession of love, the song is like a fleeting glimpse of a photo pulled from a wallet; a painted miniature, in which a lover's lock of hair is enclosed with her portrait.

'Johnsburg, Illinois' is almost an audio version of a cinematic extreme close-up. It's evident that Waits's *One from the Heart* movie experience greatly informs *Swordfishtrombones*. The album resembles a studio's backlot; the songs allow us to inhabit everywhere and nowhere. Like a camera, Waits's all-seeing eye tracks underground to find secret armies of dwarves, dissolves through to a Hong Kong dockside with a drunken sailor and stops to examine a pawnshop window crammed with props, before finding a deserted main street of an Australian ghost-town. Given how much his early work paid homage to the movies, it's ironic that the album in which Waits takes his leave of the celluloid city turns out to be the most cinematic of all. *Swordfishtrombones* breaks with the old Waits world, the hard-drinking, bohemian nights of the Top-Trop, the Ivar Theatre and the Skybar. However, the album still includes two songs of farewell to Los Angeles, contrasting in tone and relationship to the city. The first, 'In the Neighborhood', has a deliberately parochial feel; Waits simultaneously highlights and celebrates the warped small-mindedness of his home. It's a freewheeling journey, ricocheting around his unruly patch on the wrong side of the tracks. 'I was trying to bring the music outdoors with tuba trombone trumpets, snare, cymbals, accordion so it had that feeling of a Felliniesque-type of marching band going down the dirt road. And with glockenspiel to give it a feeling of a kind of a demented little parade band.'[86]

Waits chose cinematographer Haskell Wexler to shoot a music video for the track. Filming the promo in Waits and Brennan's actual East LA, it's a kind of 'home movie'. Waits prances with great gusto beside a motley crew of musicians, dwarves and hulks along Union Avenue and an alley directly behind his home. Wexler used both sepia tone and a fish-eye lens to age and distort the surreal procession. Waits is dressed as a fairground hustler, leading his troupe of misfits. In one sense, the ragged band represents Waits's songs as if they were his progeny (a later album, *Orphans* (2006), reinforces this idea of songs being like cast-offs, abandoned children). 'In the Neighborhood' presents a version of Waits proud to claim parentage of his troupe of misfits. Given how the album features dwarfs, strongmen, psychotic butchers and stranded sailors, the image of Waits as the ringmaster of a freak show is perfect. Waits exploits references to such classic films as Fellini's *Otto e Mezzo* (1963), which ends with Marcello Mastroianni parading the 'cast' of his life within a circus ring, and Todd Browning's silent movie *Freaks* (1932). Waits shares the album's cover photo with the midget, Angelo Rossitto (who appeared in *Freaks*), as well as legendary strongman Lee Kolima (whom Stanley Kubrick cast in his noir *The Killing*).

Waits had asked photographer Michael Russ to come up with a new image for him. The iconic cover photo of Waits in a languid pose, wearing touched-up blush and strong eyeshadow, did just that. Waits relished the heavy make-up, foregrounding his new self-conscious theatricality. *Swordfishtrombones* released the actor within him, which had been present from the start. In 'Martha' on *Closing Time*, Waits had sung as an old man, imagining himself as a lovelorn septuagenarian. Ten years later he fully embraced the protean nature of an actor's identity.

In a spirited farewell, 'In the Neighborhood' casts off Waits's old bohemian identity, the spine of his Los Angeles decade. But, paradoxically, the song is another postcard from LA; literally, a final walk around the block as a bona fide Angeleno. Singing about Filipino girls giggling by his local church, a broken window neglected by his landlord and the sidewalk being dug up by a jackhammer, Waits remains rooted in the familiar and domestic. In an album of global imaginings, it's a pastiche of parochialism, myopic yet affectionate.

The other song of farewell to Los Angeles, 'Frank's Wild Years', is, perhaps, the most important track on *Swordfishtrombones*. Music-ally, it's straightforward; the electric organ, accompanying the song's spoken word delivery, is very different to the layered sound textures that define most of the album. The jaunty Jimmy Smith-style jazz organ matches the monologue's dark, humorous take on postwar American conformity. The track is a portrait of Frank, a second-hand office furniture salesman with a newly built bungalow, complete

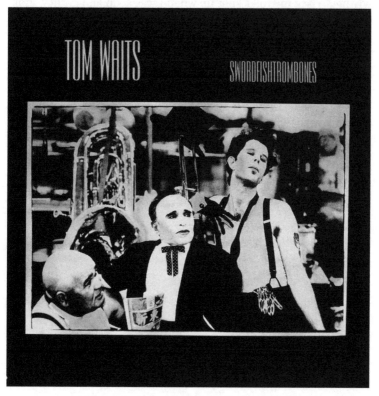

Front cover of *Swordfishtrombones* (1983).

with modern self-cleaning oven, lovely wife and Carlos, a pesky Chihuahua. Waits paints this version of a suburban LA idyll only to annihilate it. Frank 'is that little bit of the American dream that has gone straight to hell'.[87] 'Burning down the house', Frank relishes the sight of his old San Fernando life going up in bright, garish flames. He puts Los Angeles behind him, in his rearview mirror, as he hits the 101 Hollywood Freeway to head north.

Waits is finally addressing the story of his own father, who had walked out of his Whittier family life and home in 1959. Frank's desertion profoundly shaped his son's adolescence and outlook but, before 'Frank's Wild Years', Waits would mock even the thought of trying to confront such a psychologically heavy subject in his song-writing. 'Y'see my folks split up when I was a kid and . . . hey, look, let me give you $100 and I'll lie down on the couch over there, you take notes and let's see if we can get to the bottom of this.'[88]

'Frank's Wild Years' is Waits's oblique attempt to rewrite that story, transposing it into his own poetic language. The spoken-word rhythm recalls other father figures: Kerouac with his Beat prosody and Bukowski with 'The Shoelace', which Waits cited as a source for the song. Bukowski suggests that it's the little, nagging things that destroy a man's psyche:

> it's the continuing series of *small* tragedies
> that send a man to the madhouse . . .
> not the death of his love
> but a shoelace that snaps with no time left . . .
> the dread of life
> is that huge swarm of trivial shit
> that can kill quicker than cancer
> and which are always there – [89]

Despite the damage caused by his father's desertion, the song exhibits a gleeful exhilaration in Frank's revolt. 'I think there's a little bit of Frank in everyone. It's a cathartic dream.'[90] Waits wants to share the sense of freedom and release in Frank's act. Such rebellion or wildness was, after all, written into his DNA. 'In a sense I come from a family of runners. And if I had followed in my father's footsteps I'd be a runner myself, and so would my kids.'[91] There was a path that Frank Waits laid for his son that pulled him towards a crossroads. 'Frank's Wild Years' began a creative process which, over the next four years, developed the track into an album and a musical drama. As in 'Underground', it's also a metaphor for self-reinvention. Like his real and fictional Franks, Waits felt he had to cut off from his past to progress: 'It's like you start with a few colors and a certain style and you paint yourself into a corner. I didn't know how to break out unless I *set fire* to it all. And I was afraid to do that.'[92]

Waits describes his creative process with the same burning imagery he gives to 'Frank's Wild Years'. In his last LA album, Waits makes his own irrevocable break with a brutal relish and sense of reinvention. The birth of *Swordfishtrombones* could be seen as a parallel act of creative arson where he torches his LA base and past life. Waits would also get onto the Hollywood Freeway and head north, viewing the city in his rearview mirror when he and Brennan left LA for New York. It's no accident that Waits seized on fire imagery in his ode to a departure from the city. He knew how Nathaniel West, in his Los Angeles novel *The Day of the Locust*, had used burning as a thematic device. Throughout the novel, West's protagonist, the artist Homer Simpson, is painting a large tableau in the style of Goya called *The Burning of Los Angeles*. It's a key detail Joan Didion also picks up on in an essay from *Slouching towards Bethlehem* (1968). She focuses on Los Angeles in its 'burning' month of October:

> It is hard for people who have not lived in Los Angeles to realize how radically the Santa Ana figures in the local imagination. The city burning is Los Angeles's deepest image of itself; Nathaniel West perceived that in *The Day of the Locust*;

and at the time of the Watts riots, what struck the imagination most indelibly were the fires. For days one could drive the Harbor Freeway and see the city on fire, just as we had always known it would be in the end. Los Angeles weather is the weather of catastrophe, of apocalypse, the violence and the unpredictability of the Santa Ana affect the entire quality of life in Los Angeles, accentuate its impermanence, its unreliability. The wind shows us how close to the edge we are.[93]

In *Red Wind*, his short story about October in Los Angeles, Raymond Chandler wrote about how the Santa Ana winds 'make your nerves jump and your skin itch . . . Meek little wives feel the edge of the carving knife and study their husbands' necks. Anything can happen.'[94] Waits channelled this specific Angeleno sense of teetering on the edge of personal and social catastrophe in 'Frank's Wild Years'. He describes Frank's wife in deliberate noir fashion; she's a throwaway piece of used trash, a woman who knew how to shut up most of the time. Waits uses misogynistic images, which could come straight from West or Spillane.

'Frank's Wild Years' is one of Waits's finest spoken word tracks. It draws on his Kerouac-influenced attempts at the genre but has a more minimal and cinematic narrative mode. The song foreshadows much of his and Brennan's songwriting to come. Waits commented on how his wife had 'a great sense of story and of the architecture of a story'.[95] Brennan's influence on his work, from *Swordfishtrombones* onwards, would be profound. She helped separate Waits from everybody in his past, according to Howe and other LA friends. The 'Jersey Girl' became his muse and his critic. Her sharp irreverence ('she's quick – she can catch a bullet in her teeth, has a pet snake, a 64 Caddy, reads the *Wall Street Journal*, loves periodicals') made him step up a level.[96] Under her guidance and due to his re-energized creativity, Waits would go from being a neglected Californian artist to that of a world figure.

Waits went out on a limb with the recording of *Swordfishtrom-bones*. He had picked the engineer and the musicians, written the 'mission statement' for how he wanted it to sound and feel like. He admitted it was scary having to 'take responsibility for everything that goes on tape'.[97] When Waits took the tapes to Asylum there was no understanding of the quality of what he had produced. Joe Smith, the executive at Asylum/Elektra, hated it. 'This is a guy who looked like a sports announcer, so I didn't really have much of a rapport with him. I felt like I was talking to an insurance agent. He fancied himself as something of a mob boss, but he also had a little bit of a fraternity feel to him.'[98] Waits had spent a decade with the label, since David Geffen signed him up for *Closing Time*. But he'd grown frustrated with their evident disinterest. *Swordfishtrombones* proved the breaking point in the relationship:

I was at Elektra for over ten years and while I was there I spent a considerable amount of time on the road and blowing my own horn. They liked dropping my name in terms of me being a 'prestige' artist, but when it came down to it, they didn't invest a whole lot in me in terms of faith. Their identity was always more aligned with that Californian rock thing.[99]

It's remarkable that Waits and Asylum/Elektra had remained bed-fellows for so long, given the lack of any mutual empathy. 'I think they thought I was a drunk. And I was really very non-communicative. I scratched the back of my neck and I looked down at my shoes a lot, you know, and I wore old suits. They were nervous about me. But it's understandable.'[100]

With his label baffled and hostile, Waits asked to be released from his contract and the record executives agreed. Supported by Brennan, Waits looked for a label that valued him. They approached producer Chris Blackwell at Island Records. He had introduced reggae to non-Jamaican audiences and also had a reputation for supporting less commercial, more innovative artists. When the three met in a Los Feliz café, Brennan did most of the talking, persuading Blackwell to sign Waits and release *Swordfishtrombones*. 'I didn't know Tom's albums well, though I'd always loved "Tom Traubert's Blues",' Blackwell said. 'I loved the aura he projected, his presence, his extraordinary intelligence and his musical originality.'[101] Waits declared himself to be much happier on a smaller label and liked that Blackwell wasn't the average corporate executive. 'He is artistic, a philanthropist. You can sit and talk with him and you don't feel like you're at Texaco or Heineken or Budweiser. There's something operating here that has a brain, curiosity and imagination.'[102]

When *Swordfishtrombones* came out in September 1983, the musical press reviews were ecstatic. Critics latched onto its surreal, otherworldly quality. They realized that Waits had reinvented himself, pulling his music into a radically different place, although some of his fellow musicians pointed out that his musical development could be traced back : 'you could tell all of this was coming if you look back at "Red Shoes by the Drugstore".'[103]

> The music on *Swordfishtrombones* might have been different from the music he made before, but it wasn't different from his whole outlook. You could say it was like a World Music album, but it wasn't. You could say it was a new direction, but Tom was always capable of seeing all those things. It was more like something he just did finally, like he was stepping out of his own shadows.[104]

As co-producer of the 'new' Waits, *Swordfishtrombones* was also a triumph for Brennan and her successful influence over all aspects of her husband's life and work. Waits appreciated the new creative balance that she'd brought about. 'My life was getting more settled. I was staying out of bars. But my work was becoming more scary.'[105]

Conclusion:
A Strange Home of Your Own

I would rather be a failure on my terms than a success on
somebody else's. That's a difficult statement to live up to, but
then I've always believed the way you affect your audience is
more important than how many of them there are.

– Tom Waits, 1983[1]

The character of Frank, introduced in *Swordfishtrombones*,
would preoccupy Waits for the next few years. 'The tale of
an unfortunate American psychopath', as Waits described
Frank's narrative, led to the album *Franks Wild Years*, a two-act
musical revue and even a film of the stage show. 'A story about
failed dreams, about an accordion player from a small Californian
town who goes off to seek fame and fortune and ends off hoist on
his own petard . . . I would describe it as a cross between *Eraserhead*
and *It's a Wonderful Life*.'[2] Frank became a kind of anti-Waits doppel-
ganger in the singer's high-profile years after *Swordfishtrombones*;
the more Waits explored his alter ego's trajectory of failure and
decline, the more successful he seemed to become. *Franks Wild
Years* (1987) had followed the critically acclaimed *Rain Dogs* (1985)
to form an 'unofficial' trilogy of albums, initiated with *Swordfishtrombones* (1983). According to Waits, 'somehow the three [albums]
seem to go together. Frank took off in *Swordfish*, had a good time in
Rain Dogs and he's all grown up in *Franks Wild Years*. They seem to
be related – maybe not in content but at least in terms of being a
marked departure from the albums that came before.'[3] *Rain Dogs*
was the first album Waits and Brennan produced in New York,
having relocated away from LA. Waits explained the title referred to

'people who sleep in doorways . . . people who don't have credit cards . . . who don't go to church . . . who don't have a mortgage, who fly in this whole plane by the seat of their pants'.[4] However, despite the evident references to New York in *Rain Dogs* (tracks are even named 'Midtown' and 'Union Square'), songs such as 'Singapore' or 'Jockey Full of Bourbon' (which features sheets from a 'Hong Kong bed') give the album a wider international sensibility.

Rain Dogs and *Franks Wild Years* continue and deepen the transformation seen in *Swordfishtrombones*; this was no longer Tom Waits as 'Tom Waits'. Now he could be a lovesick sailor in the Far East, an angry mutant dwarf, a stranded alcoholic, a sociopath with arsonist tendencies or whatever he wanted. Under Brennan's influence, Waits could explore performance in a more Brechtian way, using modernist ideas of estrangement and foregrounding the mechanics of his diverse musical enactments. *Franks Wild Years* pushes deeper into exploring theatricality with its creation of a complex, layered persona. At the time of the album's release, Barney Hoskyns noted that the songs were 'really about performance. From the pulpit declamations of the preacher via the drinking song roar of "Innocent When You Dream" to the louche Sinatra hallucinating Las Vegas, they make up a rogues gallery of performing alter egos.'[5]

Given his shared interest with Brennan in creating his own form of musical theatre, it was no surprise that Waits would go on to become such a highly accomplished film actor. A cameo in a horror movie called *The Wolfen* (1981) saw him play his usual role of drunken pianist with a suitably uneven rendition of *Small Change*'s 'Jitterbug Boy'. But it was Francis Ford Coppola, again, who was first to realize Waits's acting potential. Having worked closely with him on *One from the Heart*, Coppola understood Waits's ability to shapeshift. He cast him as Buck Merrill in *The Outsiders* (1983), Benny, the pool hall owner in *Rumble Fish* (1983) and Irving Stark, the elegant, tuxedo-clad, stone-faced manager of *The Cotton Club* (1984). Waits described the transition from creating music to acting

Tom Waits in *Down by Law* (1986, dir. Jim Jarmusch).

as going from 'bootlegging to watch repair'.[6] His move into acting took place at the precise moment in the 1980s when his music was deepening his use of multiple personas, fracturing and reinventing his identity. Waits had finally managed to shake off the all-consuming image of 'wino man'; by 1992 he even managed to curtail his own excessive drinking and embraced sobriety. The idea of Waits no longer being a constant *habitué* of lowlife dive-bars was difficult for some critics and fans, who couldn't quite believe in a sober 'old Tom'. When Waits was asked whether he missed the booze, he claimed he had heard far better stories in AA meetings.

The influence of Brennan can be detected not only in his theatrical choices, but in every aspect of Waits's post-LA life and work. After living in New York for a while, the couple returned to California and, eventually, settled in the rural north of the state where they brought up their family in rustic seclusion. Far from becoming 'parochial' by breaking away from his Los Angeles roots and inhabiting a small Californian locality, Waits turned himself into a global artist. Brennan helped this process of Waits becoming a more international figure by 'curating' him; she pushed him to work with artists and directors who shared his avant-garde sensibilities and approach. Waits developed close relationships with several leading film directors. Jim Jarmusch (whom Waits named 'Dr Sullen') cast him as a co-lead in *Down by Law* (1986), a disembodied voice in *Mystery Train* (1989), a double act with Iggy Pop in *Coffee and Cigarettes* (2003) and a hermit called Bob in *The Dead Don't Die* (2019). Waits returned the favour, composing the film soundtrack for Jarmusch's *Night on Earth* (1991). He even played the devil incarnate in Terry Gilliam's film *The Imaginarium of Doctor Parnassus* (2009); Waits claimed he got on well with the ex-Python since they both 'drive a Buick, have a vestigial tail and horns', and 'our Mom's [*sic*] name is Alma'.[7] The range and depth of his acting ability is demonstrated in two notable performances: the limousine chauffeur Earl Piggons, who abuses his wife in *Short Cuts* (1993), Robert Altman's fine adaptation of Raymond Carver's stories; and the

Tom Waits with Jim Jarmusch on the set of *Down by Law* (1986).

Tom Waits and Iggy Pop in *Coffee and Cigarettes* (2003, dir. Jim Jarmusch).

grouchy, solitary prospector talking to an unseen pocket of gold in *The Ballad of Buster Scraggs* (2018) by the Coen Brothers.

In addition to his burgeoning film acting career (Waits has now appeared in more than thirty movies), another key collaboration was with Robert Wilson, an experimental stage director. Waits created powerfully expressive soundscapes for several of Wilson's acclaimed theatre productions; *The Black Rider* (1990), working alongside veteran Beat writer William Burroughs; a re-imagining of *Alice in Wonderland* (1992); and *Woyzeck* (2000), Georg Büchner's epic drama of alienation. Waits would also go on to release the instrumental soundtracks and songs from all these theatrical works as separate, complete albums; *The Black Rider* (1993), *Alice* (2002) and *Blood Money* (2002).

However, although in the years since he departed from Los Angeles, Waits's extraordinary musical diversity continued to grow, his recorded output became much less frequent. Waits's first decade of songwriting in Los Angeles had yielded nine original

Waits with Beat writer William Burroughs and theatre director Robert Wilson at the premiere of *The Black Rider* in the Thalia Theater, Hamburg, 1990.

albums (*Bounced Checks* was an Elektra compilation of songs drawn from earlier albums with alternate recordings). In the four decades since *Swordfishtrombones*, Waits has put out only six stand-alone albums of completely new material: *Rain Dogs* (1985), *Franks Wild Years* (1987), *Bone Machine* (1992), *Mule Variations* (1999), *Real Gone* (2004) and *Bad as Me* (2011).

Bone Machine marked another radical break in his musical development, a full stripping away of any excess instrumentation. Recorded in an old storage room with the audio battered and distorted, the album attempts to reduce everything to the near irreducible. 'Blood and death, those are my pet subjects,' Waits declared. 'It really is all about bones, cemeteries and dirty blood.'[8] The experimentation was continued in *Mule Variations*, the first album Waits produced after leaving Island Records, his recording home since *Swordfishtrombones* (Chris Blackwell, Island's founder, had resigned and Waits had no desire to be part of a conglomerate). *Mule Variations* takes the stripped-down, rural elements heard in *Bone Machine* and combines them with a country blues to create an almost new genre; what Waits called 'surrural'. 'Something somewhere between sur-real and rural. That's what these songs are. There's an element of something old about them, and yet it's kind of disorientating because it's not an old record by an old guy.'⁹ Tracks such as 'Take It with Me' and 'Georgia Lee' have a depth and timelessness; they seem to stretch right back into early twentieth-century Americana (one reason, perhaps, why *Mule Variations*, despite its blues inflections, won a Grammy for Best Contemporary Folk album). *Real Gone* came out the year after the American invasion of Iraq and, in one sense, completes another cycle or trilogy of albums. Like its two predeces-sors, the album maintains this powerful, idiosyncratic blend of the modern and the ageless. *Real Gone*'s final unadorned track, 'Day after Tomorrow', features a soldier writing home; he admits he's not fight-ing for justice and freedom, just his life and another day in the world. Such is the combined richness of Waits and Brennan's writing, the song becomes both a contemporary political commentary and a universal lament for the injustices of war.

Another seven years would pass before Waits released *Bad as Me*, his last album to date. Despite such a long gap in recording, *Bad as Me* is still full of vintage Waits; angry ('Hell Broke Luce' continues his rage against U.S. military aggression), passionate ('Kiss Me'), humane ('Pay Me', 'Chicago') and 'funny' ('Satisfied' sends up Jagger and Richards).

There has also been a sharp decline in Waits's live performances over the last few decades (in contrast to his increased worldwide media presence due to his acting). His last full concert tour, 'Glitter and Doom', was back in 2008. The constant touring of his early years has been replaced by a near complete aversion to appearing in public. Any sightings of Waits onstage have been fleeting and rare; appearing at Neil Young's Bridge House charity concert or joining veteran soul singer Mavis Staples in a rendition of 'Respect Yourself'. To compensate for his absence in performance, Waits, like other artists of his generation, has revisited and reworked his past, bringing out a monumental, sprawling three-disc box set, *Orphans: Brawlers, Bawlers and Bastards* (2006), which released 54 uncollected songs (including 32 new ones). Waits described it as 'a combination platter, rare and new. Some of it is only a few months old, and some of it is like the dough you have left over so you can make another pie.'[10]

However, Waits's music has always had an extensive life beyond his own performing. His songs have been sampled or covered by a vast array of artists including the Rolling Stones, Rod Stewart, Johnny Cash, Tim Buckley, the Ramones, 10,000 Maniacs, Bruce Springsteen, Elvis Costello, Marianne Faithful, Screamin' Jay Hawkins, the Blind Boys of Alabama, The Neville Brothers, Norah Jones, Tori Amos and Scarlett Johansson. One of his closest friends, the bluesman John Hammond Jr, released *Wicked Grin* (2001), an album composed (bar one track) entirely of Waits songs. *Come On Up to the House: Women Sing Waits*, a tribute album featuring a new generation of female singers, was released to mark the singer's seventieth birthday in 2019.

Although Waits and Brennan fiercely resisted appropriation of their work for commercials, they have allowed songs to be sampled extensively in movies and television shows ('Way Down in the Hole' from *Franks Wild Years* was a perfect choice for the title sequence track of HBO's *The Wire*). The widespread usage of Waits's music in film and TV has exposed and brought his work to new generations. By 2011, when Waits was inducted into the Rock and Roll Hall of Fame, he was routinely described as the finest post-Dylan American singer-songwriter. Barney Hoskyns went a stage further, claiming Waits to be 'as important an American artist as anyone the 20th century has produced'.[11] Not only is Waits now 'Big in Japan', as his ironic song title on *Rain Dogs* claimed, but can be said to belong to the world.

However, despite Waits becoming such a global figure and the great distance he has put between himself and his early Los Angeles-influenced, drunken Beat persona, the body of work he created while exploring the real and mythical life of the city still continues to resonate. Within his first nine albums, Los Angeles played a huge, central role in focusing his intense, poetic writing and nurturing his musical gifts. Responding to its strange, tawdry mix of sentimental dreaming and vicious social exclusion, Waits fashioned his own LA. His aesthetic response to the City of Angels, Waits's song noirs, is as lasting and distinctive as anything written by Raymond Chandler, Nathaniel West or Charles Bukowski.

The Los Angeles that Waits observed, imagined and recorded between 1973 and 1983 hardly exists any more. In fact, as Waits himself observed, it was being demolished even while he sang about it:

> If you live in Los Angeles things change so rapidly . . . if you leave town for two or three months, chances are they'll tear down the gas station or the donut shop or the cleaners where you go. The [Tropicana] hotel is gone, so I guess it stimulates your imagination about it once you tear down the place where it all happened. The stories get taller as the building gets shorter.[12]

Much of East LA, where Waits lived and celebrated in his music, is now unrecognizable. Gentrified, Silverlake has become an anodyne hipster hangout. The annual 'Crawling down Cahuenga' tour, which pays homage to Waits's LA by visiting sites associated with him, stops at the alley where the 'In the Neighborhood' video was shot. But the buildings have been bulldozed and the road is an unremarkable, uneven piece of tarmac. The Tropicana, with its infamous blackened pool and Waits's crammed apartment, has long been replaced by an anonymous Ramada Inn. The Troubadour club and the Ivar Theatre, key places Waits performed at or wrote about, are still in use, but their musical vitality has long since gone.

However, something of Waits's Los Angeles can still be witnessed today. Downtown, on Skid Row, the conditions and lives of LA's homeless, whom he sang about, are still as harsh and unforgiving. 'Tom Traubert's Blues' and 'On the Nickel', which bear witness to the suffering of the poor and downtrodden, resonate as much today as when they were recorded. Music, as Waits pointed out, is the closest thing to time travel: 'The studio is torn down, all the people who played on [these tracks] are dead, the instruments have been sold off. But you are listening to a moment that happened in time years ago and you are hearing it just as sharp as when it was made.'[13] Although *Song Noir* has traced the way Waits as an artist moved away from the 'literalism' of LA's street poetry, which dominated his first decade, I have also tried to show how this work retains its power and acts as a time capsule. Los Angeles grounded Waits and helped to make him an artist; it also threatened to unmake him when he confused the real and the imagined, the mask and the self. 'You have to be very clear about who you are and who it is you're projecting, but the two got very confusing. I got swept away with it, then felt I had to live up to something.'[14]

Waits felt an overwhelming need to bid farewell to Los Angeles and reinvented himself with the freedom of an actor. His exasperation or disquiet with the city by the time of *Heartattack and Vine* is palpable. Despite a myriad of cultural influences associated with the city, Waits felt he'd exhausted Los Angeles. The sense of creative release and farewell on *Swordfishtrombones*, which, although recorded in Hollywood, is not another LA album, is evident and exhilarating. Waits, with Brennan's help, found his way through to the dialectical freedom found in the work of Brecht and Weill. Putting on new identities, he could perform his version of a musical theatre where sound and lyric combine to define a character's sense of their world. It's a freedom from which he's never looked back. After Captain Beefheart died in 2010, Waits wrote a fine memorial poem, 'Don Is Like the Bones in a Watermelon'. He imagines traces of Beefheart being found in the natural sounds of the Mohave desert where the singer lived and died; the croak of a frog or the vibrations of a hollow tree. The poem's last lines hint at what Waits learnt and took from his fellow Californian iconoclast:

> Do not follow him
> Just take what clues he left and with them, go and build
> A strange home of your own.[15]

The words Waits chose for Beefheart feel appropriate for himself. In the years since he left Los Angeles behind in his creative wake, Waits continued on his idiosyncratic personal odyssey as an artist. He has never followed Beefheart's path or anyone else's. He took what clues were left and, with them, built a strange home of his own.

Chronology

7 December 1949 Birth of Thomas Alan Waits, son of Jesse Frank and
  Alma Waits

1949–59 Family lives at North Pickering Avenue, and then Kentucky Avenue,
  Whittier

1954–9 Attends Jordan Elementary School, Whittier

1959 Frank Waits leaves Whittier home. Tom's parents permanently separate

1960 Alma Waits relocates the family to Chula Vista, near San Diego,
  Southern California

1960–68 Attends O'Farrell Jnr High School and Hilltop High School, Chula
  Vista

1962 Sees James Brown and the Famous Flames at Balboa Park, San Diego

4 December 1964 Sees Bob Dylan perform at San Diego State University

1965–70 Starts part-time work at Napoleone's Pizza House, National City

1966 Forms The Systems, a school band that plays covers of soul music

1966 Buys his first car, a 1955 Buick Roadmaster (inspiration for his song
  'Ol' '55')

1968 Becomes fascinated with Jack Kerouac and other Beat writers

1968 Enrolls at Southwest Community College, Chula Vista, to study
  photography

1969 Works as an occasional doorman at the Heritage Club, San Diego

1969–71 Plays various folk club venues in San Diego and wider Southern
  California area

20 November 1970 First ever paid performance, at the Heritage Club

22 May 1971 Final appearance at the Heritage Club

June 1971 Manager Herb Cohen spots him playing at Doug Weston's
  Troubadour club, in West Hollywood, Los Angeles, and offers him
  a songwriting contract

July–August 1971 First demo recordings for Herb Cohen (later released
  against his wishes in two volumes as *The Early Years*)

Early 1972 Moves to Los Angeles and rents a one-room apartment in Silverlake, which he shares with Bobi Thomas, a girlfriend from San Diego

Early 1972 David Geffen hears Waits at the Troubadour and signs him for Asylum

Early 1972 Records his debut album, *Closing Time*, at Sunset Sound studio, Los Angeles

6 March 1973 Asylum Records releases *Closing Time*

April 1973 Visits Edson Cemetery in Lowell, Massachusetts, to find Jack Kerouac's grave

April–May 1973 First tour of the USA, promoting *Closing Time* (dates included Washington DC, Massachusetts, New York, Michigan and San Francisco)

June 1973 Moves to a larger apartment, 1309 North Coronado Street, Echo Park, Los Angeles

November–December 1973 Second U.S. tour promoting *Closing Time* (opening act for Frank Zappa and The Mothers of Invention)

February 1974 Meets Chuck E. Weiss outside Ebbetts Field club, Denver, Colorado

February–August 1974 Third *Closing Time* U.S. tour (opens for Zappa again)

22 April and 13–22 May 1974 Records *The Heart of Saturday Night* at Wally Heider Studios, Cahuenga Boulevard, Los Angeles, working with producer Bones Howe for the first time

October–December 1974 First tour to promote *The Heart of Saturday Night*

30 January 1975 In-depth article on Waits in *Rolling Stone*

January–September 1975 Second tour to promote *The Heart of Saturday Night*

30 and 31 July 1975 Records *Nighthawks at the Diner*, a 'live' double album at the Record Plant studio in Los Angeles

October 1975 *Nighthawks at the Diner* album released

October 1975–May 1976 U.S. tour promoting *Nighthawks at the Diner*

May–June 1976 First, short European tour (the Netherlands, Belgium, Denmark, West Germany and the UK – two weeks at Ronnie Scott's)

June 1976 Moves to live in a two-room apartment at the Tropicana Motel (Chuck E. Weiss has a neighbouring bungalow)

15–29 July 1976 Records *Small Change* album at Wally Heider Studios.

21 September 1976 Asylum releases *Small Change*

October–December 1976 First U.S. tour to promote *Small Change*

7–22 January 1977 Tours Japan for the first time

9 April 1977 Appears on *Saturday Night Live* TV show, New York

April–May 1977 U.S. and European tour to promote *Small Change* (Germany, Finland, Netherlands and the UK)

27 May 1977 Assaulted and then arrested by plainclothes LAPD officers at Duke's coffee shop along with Chuck E. Weiss

26 July–15 August 1977 Records *Foreign Affairs* album

Summer 1977 Meets Rickie Lee Jones for the first time, outside the Troubadour

13 September 1977 Asylum releases *Foreign Affairs*

October 1977–March 1978 U.S. tour promoting *Foreign Affairs*

1–13 March 1978 Tours Japan for a second time

6 April 1978 Appears on *90 Minutes Live* – interviewed in his Tropicana apartment

24 July–26 August 1978 Records *Blue Valentine* in Wally Heider Studios

September 1978 Photo shoot for cover of *Blue Valentine* features Rickie Lee Jones and Chuck E. Weiss

5 September 1978 Asylum releases *Blue Valentine*

5 October 1978–15 December 1978 First *Blue Valentine* tour in the USA

Early 1979 Release of *Tom Waits for No One*, a short, animated film

March 1979 Release of *Rickie Lee Jones* album

17–28 April 1979 Short European tour (Copenhagen, Rotterdam, Vienna, London, Dublin, Brussels and Paris) to promote *Blue Valentine*

30 April–14 May 1979 First tour of Australia

May 1979 Rickie Lee Jones's 'Chuck E.'s in Love' released and becomes hit single

26 July 1979 Records *Tonight in Person*, BBC TV concert documentary in London

1–9 September 1979 Accompanies Rickie Lee Jones on her European tour

Late September 1979 Moves out of Tropicana apartment and into a place on Crenshaw Boulevard, East LA

Early October 1979 Splits up with Rickie Lee Jones

6 October–15 December 1979 Second *Blue Valentine* tour in the USA

31 December 1979 Meets Kathleen Brennan at New Year's Eve party

January–May 1980 Moves to live in New York, disillusioned with LA life

April 1980 Francis Ford Coppola asks Waits to write a soundtrack for *One from the Heart*

May 1980 Returns to live in Los Angeles

May 1980–May 1981 Composes *One from the Heart* soundtrack based based at the Zoetrope lot at Sunset Las Palmas studios, Hollywood, Los Angeles

June 1980 Meets Kathleen Brennan for second time at Zoetrope, falls instantly in love and is engaged within a week

16 June–15 July 1980 Records *Heartattack and Vine* album at RCA Studios on Ivar Avenue and Sunset Boulevard, Hollywood, Los Angeles

10 August 1980 Marries Kathleen Brennan at Always Forever Yours Wedding Chapel, Manchester Boulevard, Los Angeles

August 1980 Honeymoon in Tralee, County Kerry, Ireland

September 1980 Moves into new apartment with Brennan on Union Avenue, between Downtown Los Angeles and MacArthur Park, East Los Angeles

October 1980–September 1981 Records music for *One from the Heart*

8–23 November 1980 Short U.S. tour to promote *Heartattack and Vine*

1981 Asylum releases *Bounced Checks*, a compilation album of alternate versions and one unreleased track

5 March–8 April 1981 European tour to promote *Heartattack and Vine*

21 August 1981 Guest appearance with Bruce Springsteen, Los Angeles Memorial Sports Arena

10 September–21 October 1981 Australia and New Zealand tour to promote *Heartattack and Vine*

11 February 1982 *One from the Heart* movie released

February 1982 Releases *One from the Heart* soundtrack album

February 1982 Breaks with manager Herb Cohen and separates from Bones Howe

March 1982 Wins lawsuit against LAPD for assault in 1977

5–18 May 1982 U.S. tour to promote *One from the Heart*

August 1982 Produces and records *Swordfishtrombones* at Sunset Sound, Hollywood, Los Angeles

September 1982 Asylum dislikes and rejects the tapes of *Swordfishtrombones*

Early 1983 Meets Chris Blackwell from Island Records, who signs him to the label

11 April 1983 Attends Oscar ceremony as nominee for best film soundtrack

Summer 1983 Acts in films *Rumblefish* and *The Outsiders*, both directed by Coppola

1 September 1983 Island Records releases *Swordfishtrombones*

Late September 1983 Birth of his first child, a daughter called Kellesimone

18 October 1983 Appears in video for 'In the Neighborhood' filmed and directed by Haskell Wexler next to Waits and Brennan's home in East LA

Spring 1984 Leaves Los Angeles and moves to New York

References

Introduction: Crawling down Cahuenga

1 Dave Zimmer, 'Hollywood Confidential', BAM (26 February 1982), www.rocksbackpages.com, accessed 23 March 2021.
2 Leonie Cooper, 'All Aboard the Tom Waits Bus Tour' (23 April 2012), www.theguardian.com, accessed 17 October 2020.
3 Alex Pappademas, 'Fifty Years of LA Rock: An Interview with Tom Waits' (12 March 2009), www.gq.com, accessed 5 March 2020.
4 William Burroughs, '"Heart Beat": Fifties Heroes as Soap Opera', *Rolling Stone*, 309 (24 January 1980), p. 30.
5 Hannah Lack, 'Scandal, Sleaze and Punk Rock: Inside the Tropicana Motel' (5 April 2016), www.anothermag.com, accessed 17 October 2020.
6 Douglas Cape, 'Los Angeles: Troubadour', *Hitch 76: What a Long Strange Trip It's Been* (1976), www.hitch76.com, accessed 17 October 2020.
7 Rickie Lee Jones, *Last Chance Texaco: Chronicles of a Troubadour* (New York, 2021), p. 248.
8 Barney Hoskyns, 'The Marlowe of the Ivories', NME (25 May 1985), www.rocksbackpages.com, accessed 23 March 2021.
9 Mick Brown, 'My Wild Years and the Woman That Saved My Life', *The Word*, 46 (December 2006), p. 85.
10 Jack Kerouac, *On the Road* (London, 2011), p. 25.

1 Riding with Lady Luck

1 Bill Milkowski, 'Tom Waits', *Downbeat* (March 1986), www.tomwaitslibrary.info, accessed 24 September 2019.
2 Rafael Behr, 'Screamin', Hollerin', Shakin'', *The Observer* (16 March 2005), www.guardian.com, accessed 10 March 2020.
3 Ibid.

4 Tom Waits, introduction to a concert in Princeton, New Jersey
   on 16 April 1976, 'Quotes: Childhood', www.tomwaitslibrary.info,
   accessed 23 March 2021.
5 Robert Sabbag, 'Tom Waits Makes Good', *Los Angeles Times Magazine*
   (22 February 1987), p. 20.
6 Dave Lewis, 'Tom Waits: A Sobering Experience', *Sounds*
   (August 1979), p. 32.
7 Barney Hoskyns, *Lowside of the Road: A Life of Tom Waits*
   (London, 2009), p. 7.
8 George Vargas, 'Tom Waits Interview', *San Diego Union
   Tribune* (3 October 2004), www.tomwaitsfan.com, accessed
   23 March 2021.
9 Francis Thumm, 'Tom's Wild Years', *Interview* (October 1988),
   p. 110.
10 Mick Brown, 'My Wild Years and the Woman That Saved My Life',
   in *Tom Waits on Tom Waits: Interviews and Encounters*,
   ed. Paul Maher Jr (Chicago, IL, 2011), p. 430.
11 Tom Waits, introducing 'Kentucky Avenue' at the Apollo Theatre
   in London in 1981, 'Live Monologues/Cues/Intros', www.
   tomwaitslibrary.info, accessed 2 December 2019.
12 'Tom Foolery: Swapping Stories with Inimitable Tom Waits',
   Buzz (May 1993), www.tomwaitslibrary.info, accessed
   3 December 2019.
13 Edwin Pouncey, 'Swordfish Out of Water', *Sounds* (5 November
   1983), www.rocksbackpages.com, accessed 23 March 2021.
14 Sean O'Hagan, 'Off Beat', *The Observer* (29 October 2006),
   www.guardian.com, accessed 19 December 2019.
15 Barney Hoskyns, 'Tom Waits: The *Mojo* Interview', *Mojo*
   (April 1999), p. 75.
16 Hoskyns, *Lowside of the Road*, p. 17.
17 Hoskyns, 'Tom Waits', p. 75.
18 Brown, 'My Wild Years', pp. 425–41.
19 Patrick Humphries, 'Heart of Saturday Morning', *Melody Maker*
   (14 March 1981), p. 36.
20 Sylvie Simmons, 'The *Mojo* Interview: Tom Waits Speaks',
   in *Tom Waits on Tom Waits*, p. 368.
21 Nigel Williamson, 'Dirt Music', *Sydney Morning Herald*
   (27 April 2002), www.smh.com.au, accessed 16 December 2019.
22 Bruna Lombardi, 'Interview with Tom Waits' (2009), from the
   series *Gente De Expressão*, www.tomwaitslibrary.info, accessed
   19 December 2019.

23 Jim Jarmusch, 'Tom Waits Meets Jim Jarmusch', in *Innocent When You Dream: Tom Waits, the Collected Interviews*, ed. Mac Montandon (London 2007), pp. 167–204.

24 Sylvie Simmons, 'The *Mojo* Interview', pp. 366–76.

25 Mark Richard, 'The Music of Chance', *Spin* (June 1994), p. 52.

26 Thumm, 'Tom's Wild Years', p. 110.

27 Rip Rense, 'Tom Waits: A Q&A about *Mule Variations*', *Performing Songwriter* (July–August 1999), www.tomwaitslibrary.info, accessed 28 December 2019.

28 Mick Brown, 'Tom Waits, Hobo Sapiens', *Telegraph Magazine* (11 April 1999).

29 Tom Waits, 'It's Perfect Madness', *The Observer* (20 March 2005), www.guardian.com, accessed 24 September 2019.

30 Gavin Martin, 'Everything Goes to Hell', *Uncut* (June 2002), www.rocksbackpages.com, accessed 23 March 2021.

31 Dan Forte, 'Tom Waits: Off-Beat Poet and Pianist', *Contemporary Keyboard* (April 1977), www.tomwaitsfan.com, accessed 2 January 2020.

32 Robert Hilburn, 'Pop Music: Tracking an Elusive Character', *Los Angeles Times (Calendar)* (6 June 1999), p. 58.

33 Hoskyns, *Lowside of the Road*, p. 30.

34 Terry Gross, 'Tom Waits: On "Alice" and "Blood Money"', interview on National Public Radio (21 May 2002), www.npr.org, accessed 21 February 2020.

35 Tom Waits interview with WAMU radio, 18 April 1975.

36 Stan Soocher, 'Tom Waits for No One', *Circus Weekly* (23 January 1979), in *Tom Waits on Tom Waits*, p. 108.

37 David Fricke, 'The Resurrection of Tom Waits', *Rolling Stone*, 815 (24 June 1999), p. 40.

38 Hoskyns, 'Tom Waits', p. 76.

39 Hoskyns, *Lowside of the Road*, p. 31.

40 Ibid.

41 David McGee, 'Smelling Like a Brewery, Lookin' Like a Tramp', interview with Tom Waits, *Rolling Stone*, 231 (27 January 1977), p. 12.

42 Behr, 'Screamin', Hollerin', Shakin''.

43 Kristine McKenna, 'One from the Heart and One for the Road', *NME* (1 October 1983), p. 39.

44 O'Hagan, 'Off Beat'.

45 Jack Kerouac, *On the Road* (New York, 1999), pp. 169–70.

46 Jay Jacobs, *Wild Years: The Myth and Music of Tom Waits* (Toronto, 2006), p. 31.

47 Hoskyns, 'Tom Waits', p. 76.

48 Jonathan Valania, 'It's Last Call Somewhere in the World', *Magnet* (October/November 2004), p. 72.

49 Terry Gross, Interview with 'Tom Waits'.

50 Mick Brown, 'My Wild Years', p. 432.

51 McKenna, 'One from the Heart and One for the Road', p. 24.

52 Rich Wiseman, 'Tom Waits, All Night Rambler', *Rolling Stone* (30 January 1975), p. 18.

53 Steve Lake, 'Waits: Last Great White Hope', *Melody Maker* (4 October 1975), www.tomwaitslibrary.info, accessed 19 December 2019.

54 John Nova Lomax, 'God, Texas and Tom Waits' (18 June 2008), www.houstonpress.com, accessed 9 January 2020.

55 Bob Webb, 'Tom Waits at the Heritage', www.tomwaitslibrary.info, accessed 9 January 2020.

56 Rich Trenbeth, 'The Ramblin' Street Life Is the Good Life for Tom Waits', in *Tom Waits on Tom Waits*, p. 81.

57 Hoskyns, *Lowside of the Road*, p. 45.

58 Brown, 'Tom Waits: Hobo Sapiens', p. 53.

59 Patrick Humphries, *The Many Lives of Tom Waits* (London, 2007), p. 38.

60 Peter O'Brien, 'Watch Out for 16-Year-Old Girls Wearing Bell Bottoms', in *Innocent When You Dream*, pp. 11–19.

61 Adam Sweeting, 'Tom Waits: A Mellower Prince of Melancholy', *The Guardian* (15 September 1992), www.rocksbackpages.com, accessed 9 January 2020.

62 'Tom Foolery: Swapping Stories with Inimitable Tom Waits', *Buzz* (May 1993), www.tomwaitslibrary.info, accessed 9 January 2020.

63 Humphries, *The Many Lives of Tom Waits*, p. 39.

64 Marc Eliot, *To the Limit: The Untold Story of the Eagles* (New York, 1997), p. 34.

65 Ibid., p. 40.

66 Hoskyns, 'Tom Waits', *Mojo* (April 1999), p. 78.

67 Todd Everett, 'Tom Waits: Not So Much a Poet, More a Purveyor of Inspirational Dialogue', NME (29 November 1975), www.rocksbackpages.com, accessed 23 March 2021.

68 Ibid.

69 Wiseman, 'Tom Waits', p. 18.

70 Kenny Weissberg, 'Tom Waits: Saturday Night Seeker', *Colorado Daily* (18 February 1974), in *Tom Waits on Tom Waits*, p. 19.

71 Stan Soocher, 'Tom Waits for No-One', in *Tom Waits on Tom Waits*, p. 108.
72 Humphries, *The Many Lives of Tom Waits*, p. 43.
73 Ibid., p. 32.
74 Soocher, 'Tom Waits for No-One', p. 108.
75 Wiseman, 'Tom Waits', p. 18.
76 Jonathan Valania, 'It's Last Call Somewhere in the World', *Magnet* (October/November 2004), p. 72.
77 Soocher, 'Tom Waits for No-One', pp. 107–8.
78 Humphries, 'Heart of Saturday Morning', p. 11.
79 Barney Hoskyns, 'Tom Waits', audio interview (28 January 1999), www.rocksbackpages.com, accessed 23 March 2021.
80 David McGee, 'Smelling Like a Brewery, Lookin' Like a Tramp', interview with Tom Waits in *Rolling Stone*, 231 (27 January 1977), pp. 12 and 15.
81 Wiseman, 'Tom Waits', p. 18.
82 Nathaniel West, *Miss Lonelyhearts and the Day of the Locust* (New York, 2009), p. 178.
83 Hoskyns, *Lowside of the Road*, p. 71.
84 Hoskyns, 'Tom Waits', audio interview.
85 Hoskyns, 'Tom Waits', p. 78.
86 Hoskyns, *Lowside of the Road*, p. 71.
87 Ibid., p. 79.
88 Ibid., p. 75.
89 Jacobs, *Wild Years*, p. 38.
90 Barney Hoskyns, *Hotel California: The True-Life Adventures of Crosby, Stills, Nash, Young, Mitchell, Taylor, Browne, Ronstadt, Geffen, the Eagles, and Their Many Friends* (Hoboken, NJ, 2006), p. 132.
91 Hoskyns, *Lowside of the Road*, p. 76.
92 Jeff Walker, 'Tom Waits: Thursday Afternoon, Sober as a Judge', *Music World* (1 June 1973), www.rocksbackpages.com, accessed 24 March 2021.
93 Fred Goodman, *The Mansion on the Hill: Dylan, Young, Geffen, Springsteen and the Head-On Collision of Rock and Commerce* (New York, 1998), p. 142.
94 Barney Hoskyns, 'Long Gone: Tom Waits Talks' (3 September 2004), www.rocksbackpages.com, accessed 23 March 2021.
95 Walker, 'Tom Waits'.
96 Fred Dellar, 'Would You Say This Man Was Attempting to Display an Impression of Sordid Bohemianism?', NME (5 June 1976), www.rocksbackpages, accessed 23 March 2021.

97 Tom Waits, introducing 'Virginia Avenue' at Boston Music Hall on 21 March 1976, 'Live Monologues/Cues/Intros', www.tomwaitslibrary.info, accessed 15 March 2020.

98 Reyner Banham, *Los Angeles: The Architecture of Four Ecologies* [1971], with an introduction by Anthony Vidler (Berkeley, CA, 2001), p. 195.

99 Joan Didion, *Play It as It Lays* [1970] (New York, 2005), p. 16.

100 Kristine McKenna, 'One from the Heart and One for the Road', NME (1 October 1983), p. 24.

101 Ibid.

102 O'Brien, 'Watch Out for 16-Year-Old Girls Wearing Bell Bottoms', p. 14.

103 Ibid.

104 Tom Waits, concert introduction, Boston Music Hall, 21 March 1976, in Jacobs, *Wild Years*, p. 40.

105 Jacobs, *Wild Years*, p. 40.

106 Ibid., p. 42.

107 Ibid., p. 46.

108 Hoskyns, *Lowside of the Road*, p. 84.

109 Ibid.

110 Stephen Holden, 'Closing Time' (26 April 1973), www.rollingstone.com, accessed 13 January 2021.

111 Hoskyns, *Lowside of the Road*, p. 53.

112 Humphries, *The Many Lives of Tom Waits*, p. 49.

113 Hoskyns, *Lowside of the Road*, pp. 66–7.

114 Richard Cromelin, 'Waits: Personality without Pretension', *Los Angeles Times (Calendar)* (14 March 1976), p. 64.

2 Neon Buzzin'

1 Jack Kerouac, *On the Road* (New York, 2011), p. 77.

2 Jay Jacobs, *Wild Years: The Myth and Music of Tom Waits* (Toronto, 2006), pp. 43–4.

3 John Dullaghan (dir.), *Bukowski: Born into This* (2003).

4 Ibid.

5 Ibid.

6 Charles Bukowski, *Confessions of a Man Insane Enough to Live with Beasts* [1965] (Los Angeles, CA, 1973), p. 168.

7 Dullaghan, *Bukowski*.

8 Charles Bukowski, *Post Office* (New York, 2014), p. 192.

9 Ibid., p. 89.

10 Mick Brown, 'My Wild Years and the Woman That Saved My Life', *The Word*, 46 (December 2006), p. 94.

11 Barney Hoskyns, *Lowside of the Road: A Life of Tom Waits* (London, 2009), p. 97.

12 Jack Kerouac, *Visions of Cody* (New York, 1972), p. 85.

13 Hoskyns, *Lowside of the Road*, p. 97.

14 Dan Daley, '"Bones" Howe & Tom Waits: The Odd Couple?' (February 2004), www.soundonsound.com, accessed December 2019.

15 Hoskyns, *Lowside of the Road*, p. 105.

16 Bones Howe, conversation with author, November 2019.

17 Ibid.

18 Ibid.

19 Ibid.

20 Ibid.

21 Ibid.

22 Jacobs, *Wild Years*, p. 53.

23 Hoskyns, *Lowside of the Road*, pp. 148–9.

24 Howard Larman, 'Interview with Tom Waits, *FolkScene* KPFK' (23 July 1974), in *Tom Waits on Tom Waits: Interviews and Encounters*, ed. Paul Maher Jr (Chicago, IL, 2011), p. 24.

25 Ibid.

26 Ibid., p. 9.

27 Ibid., p. 23.

28 Hoskyns, *Lowside of the Road*, p. 110.

29 Jacobs, *Wild Years*, pp. 55–6.

30 Sylvia Simmons, 'The *Mojo* Interview: Tom Waits Speaks', in *Tom Waits on Tom Waits*, p. 370.

31 Hoskyns, *Lowside of the Road*, p. 99.

32 Ibid., pp. 123–4.

33 Ibid., p. 120.

34 Ibid., p. 127.

35 Fred Dellar, 'Would You Say This Man Was Attempting to Display an Impression of Sordid Bohemianism?', NME (5 June 1976), www.rocksbackpages.com, accessed 23 March 2021.

36 Simmons, 'The *Mojo* Interview', p. 370.

37 David McGee, 'Smelling Like a Brewery, Lookin' Like a Tramp', *Rolling Stone*, 231 (27 January 1977), p. 15.

38 Barry Miles, *Zappa: A Biography* (London, 2004), p. 299.

39 Barney Hoskyns, 'Tom Waits: The *Mojo* Interview', *Mojo* (April 1999), p. 78.

40 Simmons, 'The *Mojo* Interview', p. 369.

41 David Fricke, 'The Resurrection of Tom Waits', *Rolling Stone*, 815 (24 June 1999), p. 40.

42 Hoskyns, *Lowside of the Road*, p. 118.

43 Todd Everett, 'Tom Waits: Not So Much a Poet, More a Purveyor of Inspirational Dialogue', *nme* (29 November 1975), www.rocksbackpages.com, accessed 23 March 2021.

44 Don Roy King, email to Blue Valentines (2 July 1999), 'Comments/ Anecdotes on Waits', www.tomwaitslibrary.info, accessed 2 November 2019.

45 Betsy Carter and Peter S. Greenwood, 'Sweet & Sour', *Newsweek* (14 June 1976), p. 84.

46 Patrick Humphries, 'Heart of Saturday Morning', *Melody Maker* (14 March 1981), p. 11.

47 Fricke, 'The Resurrection of Tom Waits', p. 40.

48 Jack Kerouac, 'Introduction', in Robert Frank, *The Americans* (New York, 1986), p. 5.

49 Marco Barla, 'Los Angeles Is Poetry', in *Tom Waits on Tom Waits*, p. 37.

50 Lou Curtiss, 'From Bouncing to Hooting to Playing the Band', *San Diego Reader* (13 January 1974), in *Tom Waits on Tom Waits*, p. 14.

51 Patrick Humphries, *The Many Lives of Tom Waits* (London, 2007), p. 61.

52 Dellar, 'Would You Say This Man Was Attempting to Display an Impression of Sordid Bohemianism?'

53 Humphries, *The Many Lives of Tom Waits*, p. 60.

54 McGee, 'Smelling Like a Brewery', p. 15.

55 Marv Hohman, 'Bitin' the Green Shiboda with Tom Waits' (17 June 1976), in *Downbeat: The Great Jazz Interviews: A 75th Anniversary Anthology*, ed. Franck Alkyer and Ed Enright (New York, 2009), p. 169.

56 Hoskyns, *Lowside of the Road*, p. 131.

57 Steve Oney, 'Twenty Questions: Tom Waits', *Playboy* (March 1988), p. 129.

58 Barla, 'Los Angeles Is Poetry', p. 36.

59 Rich Wiseman, 'Tom Waits, All Night Rambler', *Rolling Stone* (30 January 1975), p. 18.

60 Howe, conversation with author.

61 Hoskyns, *Lowside of the Road*, p. 132.

62 Tom Waits, spoken introduction to 'On a Foggy Night', *Nighthawks at the Diner* (1975).

63 Jacobs, *Wild Years*, p. 61.
64 Daley, '"Bones" Howe & Tom Waits'.
65 Jacobs, *Wild Years*, p. 61.
66 Howard Larman, 'Interview with Tom Waits', KPFK Unplugged Radio Session (23 July 1974), in *Tom Waits on Tom Waits*, p. 21.
67 Hoskyns, *Lowside of the Road*, p. 181.
68 Tom Waits, 'WAMU Radio Interview, 18 April 1975', www.tomwaitslibrary.info, accessed December 2019.
69 Tom Waits, spoken introduction to 'On a Foggy Night', *Nighthawks at the Diner* (1975).
70 Waits, 'WAMU Radio Interview'.
71 Carter and Greenwood, 'Sweet & Sour', p. 84.
72 Tom Waits, '*The Heart of Saturday Night* Press Release, 1974', in *Innocent When You Dream: Tom Waits, The Collected Interviews*, ed. Mac Montandon (London, 2007), p. 4.

3 Everything's Broken

1 Richard Cromelin, 'Waits: Personality without Pretension', *Los Angeles Times (Calendar)* (14 March 1976), p. 64.
2 Jason Solomon, 'RIP: Remembering Chuck E. Weiss', www.westword.com (24 July 2021), accessed 5 August 2021.
3 'Chuck E. Weiss and Rickie Lee Jones', www.tomwaitslibrary.info, accessed 10 September 2020.
4 Barney Hoskyns, *Lowside of the Road: A Life of Tom Waits* (London, 2009), p. 138.
5 Ibid., p. 125.
6 Ibid., p. 190.
7 Tom Waits, introducing 'Jitterbug Boy' at West Chester Jazz Festival on 2 October 1976, 'Live Monologues/Cues/Intros', www.tomwaitslibrary.info, accessed 15 March 2020.
8 Jay Jacobs, *Wild Years: The Myths and Music of Tom Waits* (Toronto, 2006), p. 68.
9 Mick Brown, 'Warm Beer, Cold Women', *Sounds* (12 June 1976), www.rocksbackpages.com, accessed 24 March 2021.
10 Hoskyns, *Lowside of the Road*, p. 151.
11 Jacobs, *Wild Years*, p. 204.
12 Marv Hohman, 'Bitin' the Green Shiboda with Tom Waits' (17 June 1976), in *Downbeat: The Great Jazz Interviews. A 75th Anniversary Anthology*, ed. Franck Alkya and Ed Enright (New York, 2009), p. 169.

13 Hoskyns, *Lowside of the Road*, pp. 170–71.

14 Ibid., p. 165.

15 Hal Willner, sleeve notes for *Tom Waits: Used Songs, 1973–1980* (2001).

16 Hoskyns, *Lowside of the Road*, p. 141.

17 Dave Marsh, 'Tom Waits: Reno Sweeney's', *Rolling Stone* (23 October 1975), www.rocksbackpages.com, accessed 24 March 2021.

18 David Koepp, 'The Odyssey of Tom Waits: The Raspy Voiced Piano Man Has Time for the Future', *Circus* (22 December 1977), www.tomwaitslibrary.info, accessed 15 March 2020.

19 Bones Howe, conversation with author, November 2019.

20 Bill Flanagan, *Written in My Soul: Interviews with Rock's Great Songwriters* (New York, 1987).

21 David McGee, 'Smelling Like a Brewery, Lookin' Like a Tramp', interview with Tom Waits in *Rolling Stone*, 231 (27 January 1977), p. 15.

22 Tom Waits, introducing 'Jitterbug Boy' at State Theatre in Sydney on 2 May 1979, 'Live Monologues/Cues/Intros', www.tomwaitslibrary.info, accessed 15 March 2020.

23 Cab Calloway, 'Call of the Jitterbug' (1934).

24 McGee, 'Smelling Like a Brewery, Lookin' Like a Tramp', p. 15.

25 Billy Wilder and Charles Brackett, *Sunset Boulevard: The Complete Screenplay* (Los Angeles, CA, 1999), p. 18.

26 Ross Maclean, 'The Ivar Theatre', www.tomwaitslibrary.info, accessed 10 September 2020.

27 Brian Case, 'Tom Waits: Wry and Danish to Go', *Melody Maker* (5 May 1979), p. 17.

28 Bob Claypool, 'For Waits City Life Is Small Change', *Houston Post* (12 December 1976), www.tomwaitslibrary.info, accessed 10 March 2020.

29 David Hepworth, 'Waits Refuses to Face His Critics', NME (20 November 1976), www.rocksbackpages.com, accessed 24 March 2021.

30 Hoskyns, *Lowside of the Road*, pp. 162–3.

31 Barney Hoskyns, 'Interview with Tom Waits' (28 January 1999), www.rocksbackpages.com, accessed 23 March 2021.

32 Rich Trenbeth, 'The Ramblin' Street Life Is the Good Life for Tom Waits', *Country Rambler* (30 December 1976), in *Tom Waits on Tom Waits: Interviews and Encounters*, ed. Paul Maher Jr (Chicago, IL, 2011), p. 81.

33 Mikel Jollett, 'Tom Waits on Harry Partch, Charles Bukowski, Myths, Rap and Nerds', *SOMA* (July 2002), www.tomwaitslibrary.info, accessed 20 March 2020.
34 Ibid.
35 Hoskyns, *Lowside of the Road*, p. 146.
36 McGee, 'Smelling Like a Brewery, Lookin' Like a Tramp', p. 15.
37 Robert Ward, 'Play It Again, Tom', in *Tom Waits on Tom Waits*, p. 56.
38 McGee, 'Smelling Like a Brewery, Lookin' Like a Tramp', p. 15.
39 Ibid.
40 Alex Pappademas, 'Fifty Years of LA Rock: Interview with Tom Waits' (12 March 2009), www.gq.com, accessed 5 March 2020.
41 Paul Morrissey (dir.), *Andy Warhol's Heat* (1972).
42 Jacobs, *Wild Years*, p. 45.
43 Ibid.
44 Bruna Lombardi, 'Interview with Tom Waits', from the series *Gente De Expressão*, www.tomwaitslibrary.info, accessed 20 March 2020.
45 Ibid.
46 Hoskyns, *Lowside of the Road*, p. 157.
47 Ibid., p. 158.
48 Charles Schwab, sleeve notes for *Tom Waits: Used Songs, 1973–1980* (2001).
49 John Lamb, 'Tom Waits for No One' (no publication date), www.tomwaitslibrary.info, accessed 5 March 2020.
50 Grover Lewis, 'Bette Bounces Back', *New West* (13 March 1978), p. 22.
51 Ibid.
52 Trenbeth, 'The Ramblin' Street Life Is the Good Life for Tom Waits', pp. 77–82.
53 Cromelin, 'Waits: Personality without Pretension', p. 64.
54 Hoskyns, *Lowside of the Road*, pp. 159–60.
55 Ibid., p. 160.
56 Ibid., p. 138.
57 Howe, conversation with author, November 2019.
58 Hoskyns, *Lowside of the Road*, p. 160.
59 Howe, conversation with author, November 2019.
60 Ibid.
61 Case, 'Tom Waits', p. 17.
62 Sam Fuller (dir.), *Pickup on South Street* (1953).
63 Koepp, 'The Odyssey of Tom Waits'.

64 The novel is collected with other works in Joseph Mitchell, *Up in the Old Hotel*, with an introduction by William Fiennes (London, 2012), quotation p. 483.

65 Tom Waits, introducing 'Muriel' at the Apollo Victoria Theatre in London, 20/21 March 1981, 'Live Monologues/Cues/Intros', www.tomwaitslibrary.info, accessed 15 March 2020.

66 Muriel Panatela Extra Cigars advertisement (1965), www.youtube.com, accessed March 2020.

67 Bruce Weber, 'Edie Adams, Actress and Singer (and Flirt with a Cigar) Dies at 81' (16 October 2008), www.nytimes.com, accessed 10 March 2020.

68 Lewis, 'Bette Bounces Back', p. 22.

69 Richard J. Pietschmann, 'Tom Waits: Skid Row', *Playgirl* (November 1978), p. 70.

70 Billy Wilder and Raymond Chandler, *Double Indemnity*: *The Complete Screenplay* (Los Angeles, CA, 2000), pp. 17–18.

71 Jack Kerouac, *Visions of Cody* (New York, 1993), p. 39.

72 Hoskyns, *Lowside of the Road*, p. 187.

73 Case, 'Tom Waits', p. 17.

74 Kristine McKenna, 'One from the Heart and One for the Road', NME (1 October 1983), p. 24.

75 Case, 'Tom Waits', p. 17.

76 R. Rayner, 'Dog Day Afternoon', *Time Out* (3 October 1985), www.tomwaitslibrary.info, accessed 10 March 2020.

77 Tom Waits, introducing 'Burma-Shave' at Austin City Limits on 5 December 1978, 'Live Monologues/Cues/Intros', www.tomwaitslibrary.info, accessed 15 March 2020.

78 Rayner, 'Dog Day Afternoon'.

79 'Tom Foolery: Swapping Stories with Inimitable Tom Waits', *Buzz* (May 1993), www.tomwaitslibrary.info, accessed 10 March 2020.

80 A study of these signs is to be found in Frank Rowsome Jr, *The Verse by the Side of the Road: Story of the Burma-Shave Signs and Jingles* (New York, 1979).

81 Hoskyns, *Lowside of the Road*, p. 191.

82 Mike Davis, *City of Quartz: Excavating the Future in Los Angeles* (London, 1990), p. 40.

83 Ibid., p. 41.

84 Hoskyns, *Lowside of the Road*, p. 177.

85 Mick Brown, 'Tom Waits: Hobo Sapiens', *Telegraph Magazine* (11 April 1999), p. 55.

86 Barney Hoskyns, 'The Marlowe of the Ivories, NME (25 May 1985), www.rocksbackpages.com, accessed 10 March 2020.

87 Rickie Lee Jones, *Last Chance Texaco: Chronicles of a Troubadour* (New York, 2021), p. 248.

88 Jim Jarmusch, 'Tom Waits Meets Jim Jarmusch', *Straight No Chaser*, 1/20 (25 February 2000), www.tomwaitslibrary.info, accessed 11 March 2020.

89 Delores Ziebarth, 'Tom Waits Arrested in LA', *Rolling Stone*, 243 (14 July 1977), p. 15.

90 Ibid.

91 'Random Notes', *Rolling Stone*, 245 (11 August 1977), p. 31.

92 Ziebarth, 'Tom Waits Arrested in LA', p. 15.

93 Jarmusch, 'Tom Waits Meets Jim Jarmusch'.

94 Steve Pond, 'Tom Waits on *One from the Heart*' (1 April 1982), www.rollingstone.com, accessed 15 March 2020.

4 I'm Never Going Home

1 David Koepp, 'The Odyssey of Tom Waits: The Raspy Voiced Piano Man Has Time for the Future', *Circus* (22 December 1977), www.tomwaitslibrary.info, accessed 15 March 2020.

2 Clark Peterson, 'Sleazy Rider: A Man Who Works at Being Derelict', *Relix* (June 1978), www.tomwaitslibrary.info, accessed April 2020.

3 'Chuck E. Weiss and Rickie Lee Jones', www.tomwaitslibrary.info, accessed 15 March 2020.

4 Timothy White, *Rock Lives: Profiles and Interviews* (New York, 1991), p. 679.

5 Barney Hoskyns, *Lowside of the Road: A Life of Tom Waits* (London, 2009), p. 194.

6 Rickie Lee Jones, *Last Chance Texaco: Chronicles of a Troubadour* (New York, 2021), p. 242.

7 Rickie Lee Jones, promotional material on *Flying Cowboys* CD (1989).

8 Timothy White, 'Rickie Lee Jones: A Walk on the Jazz Side of Life', *Rolling Stone*, 279 (9 August 1979), p. 42.

9 White, *Rock Lives*, p. 682.

10 White, 'Rickie Lee Jones', p. 42; quote from press pack for Rickie Lee Jones, *Flying Cowboys* (1989).

11 Jones, *Last Chance Texaco*, p. 238.

12 White, *Rock Lives*, p. 679.

13 Jones, *Last Chance Texaco*, p. 249.

14 White, *Rock Lives*, p. 679.

15 Ibid.
16 Rickie Lee Jones in *Chuck E.'s in Love: The Story behind the Song*, in *Top 2000 a Go-Go* (2015), www.youtube.com, accessed April 2021; Jones, *Last Chance Texaco*, p. xv.
17 White, 'Rickie Lee Jones', p. 43.
18 Rob Hughes, 'Interview with Rickie Lee Jones', *Uncut* (April 2007), www.tomwaitslibrary.info, accessed April 2020.
19 White, 'Rickie Lee Jones', p. 45.
20 'Chuck E. Weiss and Rickie Lee Jones'.
21 Jones, *Last Chance Texaco*, p. xiv.
22 Ibid., p. 249.
23 Ibid., p. 268.
24 Andy Gill, 'The Devil in Miss Jones', *The Independent* (16 January 2004), www.rocksbackpages, accessed 29 March 2021.
25 Hoskyns, *Lowside of the Road*, p. 197.
26 Jones, *Last Chance Texaco*, p. 267.
27 Ibid., p. 312.
28 Mikael Gilmore, 'Tom Waits for His Next Album', *Rolling Stone* (7 September 1978), p. 17.
29 Ibid.
30 Charley Delisle, 'Waits Bringing New Band, Same Old Clothes', in *Tom Waits on Tom Waits: Interviews and Encounters*, ed. Paul Maher Jr (Chicago, IL, 2011), p. 106.
31 Barney Hoskyns, 'The Marlowe of the Ivories', NME (25 May 1985), www.rocksbackpages.com, accessed 29 March 2021.
32 Hoskyns, *Lowside of the Road*, p. 207.
33 Jones, *Last Chance Texaco*, p. 274.
34 Ibid., p. 278.
35 Ibid.
36 Stan Soocher, 'Tom Waits for No One', in *Tom Waits on Tom Waits*, p. 107.
37 Greg Linder, 'Tom Waits: Little Murders', in *Twin Cities Reader* (17 November 1978), www.tomwaitslibrary.info, accessed 15 March 2020.
38 Ibid.
39 White, 'Rickie Lee Jones', p. 41.
40 Liam Lacey, 'Tom Waits Is Having a Devil of a Time' (21 December 2009), www.theglobeandmail.com, accessed 12 March 2020.

41 Sylvie Simmons, 'The *Mojo* Interview: Tom Waits Speaks', in *Tom Waits on Tom Waits*, p. 372.

42 Hoskyns, *Lowside of the Road*, p. 203.

43 Ibid., p. 225.

44 Rob Hughes, 'Rickie Lee Jones: Booze Valentine', *Uncut* (April 2007), p. 78.

45 Hoskyns, *Lowside of the Road*, p. 222.

46 White, *Rock Lives,* p. 690.

47 Hoskyns, *Lowside of the Road*, p. 194.

48 White, *Rock Lives,* p. 679.

49 Jones, *Last Chance Texaco*, p. 268.

50 White, *Rock Lives,* p. 679.

51 Jones, *Last Chance Texaco*, p. 268.

52 Ibid., p. 312.

53 Ibid., p. 313.

54 Simon Hattenstone, 'The Devil and Miss Jones' (18 October 2003), www.theguardian.com, accessed 18 March 2021.

55 Mick Brown, 'Life on the Edge: Rickie Lee Jones', *Telegraph Magazine* (26 August 2000), p. 49.

56 Jay Jacobs, *Wild Years: The Music and Myth of Tom Waits* (Toronto, 2006), p. 90.

57 Richard J. Pietschmann, 'Tom Waits: Skid Row', *Playgirl* (November 1978), p. 70.

58 Gavin Martin, 'Tom Waits: Everything Goes to Hell', *Uncut* (June 2002), www.rocksbackpages.com, accessed March 2021.

59 Hoskyns, *Lowside of the Road*, p. 228.

60 Sean O'Hagan, 'Off Beat', *The Observer* (29 October 2006), www.theguardian.com, accessed 19 December 2019.

61 Jones, *Last Chance Texaco*, p. 320.

62 Hoskyns, 'The Marlowe of the Ivories'.

63 Patrick Humphries, 'Heart of Saturday Morning', *Melody Maker* (14 March 1981), p. 11.

64 Dave Zimmer, 'Hollywood Confidential', BAM (26 February 1982), www.rocksbackpages.com, accessed 23 March 2021.

65 Koepp, 'The Odyssey of Tom Waits'.

66 Stephen K. Peeples, 'Tom Waits Q&A: *Heartattack and Vine*', in *Tom Waits on Tom Waits*, p. 118.

67 Patrick Humphries, *The Many Lives of Tom Waits* (London, 2007), p. 135.

68 Peeples, 'Tom Waits Q&A: *Heartattack and Vine*', p. 117.

69 Ibid., p. 116.

70 Nick Kent, 'Tom Waits: Heartattack and Vine', NME (11 October 1980), www.rocksbackpages.com, accessed 29 March 2021; Humphries, *The Many Lives of Tom Waits*, p. 139.

71 Humphries, *The Many Lives of Tom Waits*, p. 139.

72 Ibid., p. 111.

73 Simmons, 'The *Mojo* Interview', p. 373.

74 Humphries, 'Heart of Saturday Morning', p. 11.

75 Dave Zimmer, 'Hollywood Confidential', BAM (26 February 1982), sidebar on 'One from the Heart', www.tomwaitslibrary.info, accessed 23 March 2021.

5 In the Neighborhood

1 Mick Brown, 'He's a Coppola Swell', *The Guardian* (17 March 1981), p. 9.

2 Dave Zimmer, 'Hollywood Confidential', BAM (26 February 1982), www.rocksbackpages.com, accessed 23 March 2021.

3 Ibid.

4 Barney Hoskyns, 'Tom Waits: The *Mojo* Interview', *Mojo* (April 1999), p. 80.

5 'A Conversation with Tom Waits', Island Records promo material for *Swordfishtrombones* (1983), in *Tom Waits on Tom Waits: Interviews and Encounters*, ed. Paul Maher Jr (Chicago, IL, 2011), pp. 130–36.

6 Stephen K. Peeples, 'Tom Waits Q&A: *Heartattack and Vine*' (4 September 1980), in *Tom Waits on Tom Waits*, pp. 114–26.

7 Patrick Humphries, 'Heart of Saturday Morning', *Melody Maker* (14 March 1981), p. 11.

8 Zimmer, 'Hollywood Confidential'.

9 Ibid.

10 Ibid.

11 Patrick Humphries, *The Many Lives of Tom Waits* (London, 2007), p. 125.

12 Bones Howe, conversation with author, November 2019.

13 Humphries, 'Heart of Saturday Morning', p. 11.

14 Zimmer, 'Hollywood Confidential'.

15 Barney Hoskyns, *Lowside of the Road: A Life of Tom Waits* (London, 2009), p. 239.

16 Humphries, *The Many Lives of Tom Waits*, p. 129.

17 Howe, conversation with author.

18 Clare Barker, 'Make Mine a Double', *Black + White* (June/July 2002), www.tomwaitslibrary.info, accessed 15 March 2021.

19 Gavin Martin, 'Everything Goes to Hell', *Uncut* (June 2002), www.rocksbackpages.com, accessed 29 March 2021.

20 Elizabeth Gilbert, 'Play It Like Your Hair's on Fire', *GQ* (June 2002), tomwaitslibrary.com, accessed 31 March 2021.

21 Humphries, 'Heart of Saturday Morning', p. 11.

22 Gilbert, 'Play It Like Your Hair's on Fire'.

23 Jim Jarmusch, 'Tom Waits Meets Jim Jarmusch', *Straight No Chaser* (October 1992), in *Innocent When You Dream: Tom Waits, the Collected Interviews*, ed. Mac Montandon (London, 2007), pp. 167–204.

24 Hoskyns, *Lowside of the Road*, p. 255.

25 Elliot Murphy, 'Drifter Finds a Home', *Rolling Stone*, 466 (January 1986), p. 20.

26 Peeples, 'Tom Waits Q&A: *Heartattack and Vine*', pp. 114–26.

27 Hoskyns, *Lowside of the Road*, p. 252.

28 Richard Grant, 'Bard of the Bizarre', *Telegraph Magazine* (October 2005), www.tomwaitslibrary.info, accessed 31 March 2021.

29 'The Making of *One from the Heart*', TV documentary for TF1 (France, 1982), www.tomwaitslibrary.info, accessed 31 March 2021.

30 Zimmer, 'Hollywood Confidential'.

31 Brown, 'He's a Coppola Swell', p. 9.

32 Howe, conversation with author.

33 Ibid.

34 Sheila Benson, '*One from the Heart*: Less of a Tug Today', *Los Angeles Times (Calendar)* (1 March 1990), p. F2.

35 Ibid.

36 Richard Rayner, 'Dog Day Afternoon', *Time Out* (3 October 1985), www.tomwaitslibrary.info, accessed 31 March 2021.

37 Hoskyns, 'Tom Waits', p. 82.

38 Hoskyns, *Lowside of the Road*, p. 271.

39 Zimmer, 'Hollywood Confidential'.

40 Hoskyns, *Lowside of the Road*, p. 271.

41 Hoskyns, 'Tom Waits', p. 79.

42 Howe, conversation with the author.

43 Dan Daley, '"Bones" Howe & Tom Waits: The Odd Couple?', *Sound on Sound* (February 2004), www.soundonsound.com, accessed 23 March 2021.

44 Zimmer, 'Hollywood Confidential'.

45 Francis Thumm, 'Tom's Wild Years', *Interview* (October 1988), p. 112.

46 Ibid.

47 Michael Evans, 'Tom Waits: The Restless Iconoclast',
   The Oregonian (15 December 1999), www.tomwaitslibrary.info,
   accessed 31 March 2021.

48 John Robinson, 'Captain Beefheart and His Magic Band: *Trout Mask
   Replica*' (6 December 2013), www.uncut.co.uk, accessed
   19 March 2021.

49 Tom Waits and Kathleen Brennan, 'On Captain Beefheart . . .'
   (21 December 2010), www.tomwaits.com, accessed
   20 March 2021.

50 Richard Cromelin, 'Don Van Vliet Dies, 1941–2010: Pivotal Figure
   in Avant-Garde Rock', *Los Angeles Times* (18 December 2010),
   pp. AA1 and AA6.

51 Karin Schoemer, 'Holding On: A Conversation with Tom Waits',
   Newsweek (24 April 1999), in *Innocent When You Dream*, p. 267.

52 Sylvie Simmons, 'Tom Waits Speaks', *Mojo* (October 2004),
   www.rocksbackpages.com, accessed 31 March 2021.

53 Jay Jacobs, *Wild Years: The Music and Myth of Tom Waits* (Toronto,
   2006), p. 117 (ellipses in original).

54 Rip Rense, '*Bone Machine* Press Kit' (13 December 1992),
   www.tomwaitslibrary.info, accessed 1 April 2021.

55 Steve Oney, 'Twenty Questions: Tom Waits', *Playboy* (March 1988),
   p. 129.

56 George Varga, 'Interview with Tom Waits', *San Diego Union-Tribune*
   (3 October 2004), tomwaitslibrary.com, accessed
   31 March 2021.

57 Thumm, 'Tom's Wild Years', p. 112.

58 Nigel Williamson, 'Dirt Music', *Sydney Morning Herald*
   (27 April 2002), www.smh.com.au, accessed 31 March 2021.

59 Mikel Jollett, 'Tom Waits', SOMA (July 2002),
   www.tomwaitslibrary.info, accessed March 2020.

60 David Fricke, 'The Resurrection of Tom Waits', *Rolling Stone*, 815
   (24 June 1999), p. 39.

61 Kid Millions, 'The Beat Goes On', *Rock Bill* (October 1983),
   www.tomwaitslibrary.info, accessed 31 March 2021.

62 Thumm, 'Tom's Wild Years', p. 112.

63 Ibid.

64 'A Conversation with Tom Waits', p. 130.

65 Ibid.

66 Ibid.

67 Hoskyns, *Lowside of the Road*, p. 286.

68 'A Conversation with Tom Waits', p. 131.

69 Millions, 'The Beat Goes On'.

70 Barney Hoskyns, 'Variations on Tom Waits', *The Independent* (May 1999), www.rocksbackpages.com, accessed 16 June 2021.

71 'A Conversation with Tom Waits', p. 131.

72 Edward Pouncey, 'Swordfish Out of Water', *Sounds* (15 November 1983), www.rocksbackpages.com, accessed 31 March 2021.

73 'A Conversation with Tom Waits', p. 133.

74 Pouncey, 'Swordfish Out of Water'.

75 'Waits on Identity, the Creative Process, and *Swordfishtrombones*', in *Tom Waits on Tom Waits*, p. 149.

76 Barney Hoskyns, *Lowside of the Road*, p. 279.

77 'A Conversation with Tom Waits', p. 132.

78 Ibid.

79 Greil Marcus, *The Old Weird America: The World of Bob Dylan's Basement Tapes* (New York, 2011), p. 85.

80 Kid Millions, 'Waits on Bagpipes and the Writing Process', in *Tom Waits on Tom Waits*, p. 141.

81 'Waits on Identity', p. 149.

82 'A Conversation with Tom Waits', pp. 130–36.

83 Richard Grant, 'Bard of the Bizarre', *Telegraph Magazine* (4 October 2004), www.tomwaitslibrary.info, accessed November 2020.

84 Pete Silverton, 'The Lie in Waits', *Vox* (23 October 1992), www.rocksbackpages.com, accessed 1 April 2021.

85 Varga, 'Interview with Tom Waits'.

86 'A Conversation with Tom Waits', p. 133.

87 Barney Hoskyns, 'The Marlowe of the Ivories', *NME* (25 May 1985), www.rocksbackpages.com, accessed March 2020.

88 Gavin Martin, 'Hard Rain', *NME* (19 October 1985), www.rocksbackpages.com, accessed 1 April 2021.

89 Charles Bukowski, 'The Shoelace', *Essential Bukowski* (New York 2018), p. 71.

90 Hoskyns, 'The Marlowe of the Ivories'.

91 Mick Brown, 'My Wild Years and the Woman That Saved My Life', *The Word*, 46 (December 2006), p. 91.

92 Bill Forman, 'Better Waits Than Ever', in *Tom Waits on Tom Waits*, p. 194.

93 Joan Didion, 'Los Angeles Notebook', in *We Tell Ourselves Stories in Order to Live: Collected Nonfiction* (New York, 2006), p. 164.

94 Raymond Chandler, 'Red Wind', in *Collected Stories* (New York 2002), p. 685.

95 Thumm, 'Tom's Wild Years', p. 112.
96 Ibid.
97 Terry Gross, Tom Waits: On "Alice" and "Blood Money", interview
   on National Public Radio (21 May 2002), www.npr.org, accessed
   21 February 2020.
98 Mark Kemp, 'Weird Science', *Harp* (December 2006),
   www.rocksbackpages, accessed 1 April 2021.
99 Kristine McKenna, 'One from the Heart and One for the Road', NME
   (1 October 1983), p. 39.
100 Gross, 'Tom Waits'.
101 Hoskyns, *Lowside of the Road*, p. 293.
102 Martin, 'Hard Rain'.
103 Hoskyns, *Lowside of the Road*, p. 285.
104 Ibid., p. 294.
105 Fricke, 'The Resurrection of Tom Waits', p. 40.

Conclusion: A Strange Home of Your Own

1 Robert Elms, 'Skid Romeo', *The Face* (September 1983), in
  Tom Waits on Tom Waits: Interviews and Encounters, ed. Paul Maher Jr
  (Chicago, IL, 2011), pp. 136–40.
2 Barney Hoskyns, 'The Marlowe of the Ivories', NME (25 May 1985),
  p. 28.
3 Rip Rense, 'From the Set of Ironweed', tourbook for *Frank's
  Wild Years* (1987), www.tomwaitslibrary.info, accessed
  6 April 2021.
4 Michael Terson, 'TV Interview with Tom Waits', CBC (stereo),
  Canada (late 1985), in *Tom Waits on Tom Waits*, pp. 168–80.
5 Barney Hoskyns, '*Tom Waits: Frank's Wild Years*', NME (August 1987),
  www.rocksbackpages.com, accessed 6 April 2021.
6 Hoskyns, 'The Marlowe of the Ivories'.
7 Steve Inskeep, 'Waits Is Devilish in *Imaginarium of Doctor Parnassus*',
  Morning Edition (28 December 2009), www.npr.org, accessed
  6 April 2021.
8 Michael Fuchs Gambock, 'Ghost in the Machine', *Rock World*
  (October 1992), www.tomwaitslibrary.info, accessed 6 April 2021.
9 Rip Rense, 'Tom Waits: A Q&A about *Mule Variations*', Anti Records
  promotional material (April 1999), www.tomwaitslibrary.
  info, accessed 6 April 2021.
10 Sean O'Hagan, 'Off Beat', *The Observer* (29 October 2006),
   www.theguardian.com, accessed 6 April 2021.

11 Barney Hoskyns, *Lowside of the Road* (London, 2009), p. xxv.
12 Jay Jacobs, *Wild Years: The Music and Myth of Tom Waits* (Toronto, 2006), p. 117.
13 Tim Adams, 'Tom Waits: "I Look Like Hell but I'm Going to See Where It Gets Me"' (23 October 2011), www.guardian.com, accessed 6 April 2021.
14 Mick Brown, 'He's a Coppola Swell: Tom Waits', *The Guardian* (March 1981), p. 9.
15 Published in a booklet that came with the boxset release, *Captain Beefheart: Sun Zoom Spark: 1970 to 1972* (2014), p. 11.

Select Bibliography

Algren, Nelson, *A Walk on the Wild Side* (New York, 1990)
—, *The Man with the Golden Arm* (New York, 1996)
Babitz, Eve, *Eve's Hollywood* (New York, 2015)
—, *Slow Days, Fast Company: The World, the Flesh, and LA* (New York, 2016)
Banham, Rayner, *Los Angeles: The Architecture of Four Ecologies* [1971],
    with an introduction by Anthony Vidler (Berkeley, CA, 2001)
Barla, Marco, 'Los Angeles Is Poetry', in *Tom Waits on Tom Waits:
    Interviews and Encounters,* ed. Paul Maher Jr (Chicago, IL, 2011)
Brown, Mick, 'Warm Beer, Cold Women', *Sounds* (12 June 1976),
    www.rocksbackpages.com, accessed 24 March 2021
—, 'Tom Waits: Hobo Sapiens', *Telegraph Magazine* (11 April 1999),
    pp. 50–57
—, 'Life on the Edge: Rickie Lee Jones', *Telegraph Magazine* (26 August
    2000), p. 49
—, 'My Wild Years and the Woman That Saved My Life', *The Word*, 46
    (December 2006), pp. 84–94
Bruce, Lenny, *How to Talk Dirty and Influence People: An Autobiography*
    (Boston, MA, 2016)
Bukowski, Charles, *Confessions of a Man Insane Enough to Live with Beasts*
    (Los Angeles, CA, 1973)
—, *Factotum* (New York, 2002)
—, *Post Office* (New York, 2014)
—, 'The Shoelace', in *Essential Bukowski* (New York, 2018)
Burroughs, William, '"Heart Beat": Fifties Heroes as Soap Opera',
    Rolling Stone, 309 (24 January 1980), p. 30
Carter, Betsy, and Peter S. Greenwood, 'Sweet & Sour', *Newsweek*
    (14 June 1976), p. 84
Case, Brian, 'Tom Waits: Wry and Danish to Go', *Melody Maker*
    (5 May 1979), p. 17

Chandler, Raymond, *The Big Sleep* (New York, 1988)
—, *Farewell My Lovely* (New York, 1988)
—, 'Red Wind', in *Collected Stories* (New York, 2002)
'Chuck E. Weiss and Rickie Lee Jones', www.tomwaitslibrary.info,
    accessed 15 March 2020
Claypool, Bob, 'For Waits City Life Is Small Change', *Houston Post*
    (12 December 1976), www.tomwaitslibrary.info, accessed
    10 March 2020
Cromelin, Richard, 'Waits: Personality without Pretension', *Los Angeles
    Times (Calendar)* (14 March 1976), p. 64
Cooper, Leonie, 'All Aboard the Tom Waits Bus Tour', *The Guardian*
    (23 April 2012), www.theguardian.com, accessed 17 October 2020
Curtiz, Michael (dir.), *Angels with Dirty Faces* (1938)
Daley, Dan, '"Bones" Howe & Tom Waits: The Odd Couple?'
    (February 2004), www.soundonsound.com, accessed
    December 2019
Davis, Mike, *City of Quartz: Excavating the Future in Los Angeles*
    (London, 1990)
Delisle, Charley, 'Waits Bringing New Band, Same Old Clothes',
    in *Tom Waits on Tom Waits: Interviews and Encounters*, ed.
    Paul Maher Jr (Chicago, IL, 2011)
Dellar, Fred, 'Would You Say This Man Was Attempting to Display
    an Impression of Sordid Bohemianism?', NME (5 June 1976),
    www.rocksbackpages.com, accessed 23 March 2021
Didion, Joan, *Play It as It Lays* [1970] (New York, 2005)
—, 'Los Angeles Notebook', in *We Tell Ourselves Stories in Order to Live:
    Collected Nonfiction* (New York, 2006)
Dullaghan, John (dir.), *Bukowski: Born into This* (2003)
Eliot, Marc, *To the Limit: The Untold Story of the Eagles* (New York, 1997)
Everett, Todd, 'Tom Waits: Not So Much a Poet, More a Purveyor
    of Inspirational Dialogue', NME (29 November 1975),
    www.rocksbackpages.com, accessed 23 March 2021
Fante, John, *Ask the Dust* (New York, 2006)
Flanagan, Bill, *Written in My Soul: Interviews with Rock's Great Songwriters*
    (New York, 1987)
Fricke, David, 'The Resurrection of Tom Waits', *Rolling Stone*, 815
    (24 June 1999), pp. 39–40
Fuller, Sam (dir.), *Pickup on South Street* (1953)
Gardner, Leonard, *Fat City* (New York, 2015)
Gill, Andy, 'The Devil in Miss Jones', *The Independent* (16 January 2004),
    www.rocksbackpages, accessed 29 March 2021

Gilmore, Mikael, 'Tom Waits for His Next Album', *Rolling Stone*
    (7 September 1978), p. 17

Goodman, Fred, *The Mansion on the Hill: Dylan, Young, Geffen, Springsteen*
    and the Head-On Collision of Rock and Commerce (New York, 1998)

Hattenstone, Simon, 'The Devil and Miss Jones' (18 October 2003),
    www.theguardian.com, accessed 18 March 2021

Hayes, Alfred, *In Love* (New York, 2013)

Hohman, Marv, 'Bitin' the Green Shiboda with Tom Waits' (17 June
    1976), in *Downbeat: The Great Jazz Interviews. A 75th Anniversary*
    Anthology, ed. Franck Alkya and Ed Enright (New York, 2009)

Hoskyns, Barney, 'The Marlowe of the Ivories', *nme* (25 May 1985),
    www.rocksbackpages.com, accessed 10 March 2020

—, 'Tom Waits', audio interview (28 January 1999),
    www.rocksbackpages.com, accessed 23 March 2021

—, 'Tom Waits: The *Mojo* Interview', *Mojo* (April 1999), pp. 72–85

—, 'Long *Gone*: Tom Waits Talks' (3 September 2004),
    www.rocksbackpages.com

—, *Hotel California: The True-Life Adventures of Crosby, Stills, Nash, Young,*
    Mitchell, Taylor, Browne, Ronstadt, Geffen, the Eagles, and Their Many
    Friends (Hoboken, nj, 2006)

—, *Lowside of the Road: A Life of Tom Waits* (London, 2009)

Hughes, Dorothy B., *In a Lonely Place* (New York, 2017)

Hughes, Rob, 'Rickie Lee Jones: Booze Valentine', *Uncut* (April 2007),
    pp. 76–9

Humphries, Patrick, 'Heart of Saturday Morning', *Melody Maker*
    (14 March 1981), pp. 11 and 36

—, *The Many Lives of Tom Waits* (London, 2007)

Jacobs, Jay, *Wild Years: The Myths and Music of Tom Waits* (Toronto,
    2006)

Jarmusch, Jim, 'Tom Waits Meets Jim Jarmusch', in *Innocent When You*
    Dream: Tom Waits, the Collected Interviews, ed. Mac Montandon
    (London, 2007), pp. 167–204

Jollett, Mikel, 'Tom Waits on Harry Partch, Charles Bukowski, Myths,
    Rap and Nerds', *soma* (July 2002), www.tomwaitslibrary.info,
    accessed 20 March 2020

Jones, Rickie Lee, *Last Chance Texaco: Chronicles of a Troubadour*
    (New York, 2021)

Kerouac, Jack, *On the Road* [1957] (London, 2011)

—, *Visions of Cody* (New York, 1972)

—, 'Introduction', in Robert Frank, *The Americans* (New York, 1986),
    p. 5

King, Don Roy, email to Blue Valentines (2 July 1999), 'Comments/ Anecdotes on Waits', www.tomwaitslibrary.info, accessed 2 November 2019

Klein, Norman M., *The History of Forgetting: Los Angeles and the Erasure of Memory* (New York, 2008)

Koepp, David, 'The Odyssey of Tom Waits: The Raspy Voiced Piano Man Has Time for the Future', *Circus* (22 December 1977), www.tomwaitslibrary.info, accessed 15 March 2020

Lacey, Liam, 'Tom Waits Is Having a Devil of a Time' (21 December 2009), www.theglobeandmail.com, accessed 12 March 2020

Lamb, John, 'Tom Waits for No One' (no publication date), www.tomwaitslibrary.info, accessed 5 March 2020

Larman, Howard, 'Interview with Tom Waits', *FolkScene* KPFK (21 September 1973), in *Tom Waits on Tom Waits: Interviews and Encounters*, ed. Paul Maher Jr (Chicago, IL, 2011)

—, 'Interview with Tom Waits', *FolkScene* KPFK (23 July 1974), in *Tom Waits on Tom Waits: Interviews and Encounters*, ed. Paul Maher Jr (Chicago, IL, 2011), p. 24

Lewis, Grover, 'Bette Bounces Back', *New West* (13 March 1978), p. 22

Linder, Greg, 'Tom Waits: Little Murders', in *Twin Cities Reader* (17 November 1978), www.tomwaitslibrary.info, accessed 15 March 2020

McCullers, Carson, *The Heart Is a Lonely Hunter* (New York, 1992)

—, *Reflections in a Golden Eye* (New York, 2000)

—, *The Ballad of the Sad Café and Other Stories* (New York, 2005)

McGee, David, 'Smelling Like a Brewery, Lookin' Like a Tramp', interview with Tom Waits in *Rolling Stone*, 231 (27 January 1977)

McKenna, Kristine, 'One from the Heart and One for the Road', NME (1 October 1983), p. 24

Marcus, Greil, *The Old Weird America: The World of Bob Dylan's Basement Tapes* (New York, 2011)

Marsh, Dave, 'Tom Waits: Reno Sweeney's', *Rolling Stone* (23 October 1975), www.rocksbackpages.com, accessed 24 March 2021

Miles, Barry, *Zappa: A Biography* (London, 2004)

Mitchell, Joseph, *Up in the Old Hotel*, with an introduction by William Fiennes (London, 2012)

Morrissey, Paul (dir.), *Heat* (1972)

O'Hagan, Sean, 'Off Beat', *The Observer* (29 October 2006), www.theguardian.com, accessed 19 December 2019

Oney, Steve, 'Twenty Questions: Tom Waits', *Playboy* (March 1988), p. 129

Pancake, Breece D'J, *The Stories of Breece D'J Pancake* (New York, 2002)

Pappademas, Alex, 'Fifty Years of LA Rock: Interview with Tom Waits' (12 March 2009), www.gq.com, accessed March 2020

Peeples, Stephen K., 'Tom Waits Q&A: *Heartattack and Vine*', in *Tom Waits on Tom Waits: Interviews and Encounters*, ed. Paul Maher Jr (Chicago, IL, 2011), pp. 114–26

Pietschmann, Richard J., 'Tom Waits: Skid Row', *Playgirl* (November 1978), p. 70

Pond, Steve, 'Tom Waits on *One from the Heart*' (1 April 1982), www.rollingstone.com, accessed 15 March 2020

Ray, Nicholas (dir.), *They Live by Night* (1948)

Rayner, R., 'Dog Day Afternoon', *Time Out* (3 October 1985), www.tomwaitslibrary.info, accessed 18 March 2020

Rechy, John, *City of Night* (New York, 2013)

Runyon, Damon, *Guys and Dolls and Other Writings* (New York, 2008)

Schwab, Charles, sleeve notes for *Tom Waits: Used Songs, 1973–1980* (2001)

Simmons, Sylvie, 'The *Mojo* Interview: Tom Waits Speaks', in *Tom Waits on Tom Waits: Interviews and Encounters*, ed. Paul Maher Jr (Chicago, IL, 2011), pp. 366–76

Soocher, Stan, 'Tom Waits for No-One', in *Tom Waits on Tom Waits: Interviews and Encounters*, ed. Paul Maher Jr (Chicago, IL, 2011), pp. 107–8

Smay, David, *Swordfishtrombones* (New York, 2011)

Stallone, Sylvester (dir.), *Paradise Alley* (1978)

Stanford, Frank, *The Light the Dead See: Selected Poems* (New York, 1991)

Thumm, Francis, 'Tom's Wild Years', *Interview* (October 1988), pp. 110–12

'Tom Foolery: Swapping Stories with Inimitable Tom Waits', *Buzz* (May 1993), www.tomwaitslibrary.info, accessed 10 March 2020

Trenbeth, Rich, 'The Ramblin' Street Life Is the Good Life for Tom Waits', *Country Rambler* (30 December 1976), in *Tom Waits on Tom Waits: Interviews and Encounters*, ed. Paul Maher Jr (Chicago, IL, 2011), pp. 77–84

Waite, Ralph (dir.), *On the Nickel* (1980)

Waits, Tom, '*The Heart of Saturday Night* Press Release, 1974', in *Innocent When You Dream: Tom Waits, the Collected Interviews*, ed. Mac Montandon (London, 2007), pp. 3–4

—, 'Interview with Waits', KPFK radio (23 July 1974), in *Tom Waits on Tom Waits: Interviews and Encounters*, ed. Paul Maher Jr (Chicago, IL, 2011), pp. 20–26

—, Spoken introduction to 'On a Foggy Night', *Nighthawks at the Diner* (1975)

—, 'WAMU Radio Interview, 18 April 1975', www.tomwaitslibrary.info,
    accessed December 2019

—, *The Early Years: The Lyrics of Tom Waits, 1971–1982* (NewYork, 2007)

Ward, Robert, 'Play It Again, Tom', in *Tom Waits on Tom Waits: Interviews
    and Encounters*, ed. Paul Maher Jr (Chicago, IL, 2011), pp. 51–60

Webb, Bob, *Tom Waits at the Heritage*, www.tomwaitslibrary.info,
    accessed 9 January 2020

West, Nathaniel, *Miss Lonelyhearts and the Day of the Locust*
    (New York, 2009)

White, Timothy, 'Rickie Lee Jones: A Walk on the Jazz Side of Life',
    Rolling Stone, 279 (9 August 1979), p. 42

—, *Rock Lives: Profiles and Interviews* (New York, 1991)

Wilder, Billy, and Charles Brackett, *Sunset Boulevard: The Complete
    Screenplay* (Los Angeles, CA, 1999)

—, —, and Raymond Chandler, *Double Indemnity: The Complete
    Screenplay* (Los Angeles, CA, 2000)

Williams, Tennessee, *Hard Candy: A Book of Stories* (New York, 1967)

Wiseman, Rich, 'Tom Waits, All Night Rambler', *Rolling Stone*
    (30 January 1975), p. 18

Ziebarth, Delores, 'Tom Waits Arrested in LA', *Rolling Stone*, 243
    (14 July 1977), p. 15

Zimmer, Dave, 'Hollywood Confidential', BAM (26 February 1982),
    www.rocksbackpages.com, accessed 23 March 2021

Select Discography

Closing Time
1973 Asylum 53030

Ol' '55 • I Hope That I Don't Fall in Love with You • Virginia Avenue • Old Shoes (& Picture Postcards) • Midnight Lullaby • Martha • Rosie • Lonely • Ice Cream Man • Little Trip to Heaven (on the Wings of Your Love) • Grapefruit Moon • Closing Time

The Heart of Saturday Night
1974 Asylum 53035

New Coat of Paint • San Diego Serenade • Semi Suite • Shiver Me Timbers • Diamonds on My Windshield • (Looking for) The Heart of Saturday Night • Fumblin' with the Blues • Please Call Me, Baby • Depot, Depot • Drunk on the Moon • The Ghosts of Saturday Night (After Hours at Napoleone's Pizza House)

Nighthawks at the Diner
1975 Asylum 63002

(Opening Intro) • Emotional Weather Report • (Intro)/ On a Foggy Night • (Intro)/Eggs and Sausage (in a Cadillac with Susan Michelson) • (Intro)/Better Off without a Wife • Nighthawk Postcards (from Easy Street) • (Intro)/Warm Beer and Cold Women • (Intro)/Putnam County • Spare Parts I (a Nocturnal Emission) • Nobody • (Intro)/Big Joe and Phantom 309 • Spare Parts II and Closing

Small Change

1976 Asylum 53050

Tom Traubert's Blues (Four Sheets to the Wind in Copenhagen) • Step Right Up • Jitterbug Boy • I Wish I Was in New Orleans • The Piano Has Been Drinking (Not Me) • Invitation to the Blues • Pasties and a G-String • Bad Liver and a Broken Heart (in Lowell) • The One That Got Away • Small Change • I Can't Wait to Get Off Work

Foreign Affairs

1977 Asylum 53068

Cinny's Waltz • Muriel • I Never Talk to Strangers • Medley: Jack & Neal/California, Here I Come • A Sight for Sore Eyes • Potter's Field • Burma-Shave • Barber Shop • Foreign Affair

Blue Valentine

1978 Asylum 53088

Somewhere • Red Shoes by the Drugstore • Christmas Card from a Hooker in Minneapolis • Romeo Is Bleeding • $29.00 • Wrong Side of the Road • Whistlin' Past the Graveyard • Kentucky Avenue • A Sweet Little Bullet from a Pretty Blue Gun • Blue Valentines

Heartattack and Vine

1980 Asylum 52252

Heartattack and Vine • In Shades • Saving All My Love for You • Downtown • Jersey Girl • Til the Money Runs Out • On the Nickel • Mr Siegal • Ruby's Arms

One from the Heart (with Crystal Gayle)

1982 CBS 37703

Opening Montage (Tom's Piano Intro/Once Upon a Town/The Wages of Love) • Is There Any Way Out of This Dream? • Picking Up after You • Old Boyfriends • Broken Bicycles • I Beg Your Pardon • Little Boy Blue • Instrumental Montage (The Tango/Circus Girl) • You Can't Unring a Bell • This One's from the Heart • Take Me Home • Presents

Swordfishtrombones
1983 Island 90095

Underground • Shore Leave • Dave the Butcher • Johnsburg, Illinois • 16 Shells from a Thirty-Ought-Six • Town with No Cheer • In the Neighborhood • Just Another Sucker on the Vine • Frank's Wild Years • Swordfishtrombone • Down, Down, Down • Soldier's Things • Gin Soaked Boy • Trouble's Braids • Rainbirds

Compilations of Elektra/Asylum Material

Bounced Checks
1981 Asylum 52 316

Heartattack and Vine • Jersey Girl • Eggs and Sausage (in a Cadillac with Susan Michelson) • I Never Talk to Strangers • The Piano Has Been Drinking (Not Me) • Whistlin' Past the Graveyard • Mr Henry • Diamonds on My Windshield • Burma-Shave • Tom Traubert's Blues (Four Sheets to the Wind in Copenhagen)

Anthology of Tom Waits
1984 Asylum 60 416

Ol' '55 • Diamonds on My Windshield • (Looking for) The Heart of Saturday Night • I Hope That I Don't Fall in Love with You • Martha • Tom Traubert's Blues (Four Sheets to the Wind in Copenhagen) • The Piano Has Been Drinking (Not Me) • I Never Talk to Strangers • Somewhere • Burma-Shave • Jersey Girl • San Diego Serenade • A Sight for Sore Eyes

Used Songs, 1973–1980
2001 Rhino 78351

Heartattack and Vine • Eggs and Sausage (in a Cadillac with Susan Michelson) • A Sight for Sore Eyes • Whistlin' Past the Graveyard • Burma-Shave • Step Right Up • Ol' '55 • I Never Talk to Strangers • Mr Siegal • Jersey Girl • Christmas Card from a Hooker in Minneapolis • Blue Valentines • (Looking for) The Heart of Saturday Night • Muriel • Wrong Side of the Road • Tom Traubert's Blues (Four Sheets to the Wind in Copenhagen)

Acknowledgements

I would like to acknowledge the special help of Jill Brodsky, daughter of the late Joel Brodsky, who generously gave us permission to use her father's iconic photograph of Tom Waits for the cover of *Song Noir*. I'd also like to thank Victoria Rose, wife of the late Mitchell Rose (a great chronicler of rock and roll), whose image of Waits in his Tropicana apartment appears in the Introduction. Special thanks go to Carlos Benitez of ACCA Gallery for his assistance, to David Jones for indefatigable photo research, and to Stuart Glennon, Nancy Huber and David Jackson for sharing a rare image of the Heritage Club in San Diego. Thanks to Hector Martinez of *Epitaph Records* for the cover images from *Foreign Affairs* and *Blue Valentine*, and photographer Elliot Gilbert for his *Blue Valentine* shots. LA artist Ed Ruscha very generously permitted the reproduction of two of his paintings, *Norm's, La Cienega, on Fire* and *Standard Station*. Robert Marchese also provided the famous image of Waits sharing a curbstone with his Troubadour crew. Thanks to the generous Barney Hoskyns, whose Waits biography is definitive and website 'Rock's Back Pages' is invaluable for research.

I'd like to thank Bones Howe, his wife Melody and children Geoff and Kathy for their warm hospitality and talking at length to me about the Tom Waits they knew, and to Toni Kasza for her helpful introductions. I'd also like to thank my editors: at Reaktion Books, John Scanlan and Michael Leaman, for their constructive comments; at the *Los Angeles Review of Books*, Tom Lutz for commissioning my piece on Waits and LA ten years ago, and Boris Dralyuk for being a constant source of valuable insights; at the *London Review of Books*, Jean McNicol for supporting my attempt to write coherent cultural criticism. On a personal note, I'd like to acknowledge a much-missed friend, David Graves (1962–1993), who, one evening in Oxford a mere 35 years ago, suggested I should listen to an album called *Swordfishtrombones*. Lastly, I'd like to thank my wife, Anneli, who, after many years of advocacy, has come to share my passion for the music of Tom Waits.

Photo Acknowledgements

The author and publishers wish to express their thanks to the below sources of illustrative material and/or permission to reproduce it. Some locations of artworks are also given below, in the interest of brevity:

Album/Alamy Stock Photo: p. 112; Art Institute of Chicago: p. 78; © Adrian Boot/Urbanimage.tv: p. 140; © Ed Caraeff/Iconic Images: p. 39; CBW/Alamy Stock Photo: pp. 64, 148; © Peter Crivello: p. 28; © Henry Diltz: p. 87; © Brad Elterman: p. 118; Everett Collection Inc/Alamy Stock Photo: p. 107; © Elliot Gilbert, photos courtesy Elliot Gilbert and Epitaph Records: pp. 129, 130; © Dave Glass: p. 73; © Stuart Glennon: p. 33; © Bob Gruen/www.bobgruen.com: p. 100; Phillip Harrington/Alamy Stock Photo: p. 55; Frederika Hoffmann/ullstein bild via Getty Images: p. 190; Robert Landau/Alamy Stock Photo: p. 6; © Jenny Lens/ punkpioneers.com: p. 124; © Los Angeles Times Photographic Archives, Special Collections, Charles E. Young Research Library, UCLA: p. 62; © Robert Marchese: p. 83; Records/Alamy Stock Photo: pp. 93, 179; © Mitchell Rose: p. 13; Roy Hankey Collection, Los Angeles Public Library: p. 91; © Ed Ruscha: pp. 77, 136; © San Diego History Center: p. 26; TCD/Prod.DB/Alamy Stock Photo: pp. 187, 189; Underwood Archives/Getty Images: p. 47; © 1981 Zoetrope Corporation, all rights reserved: p. 155.

Index

Page numbers in *italics* indicate illustrations